REMAIN CLAM!

Did you notice the title of this book? Did you notice what was wrong with it? Or did you think the title was **Remain Calm**? Don't be embarrassed if you did. MANY people, grown-ups and kids alike, make the same mistake. Why? Well, the brain wants the title to make sense. Remain Calm makes sense; Remain Clam doesn't. Also, most of us only glance at or skim things like titles, instructions or epigraphs [which is what this paragraph is]. If we do read more closely, we might read too quickly or too anxiously and flip letters automatically. This is what some dyslexic people do, and when we're stressed, we all become a little bit dyslexic: letters switch, negatives and positives flip, and up becomes down. So? Why does this matter? It matters because test makers on every level are all too aware of this tendency, which is especially common in young minds. They know if you feel rushed, stressed or distracted that you'll be prone to miss details, get things backwards or answer the question you imagine rather than the one on the page. That means it is VERY important that you find a way to quiet your mind, focus on ALL the words and, by all means, no matter what:

Remain Clam!

An ibidPREP Book

2328 Broadway, 3rd Floor

New York, NY 10024

ibidprep.com

© 2015 Stuart Servetar

2nd Edition

ISBN 978-0-9964418-0-3

REMAIN CLAM!
HUNTER EDITION

FOREWORD

2nd Ed. © ibidPREP llc

THE HUNTER TEST

The Hunter Test is an extreme example of a high-stakes standardized test. It's a one-and-done, make-or-break shot for students in 6th grade to gain admittance to Hunter College High School for the 7th grade. There is no second chance at this test, not even if you're sick on test day. On the day of the test, you will line up around the block at Hunter with students on one side of the sidewalk and parents roped off on the other. To make matters worse, of the 2,064 students who signed up to take the test in 2015, only 182 were admitted. That is an admission rate of 8.8%. Harvard's admission rate is 5.4%!

All that said, the Hunter Test need not be a terror-fueled cauldron. Students and families who allow themselves enough time to prepare for this exam can survive and thrive. I know this to be true because every year my staff and I shepherd many students through this process.

One of the first things to understand about the Hunter Test is that you don't need to score perfectly on the exam in order to be admitted. The test is designed to be difficult for everyone, and perfection is probably beyond the grasp of even the best student. But that's okay! As is the case for every test, focusing on and doing what you do best will make it manageable, and **_learning_** what you need to know will help you excel.

This book is designed to cover all the material on the test and prepare you for whatever might come your way. Used in combination with practice tests, you should gain a good sense of the test and improve your chances on it. There is one Hunter Test put out by the school. It is available here:

http://www.hunterschools.org/hs/entrance-exam

ibidPREP also has written several mock tests for the Hunter exam. They are available at the office.

If you ever have any questions about this book, the Hunter Test or any other prep issues, please feel free to reach out to us at:

info@ibidprep.com

INTRODUCTION:

TEST TAKING AND THE STUDENT MIND

2ⁿᵈ Ed. © ibidPREP llc

I grew up a classic underachiever, partly because I thought so highly of myself that nothing I could contemplate doing was good enough for me to be doing. Therefore, I often did nothing. I certainly didn't prepare for my standardized tests; I was far too arrogant for that. I know now that a couple of practice tests and some review would probably have helped me gain a lot of points. I don't want my students ever feeling as if they didn't reach for every last point. We may not always reach our goals, but it will never be for lack of trying. The goals we reach for are never soft. Many tutoring courses artificially manipulate their diagnostics to ensure the appearance of gains among their students. I prefer the challenge of challenging my students.

As fun as it might be, complaining about tests is a waste of your time, and having a negative attitude going into your tests usually leads to a negative result coming out. The best way to use your energy is by studying and learning how to get better at taking the test in front of you, in this case the Hunter Test. Remember that all tests are inherently unfair. Most are skewed toward better prepared, calmer and more confident students. If tests were not unfair or skewed, everyone would excel equally.

TEST TAKING & THE STUDENT MIND

Underachievers—a.k.a. the Slackers

Students often come to me with their minds stressed and self-images wobbling. They are filled with notions of what kind of students they are and what their potential is or isn't; they all dread becoming numbers that don't represent them. Obviously, you are not a number, but neither are you your potential. You are what you are right now.

My job is to convince my underachievers [as I had to convince myself] to try and, in so doing, begin to end their boring cycles. Even though one of the credos[1] of the underachiever is "If I ever did try, I'd ace this test," that isn't always true. No one succeeds every time; once you learn to try, it just means that you must **always** try. Though there are no guarantees of success, I can guarantee you one thing: if you **don't** try, then it is certain you **won't** succeed.

Overachievers—The Anxious Test Takers

In addition to underachievers, I also work with a lot of students caught in the grip of test anxiety. These students are usually good students and hard workers, but they often, well, stink at tests like these. Why? Because there are certain things for which we cannot prepare, namely questions and topics that require improvisational flair. This is where the slacker excels. He is *used* to being unprepared and forced to wing it.

---

[1] statement of beliefs

THE MIND IS A MUSCLE—USE IT

EVEN FOR THOSE STUDENTS WHO SEEM TO BREEZE THROUGH TESTS, IT'S NOT BECAUSE THEY NEVER THINK; IT'S BECAUSE THEY'RE USED TO THINKING AND WORKING THROUGH PROBLEMS. THE FINEST PROBLEM-SOLVING METHODS AND APPROACHES WILL NOT HELP UNLESS YOU IMPLEMENT[2] THEM. THE MIND IS INDEED A MUSCLE THAT CAN BE STRENGTHENED AND IMPROVED THROUGH USE. IF MY FLABBY BELLY CAN BE TIGHTENED WITH FEWER BAGELS AND MORE SIT-UPS, YOUR MIND CAN WRAP ITSELF AROUND FRACTIONS.

All of You

Almost all students—slackers, overachievers and every student in between—come to me with preconceived notions of their own abilities: "I suck at math," "I'm terrible at grammar," "I'm slow," etc. Most of these preconceptions have been formed through years of parent/teacher conferences or odd family dynamics: "My sister is the smart one," "I'm the reader," "I'm not so mathish." *Ugh.* Often these diagnoses have only the slightest basis in reality and, if we believe them, lead us into self-fulfilling-prophecy territory. Students are told that they are bad at math, so they stop applying themselves, and then they really *do* become bad at math. Or students have a little difficulty getting the hang of reading, so they stop reading! Instead of conforming to artificial definitions, keep your mind open to its possibilities. If you do, who knows where you can go?

Even into adolescence, most kids' minds are amorphous[3] mushes that have yet to be formed to any reasonable degree. Telling kids that they have math minds or verbal minds is about as productive or accurate as looking at a sack of flour and saying it is only ever going to be bread and then looking at another sack of flour and saying it will only ever be cookies.

---

[2] put into practice
[3] without a clearly defined shape or form

   2nd Ed. © ibidPREP llc

NO TURTLING

YOU SEE IT EVERY DAY. WE'VE TURNED INTO A NATION OF TURTLES, AND SOMEHOW WE'RE PROUD OF IT. SOMEONE ON A TALK SHOW MENTIONS MATH, AND SOMEONE ELSE WAVES HER FLIPPERS AROUND LIKE A TURTLE FLAILING ON ITS BACK: "OH, I CAN'T DO ANY OF THAT MATH STUFF. I'M JUST AWFUL AT IT. HAHAHAHAHA!" AND FOR SOME REASON THAT'S OKAY. THAT KIND OF HELPLESSNESS IN THE FACE OF SOMETHING VAGUELY CHALLENGING IS REALLY DOING GREAT THINGS FOR US INDIVIDUALLY AND AS A NATION. NOT. I'M NOT SAYING THAT MATH ISN'T HARD, OR THAT YOU'RE A NINCOMPOOP IF YOU HAVE PROBLEMS WITH IT. WHAT I AM SAYING IS, STOP FLIPPING ONTO YOUR BACK AT EVERY OBSTACLE. TRY!

Never Rush; Never Rest –Goethe[4]

The most important tool on these tests is one you all have with you all the time. It is impossible to forget to bring with you or even to lose. Have you guessed what it is?

That's right. It's your brain.

We teach students of all ages at ibidPREP, especially those awful teenagers, and one thing all students often seem to forget is: they're allowed to think! When many students get to a hard passage, section or question on a test, they freak out and feel that if they have to think or work or reread then there's something wrong. They end up panicking and rushing instead—and that's no good. There is plenty of time for these tests.

Once you trust us not to rush, life will get easier. But of course, life is not that simple. Some students, rather than think too little, think too much. Or they think they are thinking a lot, when all they are really doing is obsessing! What does that mean? When you obsess, you stick with something too long and go over and over it in your mind trying to figure it out. Sometimes, there are some things we just can't figure out, or, because we're a little too stressed, we're not really thinking about them but actually just getting stuck on them. In those situations it's VERY important to let that one question go and move on, so you can get all the OTHER questions right. One thing my experience has taught me is that the longer a student takes to figure out a question, the greater the odds are that he will get that question wrong [and waste time and lose confidence or end up rushing on the following questions]! As a general rule, take one try, two tries, three tries on a question and then move on. Live to fight another day!!

[4] Johann Wolfgang von Goethe (1749-1832) is widely considered the greatest poet in the German language.

If you focus only on the muscle groups you are strong in, then those muscles will get very strong, and the rest of you will turn to flab.

BUT I'M NOT GOOD AT TEST TAKING...

Being good at test taking is not an innate[5] trait like having brown eyes or webbed toes. Some students may have done poorly on one or two tests when they were little and have since gotten stuck with the "poor test taker" label. Some may have started out with some test-taking anxiety only to see it snowball as they've gotten older and the tests have come to have more consequences. Whatever the case, none of this means you are doomed to a life of underperforming on tests. As you read and implement the lessons in this book, you will begin to fight fear and your preconceived[6] notions with knowledge and experience. The first step in learning how to use your brilliant young mind properly is to find a way to **Remain Clam!**

HOW TO USE THIS BOOK

This book is designed to walk you through all the types of questions you will face on the Hunter Test and review the material that will be covered on it. Use this book either in conjunction with a class or a tutor or on your own [you may also even bring your parents in on the process!] There are plenty of practice questions for each facet of the test and answers to the questions are at the back. Once you have walked yourself through the book, try the test at the back. Answers to the test are also at the back of the book along with instructions on how to score and scale the exam.

To review your test, evaluate your strengths and weaknesses. Give yourself a pat on the back for every question you get right, and try to honestly figure out what you did on the problems you missed. Don't just note the correct answer and forget it. You won't learn that way.

Also try to avoid just doing test after test. If you don't review your tests and learn from your mistakes, you'll just keep making the same ones over and over. **Practice. Review. Repeat. Improve!**

---

[5] in-born, natural
[6] pre-determined, set

2nd Ed. © ibidPREP llc

CHAPTER ONE
HOW TO USE THIS BOOK &
TEST FORMAT

It's about process. As much about HOW you do something as WHAT you do. In order to distinguish among students, these tests prey on students' tendency to make careless errors, not pay attention, and RUSH! Therefore, students who learn HOW TO: pay attention, execute properly, and NOT rush—WIN!!!

Read this book, and I do mean READ, in order to prep and guide yourself in the basic knowledge required on the Hunter Test and the rigors of HOW TO TAKE TESTS. Then practice, practice, practice, but practice WELL. It doesn't help to do a lot of work if you keep making the same mistakes over and over again. Pay attention to what you're doing and try honestly try to evaluate your weaknesses [and strengths!].

Remain Clam! contains exercises for every topic and type of question on these exams. Once you have worked through every topic and type of question, please feel free to contact ibidPREP to schedule a practice test to take with us or on your own.[1]

If we send you a test to take on your own, that means getting out of your bed and off the couch. You need to find a quiet spot in which you won't be interrupted [this may involve leaving your house entirely and seeking out the sanctuary of the nearest library, school, church or ashram[2]]. It also means uncovering the last little dirty secret almost every student clings to—in order to properly test, prep, study, read, learn, look or listen to ANYTHING, you must first turn off the computer, phone and TV. If you cannot learn to create a temporary media-free zone in your life [we call it "going acoustic" in my house], YOU WILL NEVER DO YOUR BEST ON THESE TESTS.

As you finish and correct your exercises and tests, focus on the questions you get wrong [remember to give yourself a pat on the back for the ones you get right]. Don't just look at the correct answer to your incorrect questions, say "Oh yeah," and move on. Really analyze your mistakes and try to figure out why you made them in terms of the things discussed in this book. Did you rush? Did you skim? Did you panic because it looked difficult? Was it a subject/topic you need to go back and review? Tackle every wrong question one by one and really try to grasp your errors on each so that you don't continue to make those same errors for the rest of your test-taking life!

Also, please don't fall into the trap of thinking that doing a lot of tests and questions is necessarily a good thing. If you are not learning from your mistakes, then you are simply going to repeat them and not improve your performance. It is far better to do one or two tests under super-realistic conditions, analyze your results REALLY closely, and then perhaps do one more test than to do a bunch of tests, one right after the next like a crazy person!

HUNTER TEST BREAKDOWN

The Hunter Test has it all, reading, math and an essay. The questions are all multiple choice, but now you have five answer choices. Welcome to the big leagues!

The test starts with READING COMPREHENSION. You will be given a series of passages from many different kinds of writing: poetry, fiction, memoir, nonfiction, you name it. Along with each of about six passages will be anywhere from five to ten multiple choice questions for a total of 50 questions. You've been doing questions like these for as long as you've been in school, though the ones on this test may be slightly more difficult than those you've seen before.

Then comes something new, something many students find to be the most treacherous part of the exam: the essay! You've written plenty of these in your time, but the Hunter Essay is not your standard writing assign-

---

[1] info@ibidprep.com
[2] religious retreat [Hindu]

ment. The prompt here is often open-ended and usually not only allows but *requires* creativity. We'll go into this thoroughly later.

Finally the math. This section is only 30 multiple choice questions and will cover every bit of math you've ever seen. Maybe even some you haven't. But don't worry: we'll help you with all of it.

Students are allotted a total of 180 minutes [3 hours] in which to answer the questions and write the essay. Although the test booklet will recommend that students divide their time evenly among the sections, it is up to each student how she chooses to manage her time.

<u>There are no breaks given during the test.</u>

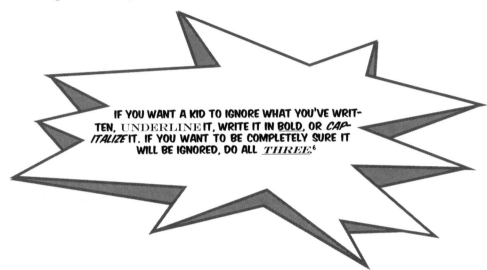

IF YOU WANT A KID TO IGNORE WHAT YOU'VE WRITTEN, UNDERLINE IT, WRITE IT IN **BOLD**, OR *CAPITALIZE* IT. IF YOU WANT TO BE COMPLETELY SURE IT WILL BE IGNORED, DO ALL *THREE*.[6]

Parents love this line because it's absolutely true. I have watched countless times as students get questions wrong and then discover that they had, in effect, answered the wrong question:
Oh, they wanted the first number that was NOT a perfect square...
—Damn, they wanted to know which was the LEAST like the author's main idea...
—Oh, they wanted PERIMETER not AREA!
—Oops.
—Did they say EXCEPT?

Oh.

---

[3] I hope by now you start to notice how often I use bold, underline and italics to indicate that something is important and you should pay attention to it. I promise I won't overdo it, if you promise to start HEARING it.

2ⁿᵈ Ed. © ibidPREP llc

ibidPREP Book Key

One of the main goals of this book is to try to get students to stop skimming through texts and tests and encourage them by any means necessary to READ ALL THE WORDS in order to better comprehend reading passages, ensure that they're answering the questions asked and get them to avoid partially correct answer choices. I firmly believe that students can and should develop the mental strength to plow through dense text no matter what.

However, to make reading this book a little more enjoyable, I have broken up our dense text by presenting it in various graphic forms. There is something of a method to our breakouts, and that format is explained below.

Brains generally feature amusing though often incredibly wise anecdotes I've gleaned from my experiences with students and in everyday life.

These spiky splashes include pithy aphorisms and reminders that I hope will stick in your mind.

Clamshells contain sets of information that you MUST KNOW in order to excel on your exam. MUST KNOW information usually covers basic knowledge that students should have come across long ago. If you haven't truly learned this info, you should do so asap. It will make your life much easier.

Gray boxes and margins indicate practice sets and exercises.

HOW TO AVOID EXAMICIDE

PART I—CARTOON CATS & OTHER CREATURES!

1. THE CAT & THE RAKE

There is an old expression:
Fool me once, shame on you; fool me twice, shame on me.

For many of my students the rule seems to be:
Fool me a thousand times, and I'll keep coming back for more.

Some students make the same mistakes over and over and over again, which is why these tests are so fond of building the same pitfalls into every section. Think of those poor cartoon cats chasing the mouse through the yard. They've been around that backyard so many times that you'd think by now they would know there is going to be a rake lying in the grass just waiting for them to step and thwack them in the head. Yet episode after episode, those cartoon cats step on the same darn rake. Don't be that cartoon cat.

2. WATER FLOWING DOWN A HILL

When contending with tests, think of yourself as water flowing down a hill [I swear this is as Zen as I'm gonna get]. When water hits a tree, it doesn't stop, head back up the hill or freak out; it merely finds a way around, under or over the tree. You should too. If your approach to a problem fails, try something else. If that doesn't work, find another hill.

I often ask my students what water flowing down a hill does when it hits a tree. Most answer the basic "Goes around," "Goes under," etc. When I asked one student, a broad-shouldered soccer player, what the water did when it encountered a tree, she told me: "It knocks the tree down." She did just fine on her tests.

2ⁿᵈ Ed. © ibidPREP llc

HOW TO AVOID EXAMICIDE

3. ADRENALINE IS GOOD FOR ONLY THREE THINGS, NONE OF WHICH IS TEST–TAKING...

Adrenaline is a magical substance. In situations of distress it can give us strength and energy unimaginable in normal circumstances. For many students, who have so many other hormones raging in their system, adrenaline surges are fairly common occurrences. Only problem is, adrenaline evolved to aid prehistoric man in peril, not 21st-century teens taking tests.

Adrenaline worked great in frightening situations when most of our frightening situations involved lions, tigers and bears or other dudes with spears. Now, however, most of our frightening situations involve accidentally posting those pics from spring break, forgetting to erase our texts—or taking standardized tests. If a caveman left his cave in the morning and right outside the cave he saw a mountain lion, his brain would shut down and adrenaline would take over. Adrenaline would give his brain one of three simple commands for his body to execute: fight, flee or freeze. That means the dude could use the adrenaline to get mad strong, pick up a rock and bash the lion [Me Kill Test Before It Kill Me], use the adrenaline to power his legs and get the heck out of there [Me Rush Through Test Before It Kill Me] or stand very, very still in the hope that the lion would not notice him [Me Freeze and Completely Choke on Test So Test Not Kill Me]. A little adrenaline bump will certainly perk you up and keep you going during test times, but a total surge is not good for most test situations because all your energy and strength is in your body and your mind is completely focused on fighting, fleeing or freezing, NOT solving complex problems.

SEE NEXT EXAMICIDE ON PAGE 140!

CHAPTER TWO

READING COMPREHENSION

2nd Ed. © ibidPREP llc

It is very important for all tests [and learning and school and life] that you have a reading life. That means that you spend some part of most every day reading something outside of school. It really does not matter what you read: books, newspapers, fiction, nonfiction, graphic novels, blogs, textbooks. Whatever you like. What does matter is that you're always paying attention to what you read and making sure that you don't let words or ideas just slide by. If there's something in your reading you don't quite follow, stop and try to figure it out, or ask your parents, teachers, friends, caregivers—anyone—what the passage or words might mean. Remember: fools think they are wise people, but wise people know they are fools! [And if you don't understand what *that* means, don't be afraid to ask!]

There is one more thing that matters in how you go about your reading life: no more being read to! I'm REALLY sorry about that because it really is a nice thing, but it's very important that you start reading to and for yourself. Why? Because it is very important that you learn to become an **active** reader who is not afraid to work through hard or boring material.

When your mom or dad or grandma or big sister or whoever reads to you, it's a little like watching TV. All this interesting stuff just sort of washes over you, and you don't have to do much [it's also a little like being a baby bird whose mom does everything including chewing your food for you]. As you start to become bigger kids and more independent students, it's time to start chewing your own food and working through your own books!

Boring Reading

Many, many students tell us that they like to read but only stuff they *like* to read. That makes a lot of sense. Unfortunately, that usually just means the fun stuff like Percy Jackson or Harry Potter or Eloise. Good stuff, but not the kind of thing you're going to find on tests. Sometimes on tests you find interesting stories, but more often you find passages about things you don't like. Some kids love reading about sea turtles, some students would rather chew their arms off than read about sea turtles. The point is, you don't get to choose. You get what you get and you don't get upset! The important thing is to always try to stay involved and engaged in your reading. It makes taking these tests that much easier, and you never know where you might just find something new or interesting!

How to Read

Most of your teachers in school try to help you with your tests. However, while teachers are very good at teaching students about history and math and spelling, they're not always so good at teaching kids about tests. That's okay, they're not supposed to be. We are. If teachers have ever told you anything about not reading passages or reading questions first or any other games like that, we'd like to ask you to forget all those tricks for now. Let us help you learn to read better instead.

If you are really, really having troubles with the reading then we'll play all kinds of games. But for now, the first way to get better at reading is to read better!

PASSAGE TYPES

We generally encounter two types of reading on the Hunter Test: nonfiction and fiction/memoir.

Nonfiction

Nonfiction passages usually comes from textbooks, magazines, newspapers or online reporting. Nonfiction writing usually involves a third-person narrator speaking relatively objectively about a topic. Passages about science, history, ideas, art and current events all fall under the heading of nonfiction, as do biographies and book reports.

WHAT TO LOOK FOR IN NONFICTION

The Three T's

The best readers are constantly asking questions of themselves and, more important, the material in front of them. "Why is this mind-numbingly boring?" "Why is that author going on for so long about this tiny thing?" "Why is he asking us this question?" "Why am I having problems getting through this part?"

Good readers do not accept confusion as a natural state while reading. If something doesn't make sense, they stop and try to figure it out. These are the points at which ALL readers need to slow down and break down what is being said. Don't worry, though; spending extra time on thorny sections is often made up for by being able to spend less time on other parts. There are indeed many parts of a reading that you may go through at a good pace because they are saying predictable things or repeating themselves.

As you are reading nonfiction, the questions you always need to have at the back of your mind are the **three T's:**

What is the **THEME** of this piece [**what** is its TOPIC]? First things first: figure out what the whole thing is about. Is it about sea turtles? Cool 4th graders hanging out prepping for a test? Or is it about pirates and how they fix their hair? Make sure you're clear on WHAT the piece is about, then figure out:

What is the **THESIS** of the piece [**why** is the author writing this? **What** is the point the piece is trying to make about its TOPIC]? The WHY is the author's opinion or the point she is trying to make about her THEME. In other words, WHY the author has gone to all the trouble of writing the piece in the first place. Perhaps: sea turtles are amazing creatures that should be protected. Or: 4th graders prepping for a test are cool but need to practice their reading processes—how they read—if they want do well on their tests!

What is the **TONE** of the piece [**how** does the author convey her THESIS—objectively, ironically, skeptically, critically, analytically, angrily, humorously...]? This question is much easier to answer once you can tell what kind of writing it is. If it's fiction, the tone could be all kinds of things depending on the character telling the story. It could be silly or funny or even confused. If the piece is a nonfiction piece, like something from a textbook or newspaper, then most of the time the tone is going to be neutral, fairly serious and objective. If the piece is an opinion piece, the tone could be neutral, but it might also be a little angry [never too angry] or excited or even amused and humorous.

Think of tone like the tones in a pencil drawing from darkest dark to the almost bare white of a page. The darkest tones are the serious, angry, harsh tones. The grey middle tones are the neutrals, and the lightest, almost white tones are the humorous, easygoing tones.

2nd Ed. © ibidPREP llc

Although we are delighted by our students' interpretations (opinions, ideas, etc.) of the world, we are not interested in those interpretations if they are made without any foundations—if they are not based on anything. Interpreting information and texts does not mean immediately sticking your own opinion on everything that's put in front of you. It does not mean seeing everything you read through your eyes only. At ibidPREP, interpretation means taking in what is placed before you [book, film, discussion, experience] and letting all the words and information go into your brain, so you may establish what the reading is trying to say from its author's viewpoint [not your own]. Once you are able to explain what someone else's viewpoint is, then your interpretation will have a lot more strength!

INTERPRETATION

FINDING THE MAIN IDEA—THESIS

Your Assumptions Will Be Used Against You

If you get to a passage about global warming and you've already heard or read a lot about this topic, chances are your initial reaction will be, "Yeah, yeah, global warming is bad, *yada, yada, yada...*" And that's when they've got you, because these tests love, *love, love* picking passages that go against expectations. And they don't just go against expectations, they do it by first laying out what your expectation might be. I call this:

Banana, Banana, Banana, Banana, Banana, but *Really Strawberry*

Since the test makers know that most people skim, they pick readings that really penalize the skimmer. What kinds of passages penalize the skimmer? Passages that do not make their main point right off the bat, for one. I call these passages "banana, banana, banana, banana, banana, but *really* strawberry," because they start by offering one point of view [banana]. This point of view is what is known as a red herring. It does not offer the writer's point of view, but involves him or her setting out others' points of view for the main purpose of contradicting those points of view with his or her own point later in the passage. The test makers know that after our parents make the same point two or three times, we generally tune out, after which time they could be saying anything! **Do not do this here.** Once again I'll say it: this test is not a lecture from your parents. Do not treat it as such. In fact, in most reading passages the main point of the piece is not revealed until at least the end of the first paragraph and sometimes not until the beginning of the second, the middle of the second, somewhere in the third paragraph or sometimes not even until the end. Your job is to keep reading until you find the strawberry.

How to Find the Strawberry: Always Look for the "But"

One way to know when the author is finally putting forward her main point is to look for the "but" [aka the "however," the "although," the "yet," the "actually"—you get the idea.] The "but" marks the shift in the piece from the author recounting what everyone else thinks, to her laying out what the truth really is [according to her point of view, of course.]

> *Most people believe that science is a rational process based on cool, dispassionate evaluation of facts and data. The majority of books and movies portray scientists as cold, clinical beings more at home with test tubes than with other warm-blooded living creatures.* **HOWEVER**, *the truth is that most scientists are passionate, highly social beings who rely as much on feeling and intuition as they do on cold-blooded, rational evaluations of their subjects.*

How to Answer

With reading comprehension questions, it is not always possible or wise to do what kids usually do: read the question and then pick through the answers for something reasonable. First of all, it's not always clear what the question is. Second, the answer choices for the questions are often so unclear and poorly worded that by the time you get to answer choice (D), you might be hard-pressed to know what to think or to even clearly remember the question. Here's a better way to proceed:

1.   Read the question and restate it in your own words.

2.   Answer the question for yourself **BEFORE** you look at the answer choices. If you don't have an answer to the question without looking at the text, look at the text, THEN come up with an answer.

3.   Once you've determined your answer, **THEN** look at the answer choices and select the one whose meaning is closest to yours. Be careful: the answer choice may word your answer differently from what you expect.

More on tone:

Negative Tone

Be careful here. If an author is reporting or describing something that is bad or negative, that's not the same as having a negative tone about the thing. For example:

Example of Negative News, Neutral Tone:

> *Hitler killed 6,000,000 Jewish people during World War II.*

Example of Negative News, Negative Tone:

> *That twisted, weak, pathetic Hitler killed 6,000,000 Jewish people like the evil, sick, cowardly rat he was.*

See the difference?

By the same token, the occasional negative word does not mean the writer's thought is negative.

> *I ate a big fat hamburger. [Most teens stop dead at the word "fat."]*

> *We had a horribly good time at the fair.*

> *The man was awfully kind.*

WHY THE READING COMP SECTIONS ARE BORING

One year, while the first online music download site NAPSTER was still a big deal, there was a passage about it on the SAT. Not one of my students got more than one question wrong out of thirteen on that section! [And some of my students can't read shampoo instructions {lather, rinse, repeat} without getting distracted!!] The SAT test makers accidentally included a section that was interesting to its readers—they never made that mistake again!

2nd Ed. © ibidPREP llc

READING FOR DETAIL—SHE WHO DOES NOT GET BORED WINS!!!

If the critical reading passages were interesting, most students would get most questions right. Therefore, the test would not be an effective measure of differences among readers. **One way to separate students out is to present passages that are progressively more boring.**

How do the test makers succeed in boring you? Either they choose topics that are duller than watching your fingernails grow or they choose passages that are so obscurely[1] written that no one save[2] the authors' mothers could slog through the pieces. Sometimes they even select passages that are *both* deadly dull topics AND incredibly densely written! Ouch. **Your goal as a student is to refuse to be bored.**

If You Skim You're Sunk!

If you skim through the passage, you'll miss the point of the passage and misunderstand what you're being asked.

If you skim through the answers, you'll often be fooled into picking the wrong answer, usually an answer that is word for word about 80% correct but contains a word or words that make it 100% incorrect.

To avoid skimming, you first have to realize you're doing it. We all do. But you have to realize when you're not committing yourself to the passage and just trying to get through it by glossing over the surface of the piece. Chances are, if you've been going through our educational system, whether it is public or private, you've been forced to schlep through a lot of material and just cover it with your eyes. I'm telling you now that every time you skim and don't absorb the material, you're wasting your time, energy and points.

If you're ever not sure—READ SOME MORE!

The nice thing about reading comprehension is that all the answers are in the text! In math or grammar, if you have forgotten a concept or approach, you may have no way of finding it out during the exam. In reading, however, if you're not sure of a detail, instead of staring off into space, look back to the text! It's all there!! It's the same for questions regarding specific lines. If you can't determine an answer from the specific lines given, read more before or after the lines to make better sense of them!

READ ALL THE WORDS [ESPECIALLY ITALICS AT THE BEGINNINGS OF PASSAGES]

One student of mine had reading issues and processing issues and issue issues and needed extra time and

[1] not easily understood
[2] except

so on and so on. I worked with her a while before I started noticing a number of things, mostly that she was an incredibly passive reader. The words on the page scrolled past her eyes, but she never took it upon herself to process what those words were saying. Eventually, I thought I figured it out and asked her, "Do you watch much TV?" It turned out she watched about four hours of TV a night! TV is great, ridiculously good, but a lot of it is like baby bird food: all pre-chewed for you, completely passive, which is why it's so good for vegging at the end of the day. It does not, however, promote an active mind.

Eventually, I was able to cajole this student into actually letting the words on the page into her brain. Then one day it all seemed to click, her reading score shot up, AND she didn't really need the extra time [skimming really ends up taking MUCH longer than reading well]. Stunned, I asked her what had clicked for her. She blithely[3] replied, "Oh. I just started reading all the words."

Oh.

BLAH, BLAH, BLAH, GOLF!

MY YOUNGER SON NOTICED I HAD A SUNBURN. I TOLD HIM, "YEAH. I USUALLY ONLY WEAR A HAT OUTSIDE WHEN I PLAY GOLF. YESTERDAY I WAS OUTSIDE IN THE SUN, BUT I DIDN'T PLAY GOLF, SO I DIDN'T WEAR A HAT AND GOT A SUNBURN BECAUSE OF IT."

HE REPLIED, "BUT YOU DIDN'T PLAY GOLF YESTERDAY."

I LAUGHED AND SAID, "YOU KNOW, WHEN I TALKED JUST NOW ALL YOU HEARD WAS 'BLAH, BLAH, BLAH, GOLF!'"

HE LAUGHED AND GRUDGINGLY AGREED.

Hear the Words

I had another not-so-good reader who also became a VERY good reader seemingly overnight. Her secret? She started reading aloud to herself in her head [oxymoron intended]. Some readers do this naturally. The words flow through their heads on a semi-audible level, and that makes it easier for them to "hear" and understand what the author is saying. If you don't do this, try. Even if you have to actually read out loud for a little while—just make sure you're not doing this during the actual test!

---

[3] showing a cool and casual indifference

THE POINT IS NEVER...

ALTHOUGH SOMETIMES YOU READ A SENTENCE AND YOU FEEL LIKE THEY MUST BE SAYING SOMETHING LIKE:

ME LIKE CRAZY TALK, YOU CAN'T UNDERSTAND FISH PANTS BECAUSE BLADDERS ARE FULL OF SKEPTICISM...

OR

THE FLOWERS ON PLANET ZUDON ARE POISONOUS SO THAT MEAT PIES HAVE HAIR...

REMEMBER:

NO   MATTER HOW OBSCURE THE LANGUAGE OF A SENTENCE MIGHT BE, THE POINT IT IS MAKING, THOUGH OCCASIONALLY COMPLEX OR SLIGHTLY LAYERED, IS NOT!

READING FOR INFERENCES, IMPLICATION AND SUGGESTION

1. What is an inference?
   a. For the purposes of standardized tests, an inference is a two-step logical conclusion that can be drawn from the text.
   b. If you read, "The boys had not eaten all day," you might be able to infer that:
      i. They were hungry.
      ii. They had been unable to eat food.
   c. You cannot infer that:
      i. They were poor.
      ii. They were punished.
      iii. They were anorexic, etc.
2. How to determine what answer is an inference:
   a. Check answer offered.
   b. Go to passage where answer under consideration is discussed.
   c. Does the answer choice simply restate the lines cited?
   d. If "yes," then don't pick the answer.
   e. If "no," then evaluate the answer choice to see if it can be inferred from the text.

STOP THE MULTIPLE CHOICE MADNESS [AND OTHER BAD HABITS WE PICK UP IN SCHOOL]

Conventional wisdom has it that multiple choice questions are great if you're not entirely sure about what you are doing. They give you something to get you moving in the right direction. Right? Wrong. Not on these tests. If you have no idea or only a partial idea of what you're doing on a question, the answer choices are going to be there to distract, annoy, confuse you further OR sucker you into the wrong answer right away. The multiple choice answers help give you a confidence boost only when you already know what you are doing in a question.

When your teacher gives a multiple choice test, she is probably using those multiple choices to help you. The answers act as prompts that are meant to steer students toward the correct answers and reward those who, even though they may not remember the exact answer to a question, have a general sense of the topic and what are reasonably correct answers. This is NOT AT ALL what goes on in most standardized tests!

Almost every kid, when left to his or her own devices, will tackle most multiple choice problems pretty much the same way: look at the problem, get a rough idea of what's being asked, and then pick through the answers for something that looks good. I would like to break you of that habit, not because it doesn't work on the problems on which it works, but because it really doesn't work on the problems on which it doesn't work. If you don't know the answer to a question and start picking through the answers, you are very likely to pick an answer that is partially correct and therefore completely incorrect. Most standardized tests are loaded with incorrect answer choices placed there to tempt and weed out the lazy.

How to combat these false answers? Come up with your own answer first! Don't just jump to the answer choices. For reading especially: figure out your own answer to the question FIRST, before you start shopping around from among the multiple choice selections. Then pick the answer choice that is closest to your own answer. You'll save time, energy and points!

HOW TO ANSWER—AGAIN

1. **REPHRASE** the question.
2. **FIND ANSWER** in **TEXT**
3. **SELECT** best-fitting multiple choice answer.

Or—Last Resort—If All Else Fails, Select the <u>Least</u> Wrong Answer

Let's say you've read for the Three T's or STEW, read and rephrased the question and found the answer in the text, but you still can't find the equivalent to your answer among the choices; just remember that it is often the case that NONE of the answers truly hits the mark, and I'm not talking about the answers that are put in to confuse and distract you, I'm talking about the answers that are actually meant to be correct. This is why it is very important NOT to get hung up looking for the **perfect** answer; it might not be there. It is far more important to get good at choosing the least wrong answer!!

One of the best ways to find the least wrong answer is to find the **wrong wrong** answers and eliminate them. These include answers that:

- include absolutes[4] that can't be proven. An absolute USUALLY cannot be proven because, as with most things in life, there is ALMOST always an exception. [Look for answers that include words that make things NOT so absolute. Words like USUALLY and ALWAYS as used above!]
- include direct repetition of quoted text.
- are just plain dopey.
- are 80–90% correct but contain one or two words that make them 100% WRONG. If you like to just read the beginnings of answers and then grab and go, these answers will get you every time.

Eliminating bad answers can usually help you shake out one or two bad answers. The ones that are left are generally not as tough to choose from as you might think. After you've done enough practice, you can begin to smell the right answers. That's right; there is a certain odor to these kinds of answers. It smells not too vague

---

[4] Absolutes are those things we say that make it sound as if something is all one way or the other: "You ALWAYS say that!" "It is NEVER good to guess." "ALL students hate tests."

2ⁿᵈ Ed. © ibidPREP llc

but not too specific. It limits what it's saying to cover its back and is generally about 90% right.

If You're Going to Get It Wrong, Get It Wrong Quickly

Studies [mine] show that the longer a student takes to answer a reading comprehension question, the greater the odds are that that student is going to get it wrong. Therefore, if you're going to get a reading comprehension question wrong—if you have no feel for the question, if you were able to get rid of only one bad answer, if the remaining answers are all blurring together, don't agonize; don't sit there thinking "A no B no D...darn it, C." In these situations, GUESS ONE and MOVE ON [aka GTHOOT—get the heck out of there!] Some questions are just lost causes, and it's not worth suffering over them when there are others to tackle (unless you have extra time at the end of the test after you've checked all your other answers). When you guess like this, you might get it wrong, but you will save time, energy and confidence.

The other thing about wrong answers is that they often seem correct at first glance. That is, 90% of the answer seems correct, but perhaps one or two wrong or misplaced words make the entire answer wrong. Readers who skim the answers, just like readers who skim the passages, are sunk. Make sure you read through the entire answer to be certain that everything it is saying is correct:

The cotton gin was the most influential invention of the 19th century.

While it is true that the cotton gin was a very influential invention, it was invented in the 18th Century and the passage most assuredly would have mentioned that fact!

STOP FLIPPING

SO MANY STUDENTS NEVER FINISH THEIR READING SECTIONS BECAUSE THEY SIT THERE WRESTLING AMONG BAD AND WORSE ANSWERS. EVEN WORSE, THEY FLIP BACK AND FORTH AND BACK AND FORTH FROM THE READING TO THE QUESTIONS TO THE READING TO THE QUESTIONS. ONCE YOU START OVER-FLIPPING, YOU'RE DEAD. YOUR BRAIN DURING THE TEST AND, TRUTH BE TOLD, MOST TIMES, IS LIKE A COLANDER.[5] YOU WOULD NOT USE A COLANDER TO CARRY SOUP FROM THE KITCHEN TO THE TABLE. IF YOU DID, YOU WOULD PROBABLY TRY TO RUN TO THE TABLE BEFORE EVERYTHING LEAKED OUT. YOU CERTAINLY WOULDN'T GO BACK AND FORTH AND BACK AND FORTH TO THE KITCHEN TRYING TO TOP OFF THE SOUP EACH TIME. EVENTUALLY, EVERYTHING WOULD DRAIN OUT, AND YOU'D END UP IN A PUDDLE OF SOUP, CONFUSED, OUT OF TIME,   LACKING IN CONFIDENCE, SOUPLESS AND WRONG.

[5] spaghetti strainer, sieve

OTHER KINDS OF READING

You may or may not be surprised to learn, just as you may or may not have been surprised to learn that you really didn't know how to read, that there are several different types of reading you didn't know how to do. Although you should always be reading the material closely, there are a few different angles from which you should closely review the material in front of you.

FICTION & MEMOIRS

Fiction

Most of your reading in school is either from textbooks or articles. These are usually written as straightforward essays. Essays are writings on a theme [a subject] that make a point about that theme using examples and specific facts. Essays can do a bunch of other things, but their main job is to make one point and make it clearly and well.

In school and at home, you probably also read fiction, but fiction is different from your other readings. For the most part, fiction has one job, too, but its job is to tell a story. By whatever means necessary, a work of fiction tells us about something that happened. That's pretty much it.

Memoirs

Memoirs are a lot like stories, but they are meant to be true stories. These are stories that are being recalled by the people whose story it is. In the old days, we called them autobiographies—life stories told in the first person. Memoirs are basically pieces of autobiographies. When reading memoirs we read them a little bit like nonfiction, looking for the Three T's, but mostly we read them like we read fiction.

Here's how we read fiction.

FICTION & MEMOIR: STEW

Just as there are three main things to look for in most other kinds of prose passages, there are four main things to look for in fiction reading.

S—Subject
T—Tone
E—Eyesight
W—What Happened??

Let's start with a story most everyone knows.

Rapunzel

There once were a man and a woman who had angered an enchantress. She threatened the man and woman,

'You must give me the child which your wife will bring into the world; I will care for it like a mother.' When the woman gave birth, the enchantress appeared at once, gave the child the name of Rapunzel, and took it away

2ⁿᵈ Ed. © ibidPREP llc

with her.

Rapunzel grew into the most beautiful child. When she was twelve years old, the enchantress shut her into a tower in a forest It had neither stairs nor door, but at the top was a little window. When the enchantress wanted to go in, she stood beneath it and cried:

'Rapunzel, Rapunzel,

Let down your long hair.'

Rapunzel had magnificent long hair, fine as spun gold, and when she heard the voice of the enchantress she undid her long braids all the way to the ground, and the enchantress climbed up by it.

It soon came to pass that the king's son rode through the forest and passed by the tower. Then he heard Rapunzel singing, and it was so beautiful that he stood still and listened. The king's son looked for the door of the tower, but none was to be found. He rode home, but the singing had so deeply touched his heart, that every day he went out into the forest and listened to it. Once when he was thus standing behind a tree, he saw that an enchantress came there, and he heard how she cried:

'Rapunzel, Rapunzel,

Let down your long hair.'

Rapunzel let down the braids of her hair, and the enchantress climbed up to her. 'If that is the only way up, I too will try it,' he said. The next day when it began to grow dark, he went to the tower and cried:

'Rapunzel, Rapunzel,

Let down your long hair.'

Immediately the hair fell down and the king's son climbed up.

At first Rapunzel was terribly frightened, but the king's son began to talk to her quite like a friend, and told her that his heart had been so stirred that he had to see her. Then Rapunzel lost her fear, and when he asked her if she would take him for her husband, she saw that he was young and handsome. She said yes, but that she had no way to get down, since the hair ladder was attached to her head. She told the king's son to bring her silk that she could weave a ladder with, and when it was ready he would take her away.

When the special night arrived, the enchantress had stayed home, suspicious at Rapunzel's barely concealed glee. She heard the king's son calling for Rapunzel and was furious.

'Ah! you wicked child,' cried the enchantress. 'You have deceived me!' In her anger she clutched Rapunzel's beautiful tresses, wrapped them twice round her left hand, seized a pair of scissors with the right, and snip, snap, they were cut off, and the lovely braids lay on the ground.

On the same day that she cast out Rapunzel, however, the enchantress fastened the braids of hair, which she had cut off, to the hook of the window, and when the king's son came and cried:

'Rapunzel, Rapunzel,

Let down your long hair.'

She let the hair down. The king's son ascended, but instead of finding his dearest Rapunzel, he found the enchantress

'Aha!' she cried mockingly, 'Rapunzel is lost to you; you will never see her again.' The king's son was extremely sad, and in his despair he leapt down from the tower.

He escaped with his life, but the thorns into which he fell pierced his eyes. He wandered blind about the forest, weeping over the loss of his wife, but Rapunzel was wandering too, and when they found each other she knew him immediately. She hugged him and wept; two of her tears wetted his eyes and they grew clear again, and he could see with them as before. He led her to his kingdom where he was joyfully received, and they lived for a long time afterwards, happy and contented.

SUBJECT—What is the story about?

The story is about Rapunzel, a girl who an enchantress held hostage because of her magical hair.

TONE—How is the author telling the story?

The author of "Rapunzel" uses a lighthearted tone to tell the story.

To determine tone, it can be helpful to think about what the author's attitude is and to describe that attitude as a feeling. So an author may write in a reflective, wistful, regretful, affectionate or _____ tone. The list goes on.

If you are having a hard time figuring out tone, think of tone in terms of shading in pictures from dark to light. Something funny like The Diary of a Wimpy Kid might have a light tone, something scary or sad like a horror story might have a dark tone, while most articles and textbooks are written with a neutral [middle], gray tone.

The author is using a light to gray voice to describe the actions of the story.

While her voice is unbiased [neutral] when she tells the story, the events in the story are sometimes dark and dangerous. She is not really showing much opinion about what happens to Rapunzel.

EYES—Through whose EYES are we seeing the narrative unfold? Who's seeing the story?

In "Rapunzel" we see the story through Rapunzel's eyes.

To find the EYES, ask yourself:

Who is seeing the story?

A character? (first person)

An outside narrator? (third person limited)

An all-knowing observer? (third person omniscient)

What is THAT person's attitude toward the story?

Remember: Each character has his or her unique attitude [point of view], and each of these might be different from the narrator's attitude, and both of those might be different from what the author thinks. Got that? It's tough at first, but just try to notice who's telling the story, whose EYES we're seeing the story through, and what the author might be trying to tell us about what's going on.

Finally:

What Happened & Why?!

The What Happened it like the THESIS of a work of nonfiction—it's the point of the piece, which in this case is to tell us what happened and why. It's also the most IMPORTANT part of your reading.

Rapunzel is locked up in a tower by an enchantress because her long hair is magically strong. One day, a prince comes and rescues her, and they live happily ever after.

When you read fiction, your job is to follow the narrative like a detective or a reporter. You must follow all the knots and loops of the thread of the story to make sure you notice EVERYTHING and how the EVERYTHING adds up to WHAT HAPPENED!

Come to think of it, that's not a bad way to read all kinds of writing!!

In fiction, this job can be a little tricky because the author is not always making it super clear what happened. Sometimes, because the author is telling the story through the EYES of a certain character, we can't always trust what that character is telling us. Then we have to interpret what that narrator is telling us to figure out what's really happening.

What does this mean?

Does your mom ever ask you a question like:

Are you going to eat your greens?

She isn't really asking you what your plans are and whether or not you really want to eat your greens. She's really TELLING you to EAT YOUR GREENS.

Or did you ever tell your dad:

I don't need the light on...

What you were really probably saying was, "I don't want you to think I need the light on, but I really, really hope you leave it on anyway!"

This is the same thing that happens in fiction. Depending on whose eyes you're seeing the story through, figuring out what's really happening can be tricky.

Like in this passage told through the eyes of a 6th grader:

I didn't care what the bully said. Big Alice didn't scare me. I wasn't leaving the playground because she told me to. Or because I was scared of her. It was just because I knew my grandma wanted me to take out the garbage, and it was probably getting stinky, so I thought it would be a good idea to hurry home. So, I ran out of the playground as fast as my feet could carry me. I was glad to be getting away; I mean getting home to help my grandma!

Can you figure out what's really happening here? How do you know?

LITERARY DEVICES

Just like other people who make things, authors have a toolbox from which to choose. A writer's tools are called *literary devices*. As readers, keeping an eye out for those tools can help us understand what's going on in the story. Why? Because the better we understand what effect the writer is going for, the better we can understand what we read!

For example: if we, as readers, notice that the author is using a tool called **foreshadowing**, we know that the writer wants us to think about what's going to happen later. The writer is signaling the reader: *Hey! Listen up! This part is important!*

Of course, the writer's tools don't stand out as much as we might like. They're always wrapped up in the story, and if we're not paying attention, we'll miss them. That's another reason it's important to be a slow and careful reader.

Below are four of the most common literary devices to look for. Learn them so you can spot them!

- Characterization – The traits that a character displays, including actions and appearance.
  - *Snidely was a sneaky guy. He even looked a little like a weasel.*

- Conflict – The main thing preventing the protagonist [main character] from reaching his or her goal.
  - *Gertrude needed to reach the castle gate, but a giant, angry dragon stood in her way.*
  - *Danny really wanted to ace his tests, but every time the clock started he froze!*

- Mood – The feeling that the passage gives as a whole (i.e., suspenseful, foreboding, comic, soothing, hopeful, light, spooky, etc.)
  - COMIC –
    - *Kids were sitting at their desks picking their noses, making googly eyes and otherwise being knuckleheads. The teachers were yakking like, well, yaks, and the principal was stomping from room to room like a grumpy bear. Meanwhile, poor Danny was trying to concentrate on taking his test.*
  - CALM –
    - *Gertrude rode down into the valley. The soft spring breeze stirred lightly. She breathed in the scent of the newly blossoming flowers and breathed out calmly. The whole world rolled out gently before her.*

- Foreshadowing – Hints about what is going to happen later in the story.
  - *Young Abraham dreamed that he saw two trains on the same railroad track. One was heading north and the other south. They were doomed to collide. When Lincoln awoke, he sat up and exclaimed, "Good thing that never happens!"*

 2nd Ed. © ibidPREP llc

POETRY

Poetry can be imaginative, vivid, deeply felt and deeply thought. The words are usually arranged so that they have a pleasing sound or rhythm (sonnet, limerick, free verse, etc.) or in order to emphasize other particular qualities of the language.

Reading Poetry

Reading poetry even more, not less, than prose, is not about YOUR interpretation of it or what you think you see in the writing. Poetry involves a very precise use of language to make one or several points. Although it is often true that words and lines have more than one meaning, those meanings are what the author intended[6], NOT as readers may loosely guess at them. This is not to say that poets do not leave some things to a reader's imagination or interpretation, but that happens much less often than most students are led to believe and is only a piece of the poetry puzzle.

Once readers acknowledge that *all* the words count and that their meanings are intended by the poet, THEN the reader is free to delve into those meanings and to have a personal response to the material.

One nice thing about poems is that, for the most part, the entire piece is right in front of the reader, just as it is with a painting. Staying focused on the whole and parts of the piece does not require flipping back and forth between pages but rather bearing down on what's immediately in front of you.

Don't worry about how hard it seems; just read it.

Many students are intimidated by poetry. Perhaps this is because there is more prose than poetry in the world. Perhaps this is because we don't read that much poetry in schools. Perhaps this is because poets use literary devices in their writing. Whatever the reason, poetry does not need to be difficult. Although poetry is often denser than prose with more meaning packed into fewer words, as with all complex readings the best way to handle it is to break it down to smaller and smaller pieces and process those! The good thing about most poems is that though they might be densely packed with meaning and images, they are usually much shorter than prose pieces, so you can feel comfortable taking your time to break them down. So when you see a poem on the Hunter Test, you need not get tripped up by it. You need to welcome it like an old friend. (Did you catch that simile? If not, keep reading!)

There <u>are</u> right and wrong ways to read and interpret poetry!

Some students think poetry is fluffy and silly and that there is no right way to decipher it, therefore *anything* they say about poetry is correct. Wrong! Poetry is full of meaning, plots (sometimes), characters (sometimes), imagery and speakers (narrators). And just like in your prose readings, poems make a point. All the clues are there. It's your job to pay close attention to the poem and figure out what the poet (or the speaker) is saying!

Reading Poetry Is not that Different from Reading Prose

Reading poetry is a lot like reading prose: we are still reading for the three T's. We are trying to figure out what the topic of the poem is, what the point the poet is trying to make about her topic and what tone the poet is using in order to get her point across.

Literary Devices

Some questions on the Hunter Test might ask you about the names of these literary devices, but even if they don't, it helps for us to know about them so that we can better decipher poetry. Also, fiction writers and nonfiction writers can use these literary devices too! It's just that they are especially crucial to understanding poetry.

[6] planned, envisioned

1. Metaphor: comparing one thing to another thing not using "like" or "as" *(The fog was a blanket; He was a go-rilla on the basketball court).* One thing actually BECOMES the other: *"She was a pillar of strength."*

2. Simile: comparing one thing to another thing using "like" or "as" *(The fog was thick as a blanket; He was like a gorilla on the basketball court).*

3. Personification: when an idea, object or animal is given human characteristics *(The autumn leaves danced).* Personification can also involve a person becoming the embodiment of something nonhuman *(Kobe is the personification of evil; That nurse was kindness personified).*

4. Hyperbole: obvious and extreme exaggeration that is intended for effect *(I've been waiting here for an eternity).*

5. Imagery: the use of sensory words (sight, sound, smell, taste, feel) to describe an object or person. Many of the poems you'll see on your state tests involve a lot of imagery. Understanding what these images stand for or are meant to convey is HUGE.
    a. *a sky-blue blanket*
    b. *a freezing-cold greeting*

6. Foreshadowing: the author's clues or hints to events that will follow.

7. Alliteration: repetition of initial sounds *(Ask Adam for an apple; Several sweet sounds swooshed over the sea).*

8. Rhyme: regular recurrence of corresponding sounds *(The new plane flew into the deep blue).*

9. Rhythm: the beat; the pattern of stressed and unstressed syllables[7]
    (da – dum – da – dum – da – dum = *to be or not to be*)

10. Onomatopoeia: words that imitate the sounds associated with them *(buzz, beep, zoom).*

---

[7] a unit of sound that forms the whole or a part of a word; e.g., there are two syllables in *glass-es* and three in *blue-berr-y.*

2nd Ed. © ibidPREP llc

Example Poems

Read the following poems and try to answer these questions:
  A) What is the poem about? What is the point of the poem?
  B) What is the tone of the poem?
  C) Do you notice any literary devices at play in this poem?

Bed in Summer

by Robert Louis Stevenson

>   In winter I get up at night
>   And dress by yellow candlelight
>   In summer, quite the other way,
>   I have to go to bed by day.
>
>   I have to go to bed and see
>   The birds still hopping on the tree,
>   Or hear the grown-up people's feet
>   Still going past me in the street.
>
>   And does it not seem hard to you,
>   When all the sky is clear and blue,
>   And I should like so much to play,
>   To have to go to bed by day?

MULTIPLE CHOICE QUESTIONS

1. What does the speaker find to be difficult?
   A. Going to bed while the sun is out
   B. Falling asleep
   C. Finding someone to play with
   D. Not going to bed by yellow candlelight
   E. Finding the outside world as interesting as the bedroom

2. What can be inferred about the speaker's bedtime?
   A. It changes with the seasons.
   B. It is the same time all year.
   C. He has no bedtime.
   D. It is at a different time every day.
   E. It is too early for someone of the speaker's age.

3. Which of the following literary devices is used in the poem?
   A. Simile.
   B. Imagery.
   C. Onomatopoeia.
   D. Foreshadowing.
   E. Hyperbole.

4. We can infer which of the following:
   A. That the speaker is a boy.
   B. That the speaker is a girl.
   C. That the speaker is young.
   D. That the speaker lives close to the equator.
   E. That the speaker is a prisoner.

5. In the second stanza, the speaker mentions hopping birds and grown-ups walking by. This serves to:
   A. Show what is going on while the speaker is in bed.
   B. Show why it is too loud for the speaker to fall asleep.
   C. Show that the speaker fears birds and grown-ups.
   D. Show that everything outside is actually fairly boring.
   E. Show that birds are always allowed to stay up later than children.

Vespers[8]

By A.A. Milne

Little Boy kneels at the foot of the bed,
Droops on the little hands little gold head.
Hush! Hush! Whisper who dares!
Christopher Robin is saying his prayers.

God bless Mummy. I know that's right.
Wasn't it fun in the bath to-night?
The cold's so cold, and the hot's so hot.
Oh! God bless Daddy - I quite forgot.

If I open my fingers a little bit more,
I can see Nanny's dressing-gown on the door.
It's a beautiful blue, but it hasn't a hood.
Oh! God bless Nanny and make her good.

Mine has a hood, and I lie in bed,
And pull the hood right over my head,
And I shut my eyes, and I curl up small,
And nobody knows that I'm there at all.

Oh! Thank you, God, for a lovely day.
And what was the other I had to say?
I said "Bless Daddy," so what can it be?
Oh! Now I remember it. God bless Me.

Little Boy kneels at the foot of the bed,
Droops on the little hands little gold head.
Hush! Hush! Whisper who dares!
Christopher Robin is saying his prayers.

---

[8] Evening prayers

2nd Ed. © ibidPREP llc

1. The first and second stanzas are different from each other in which way?
    A. They have different rhyme patterns.
    B. They are spoken by different people.
    C. The first is more poetic than the second.
    D. They have different opinions about religion.
    E. They take place at different times of the day.

2. Why does Christopher Robin cover his head with the hood?
    A. To feel warmer.
    B. To help him focus on his prayers.
    C. To feel like nobody can see him.
    D. To make his nanny jealous because she does not have a hood.
    E. To make it easier to fall asleep.

3. What color hair can we infer that Christopher Robin has?
    A. Blonde
    B. Red
    C. Black
    D. Brown
    E. White

4. During what time of day does the poem take place?
    A. Morning
    B. Afternoon
    C. Tea time
    D. Dinner time
    E. Night

5. Christopher Robin does not ask God to bless:
    A. His nanny.
    B. Anyone.
    C. His friend.
    D. Himself.
    E. His mummy (mom).

PLAYS

Reading a play can be intimidating. There are capital letters and italics everywhere, and it's hard to tell where everybody is. The trick to remember is that plays aren't *really* meant to be read. Instead, they're guidelines for actors and directors to perform the play. Plays, like movies and TV shows, are meant to be seen!

But how helpful is that? You're stuck at a desk with sheets of paper and there's no way you can leave to go watch a play. So what do you do? **Imagine** the play in your head!

That's easier than it sounds because the playwright—the person who wrote the play—gives you clues about what the performance should look like.

The first clues to look for are called **stage directions**. Stage directions are written in *italics*. In these directions playwrights tell you where the scene takes place, who is involved, what the characters are wearing, what time of day it is and other important details about the setting and situation. Like all directions, do not ignore these! They tell a lot!

Try reading the scene below. Read the stage directions and try to imagine the setting and what's happening as you go. See the show in your head [close your eyes if you have to!]

EXAMPLE—Dramatic Text

from **He Said and She Said** by Alice Gerstenberg

[Living-room at the Haldemans. Enid Haldeman, the woman of the house, tidying and cleaning the room. Felix Haldeman, her husband, enters in hat and coat and jingling a bunch of house keys. He kisses Enid affectionately as if it were a daily habit and then tosses down the evening newspaper.]

FELIX: Hello, dear.

ENID: Felix, I asked Diana and Mrs. Packard over for dinner. You'd better hurry and wash up a bit.

FELIX: What? Am I to be the only man again?

ENID: Can't help it, darling. Mr. Packard's in Washington and all of Diana's suitors are in the trenches.

FELIX: There must be some old greybeard left somewhere to invite for Diana.

ENID: Oh, there are a few left-overs floating around but Diana doesn't like them. If she can't get the best male company she prefers female.

FELIX: Diana's a peach! She should have married one of the boys before they all went over. Poor Aubrey Laurence was madly in love with her.

ENID: Hurry up, there's soot on your cheek. *[She taps it affectionately.]*

FELIX: All right, if I have to dine with three women I'd better look my best. *[Exit down left.]*

Did you picture a living room? Did you see Enid dusting and straightening things? Could you imagine Felix wearing a coat and hat and playing with his keys? If you did, then you just read a play!

2ⁿᵈ Ed. © ibidPREP llc

Try it now with a slightly more complex scene and then answer the questions afterwards

Dramatic Text: PETER PAN Scene

(The nursery window is blown open, probably by the smallest and therefore most mischievous star, and PETER PAN *flies into the room.)*

PETER (in *a whisper)*: Tinker Bell. Tink, are you there? *(A jug lights up.)* Oh, do come out of that jug. (TINK *flashes hither and thither.)* Do you know where they put it? *(The answer comes as of a tinkle of bells; it is the fairy language.)* Which big box? This one? But which drawer? Yes, do show me.

TINK *pops into the drawer where the shadow is, but before* PETER *can reach it,* WENDY *moves in her sleep. He flies onto the mantel shelf and sits. Then, as she didn't wake, he flies to the drawer and scatters its contents to the floor. In his joy at finding his shadow, he forgets that he has closed* TINK *in the drawer. He sits on the floor with the shadow, confident that he and it will join like drops of water; they don't. Then he tries to stick it on with soap from the bathroom, and this failing also, he sits dejectedly on the floor. This wakes* WENDY.

WENDY (courteously): Boy, why are you crying?

(He jumps up and, crossing to the foot of the bed, bows. WENDY, *impressed, bows to him from the bed.)*

PETER: What is your name?

WENDY *(pleased to be saying it)*: Wendy Moira Angela Darling. What is yours?

PETER *(finding his own name too brief)*: Peter Pan.

WENDY: Is that all?

PETER *(biting his lip)*: Yes.

WENDY *(politely)*: I am so sorry.

PETER: It doesn't matter.

WENDY: Where do you live?

PETER: Second star to the right and then straight on till morning.

WENDY: What a funny address!

PETER: No, it isn't.

WENDY: I mean, is that what they put on the letters?

PETER: Don't get any letters.

WENDY: But your mother gets letters?

PETER: Don't have a mother.

WENDY: No wonder you were crying.

PETER: I wasn't crying. But I can't get my shadow to stick on.

WENDY: It has come off! How awful. *(Looking at the spot where he had lain.)* Peter, you have been trying to stick it on with soap!

PETER *(snappily)*: Well then?

WENDY: It must be sewn on.

PETER: What is 'sewn'?

WENDY: You are dreadfully ignorant.

PETER: No, I'm not.

WENDY: I will sew it on for you, my little man. But we must have more light. *(She touches something, and to his astonishment the room lights up.)* Sit here. I'm afraid it will hurt a little.

PETER *(a recent remark of hers bugging him)*: I never cry. *(She seems to attach the shadow. He tests it.)* It isn't quite itself yet.

WENDY: Perhaps I should have ironed it.

The shadows wakes and is as glad to be back with Peter as he is to have it. He and his shadow dance together. He is showing off now. He crows like a rooster.

PETER: Wendy, look, look; oh the cleverness of me!

WENDY: You conceit. Of course I did nothing!

PETER: You did a little.

2nd Ed. © ibidPREP llc

MULTIPLE CHOICE QUESTIONS

1. Read the following sentence from the passage:

   He sits on the floor with the shadow, confident that he and it will join like drops of water. Then he tries to stick it on with soap from the bathroom, and this failing also, he sits dejectedly on the floor.

   In the above stage direction, the word "dejectedly" most nearly means:
   A. sleepily.
   B. clumsily.
   C. angrily.
   D. sadly.
   E. lazily.

2. Peter is most likely feeling "astonishment" when the room lights up because:
   A. He does not know how electricity works.
   B. He is afraid he will be caught.
   C. He needs the light to find his shadow.
   D. He is jealous of Wendy.
   E. He did not think Wendy's house had electricity.

3. Peter most likely cries because:
   A. He misses his mother.
   B. He is lonely.
   C. He wasn't crying.
   D. He has shut Tinkerbell in a drawer.
   E. He can't get his shadow to stick on.

4. Read the following lines from the passage:

   PETER. Wendy, look, look; oh the cleverness of me!

   WENDY. You conceit. Of course I did nothing!

   PETER. You did a little.

   The word "conceit," as used in these lines, most nearly means:
   A. jerk.
   B. braggart.
   C. boy.
   D. thief.
   E. ingrate.

5. Peter most likely sits on the mantel in order to:
   A. Survey the room.
   B. Find Tinkerbell.
   C. Hide from Wendy.
   D. Find some soap.
   E. Get a better look at Wendy.

6. Peter most likely comes to the nursery to
   A. See it for the first time.
   B. Invite Wendy to come visit him where he lives.
   C. Find Tinkerbell.
   D. Ask Wendy to sew his shadow back on.
   E. Find his shadow.

7. Through this scene, the author conveys which idea?
   A. Though Peter seems full of himself, he is actually insecure.
   B. Though Wendy is afraid of Peter, she conquers her fear.
   C. The Darling family should probably lock their windows.
   D. Though Peter and Wendy are different, they find a way to become friends.
   E. Peter probably lost his shadow because he was too arrogant.

Mr. Badger (from *The Wind in the Willows*)

The Mole and the Rat waited patiently for what seemed a very long time, stamping in the snow to keep their feet warm. At last they heard the sound of slow, shuffling footsteps approaching the door from the inside. It seemed, as the Mole remarked to the Rat, as if someone were walking in carpet slippers that were too large for him; which was intelligent of Mole, because that is exactly what it was.

There was the noise of a bolt shot back, and the door opened a few inches, enough to show a long snout and a pair of sleepy blinking eyes.

'Now, the VERY next time this happens,' said a gruff and suspicious voice, 'I shall be exceedingly angry. Who is it THIS time, disturbing people on such a night? Speak up!'

'Oh, Badger,' cried the Rat, 'let us in, please. It's me, Rat, and my friend Mole, and we've lost our way in the snow.'

'What, Ratty, my dear little man!' exclaimed the Badger, in quite a different voice. 'Come along in, both of you, at once. Why, you must be perished. Well I never! Lost in the snow! And in the Wild Wood, too, and at this time of night! But come in with you.'

The two animals tumbled over each other in their eagerness to get inside, and heard the door shut behind them with great joy and relief.

The Badger, who wore a long dressing-gown, and whose slippers were indeed too large for him, carried a flat candlestick in his paw and had probably been on his way to bed when their summons sounded. He looked kindly down on them and patted both their heads. 'This is not the sort of night for small animals to be out,' he said paternally. 'I'm afraid you've been up to some of your pranks again, Ratty. But come along; come into the kitchen. There's a first-rate fire there, and supper and everything.'

He shuffled on in front of them, carrying the light, and they followed him, nudging each other in an anticipating sort of way, down a long, gloomy, and, to tell the truth, decidedly shabby passage, into a sort of a central hall; out of which they could dimly see other long tunnel-like passages branching, passages mysterious and without apparent end. But there were doors in the hall as well—stout oaken comfortable-looking doors. One of these the Badger flung open, and at once they found themselves in all the glow and warmth of a large fire-lit kitchen.

Mr. Badger—STEW
In complete sentences, please use the text to answer the following questions.

What is the SUBJECT of the passage [what is it about]?

_____

_____

Describe the TONE of the passage [think of dark to light]:

_____

The EYES of this passage belong to [whose eyes are we seeing the story through?]

_____

The WHAT HAPPENED & WHY of this passage are [in other words, WHY is this story worth telling?]

_____

_____

1. What causes the Rat and the Mole to visit Mr. Badger at the beginning of the story?
   A. They want to irritate him as a fun prank.
   B. They are hungry and think he has food and drink for them.
   C. They need to tell him something urgent.
   D. They need protection from wild animal predators.
   E. They lost their way in a bout of bad weather.

2. What is the reason Mr. Badger's voice changes?
   A. He has a cold so his voice is hoarse.
   B. He cannot believe the Rat and the Mole got lost.
   C. He recognizes his friend the Rat and speaks jovially.
   D. He becomes angrier that the Rat and the Mole woke him up.
   E. He sees they are in a hurry and speaks more quickly.

3. What do the Rat and the Mole do when Mr. Badger fully opens the door?
    A. They leave and find their way home.
    B. They scramble to get inside as quickly as possible.
    C. They walk through the door slowly and with trepidation.
    D. They thank him profusely and express their embarrassment.
    E. They thanked him for his generosity but found somewhere else.

4. What does the story suggest is most likely to happen next?
    A. Mr. Badger will feed them a warm, nourishing meal.
    B. Mr. Badger will kick them back out into the snow.
    C. Mr. Badger will give them warmer clothes.
    D. The Rat and the Mole will steal food from Mr. Badger's house.
    E. The Rat and the Mole will figure out how they got lost.

5. Which of the following best describes the tone of the story?
    A. Scary
    B. Angry
    C. Satirical
    D. Fantastical
    E. Serious

6. In the first paragraph the Mole tells the Rat that he hears someone with overlarge slippers behind the door. This tells the reader which of the following?
    A. The Mole judges others before he gets to know them.
    B. The Rat is someone who can't hear very well.
    C. Mr. Badger does not know how to shop for shoes.
    D. The Mole has unusually large ears.
    E. The Mole has unusually good hearing.

A SMALL BOY VISITS A MAMMOTH CAVE

When I was a kid I wanted to be a *spelunker*, which is just a fancy word for someone who goes into caves. So when I was in fourth grade and my family was taking a car trip to the Midwest from Virginia, I convinced my parents to stop at Mammoth Cave National Park in Kentucky.

Mammoth Cave is the longest known system of caves in the world. Located around the intersections of many big rivers in the hilly regions of central Kentucky, the cave's network of tunnels goes on for almost 400 miles. Every year that number grows as new outlets and passages are discovered.

My family and I arrived on a hot summer day, and I was eager to be a regular Tom Sawyer and get lost in a big cave. Unfortunately, the underground part of the park was already closed for the day, so we had to make do with some light, evening hiking through the forests along the river. That didn't excite me because I could walk through trees anywhere.

The next day also started with some disappointment. I had expected a big, unguarded hole in the ground that

I could run down as fast I could with only a flashlight to guide me. Instead, the place was very institutionalized. Nobody was going to get in without buying a ticket, and nobody was going to go anywhere down there without a guide. Period.

Worse, being a smidgy little fourth grader, I was too young to go on the mega, day-long expeditions through exciting sounding slits in the rock with names like Tall Man's Misery and Fat Man's Agony. No, I was going to be shuffling along with a great big crowd of tourists in fanny packs, just like everyone else.

We all huddled into a metal freight elevator which immediately began its rumbling flight down a tunnel cut out of the rock itself. With every yard we went down, the air cooled more and more until it felt like the cave was a massive refrigerator, and we were the food.

When the elevator clattered to a halt, our guide switched off the light before opening the door. The darkness was total. It had no shine, no layers, not one variation in its perfect black. Were it not for the alarmed voices of the other tourists, I would have thought myself all alone in the universe.

"Ready?" asked the operator. From the new location of his voice I could tell he had left the elevator. His voice echoed.

Then he pulled a big switch and the sound of clicking circuits ricocheted far away.

From that cramped darkness emerged an enormous hall of rock spanning hundreds of yards away from us. Jagged stalactites[9] hung down from the ceiling, some even merging with stalagmites coming up from the cave floor. And in the light we could see that everything was a different amazing color.

I was hooked. I've been obsessed with caves ever since. I may not spend much time spelunking, but I am a spelunker at heart. Unfortunately, many of the world's caves are in trouble. Their main residents—bats—are dying in the millions due to a poorly understood fungus commonly called White Nose Syndrome. Humans spread it, so many caves are now closed by the park service. As more and more caves may be closed in the future, now is the time to take advantage of these amazing worlds beneath our own.

Since this is a MEMOIR, in complete sentences, please use info from the text to find the STEW in the passage.

What is the SUBJECT of the passage [what is it about]?

_____

_____

Describe the TONE of the passage [think of dark to light]:

_____

[9] Downward-hanging mineral-rock formations

The EYES of this passage belong to [whose eyes are we seeing the story through?]

_____

The WHAT HAPPENED & WHY of this passage are [in other words, WHY is this story worth telling?]

_____

_____

1. The author says that the network of caves is known to be almost 400 miles long but that that length is growing every year. The author suggests which of the following reasons for that growth:
   A. Heavy rains are eroding soil and rock at the ends of the cave.
   B. Humans are discovering previously unknown passages.
   C. Climate change is changing the composition of the rock.
   D. Spelunkers are getting better at taking measurements.
   E. Humans are extending passages to improve tourists' experiences.

2. Which of the following is an example of spelunking?
   A. A young girl going to Kentucky to see the horses run the Kentucky Derby.
   B. A middle-aged man imitating his favorite fictional character.
   C. A Navy SEAL scuba diving into an underwater cave.
   D. An old farmer exploring a forest on his land.
   E. A city worker fixing a sewer line under the street.

3. Why is the narrator initially disappointed with Mammoth Cave?
   A. He won't be able to explore the cave on his own.
   B. The cave is too small.
   C. Caves just aren't really that great.
   D. Mammoth Cave was actually just a forest.
   E. It's not much like the cave Tom Sawyer explored.

4. How would the narrator's visit be different if he were a grown-up instead of a kid?
   A. He would be unable to squeeze through really tight passages.
   B. He would find caves really boring.
   C. He would be able to explore newly found passages of the cave.
   D. He would be at a high risk for spreading White Nose Syndrome.
   E. He would be able to join a much more advanced tour of the cave.

2nd Ed. © ibidPREP llc

5. Why does the author eventually like Mammoth Cave?
   A. It helps him conquer his fear of the dark.
   B. He discovers how big and beautiful it is inside.
   C. Being scared teaches him what's important.
   D. He really likes touching the stalactites.
   E. It makes him feel more content with life above ground.

6. The author suggests that caves are in trouble for which of the following reasons:
   A. Not enough tourists are interested in visiting them.
   B. They are too dangerous for people to explore safely.
   C. Disease threatens the bats who live in caves.
   D. People are now too tall and large to maintain the hard-to-reach parts of caves.
   E. Lighting them with electricity disrupts the ecosystem of the caves.

7. What does "institutionalized" most closely mean as it is used in the fourth paragraph?
   A. The park is really just one big gift shop now.
   B. Every aspect of the park is subject to rules and regulations.
   C. The cave has been physically altered to meet human needs.
   D. The cave is in trouble because of White Nose Syndrome.
   E. The cave has been outfitted with all the conveniences of home.

WATCHING A CRAFTSMAN

I was very scared. Maurice was feeding boards into a kind of saw that was totally new to me, and its blade was *very* visible. It was also very near his hands.

It was early July, and I had been working for the past two weeks as Maurice's assistant in his woodshop. The shop was located at the top of a big green hill on his farm and offered a tremendous view of a healthy valley and rolling hills covered in corn and soy.

Maurice's farm was just his hobby. His true love—and income—was in his shop. He made fine furniture, instruments, and model airplanes, and he made them perfectly. In his farmhouse just down the lane was a harpsichord exactly like one on display at the Metropolitan Museum of Art. The director of a rival museum in Washington had heard about the masterpiece, came to test it for himself, and commissioned another one on the spot.

That project was still in its very early phase, which was why Maurice needed my help. Not that I knew a thing about building anything; I can barely change a light bulb! Instead, he needed me to hold stuff and, later, if I was lucky, hand him stuff.

Today I was holding the back end of those big boards as Maurice fed them into the saw, which was called a planer. Maurice had somehow located a supply of cypress wood, which is amazing because the tree is highly protected.

Maurice was such a perfectionist that he trusted no one to make his lumber for him. So these boards we were pushing through the planer were huge and very rough. Over the next several days we passed each one through many times, taking off a tiny amount of sawdust with each pass. This way we could be sure we didn't damage the wood in any way.

Next we started to work on the wood that would form the soundboard. The soundboard is a very thin piece of wood in a piano or harpsichord or similar instrument that is placed in such a way that it magnifies the sound made by the player. It would be a long time before we would be ready to make the soundboard itself, but Maurice wanted to get the lumber ready while he had me to help him.

Just when I thought the whine of the saw was going to drive me crazy, Maurice turned off the saw and blew some sweet-smelling cypress dust out of his moustache. He lit his pipe. "Yeah," he said. "I think it's time for a break."

We went out in the fresh air and sat down on a bench overlooking the lush valley. I picked idly at some sap on my palms and waited for Maurice to speak. This was my favorite part of the day.

"The harpsichord is a way to make the past live again. The model for this harpsichord—all harpsichords really—is based on the genius of a people who no longer exist. The Flemish. Today their country is split up among the French, the Belgians, and the Dutch. We cannot visit them nor can we speak with a Flemish man, but by making their instrument the way they made it, I can learn how they thought. They were brilliant craftsmen."

One of Maurice's cows mooed at us and strolled away to find some shade. Covered in sawdust, tired to the bone, and wholly inspired, it occurred to me that I was learning more from Maurice than I did in school. Perhaps, if Maurice would accept me as an apprentice, I would not return to school at summer's end.

Since this is a MEMOIR, in complete sentences, please use info from the text to find the STEW in the passage.

What is the SUBJECT of the passage [what is it about]?

_____

_____

Describe the TONE of the passage [think of dark to light]:

_____

The EYES of this passage belong to [whose eyes are we seeing the story through?]

_____

The WHAT HAPPENED & WHY of this passage are [in other words, WHY is this story worth telling?]

_____

_____

MULTIPLE CHOICE QUESTIONS

1. The narrator had been planning to stop working for the craftsman when:
    A. Summer ended.
    B. The two had taken a trip to Flanders.
    C. The soundboard was completed.
    D. Maurice no longer needed him.
    E. He got tired of building things.

2. Mentioning the director of the museum in Washington serves:
    A. To build suspense.
    B. To show where the story takes place.
    C. To explain why the narrator is interested in working with Maurice.
    D. No purpose. The director should not be mentioned at all.
    E. To show just how skilled Maurice must be.

3. What can be inferred about the quality of store-bought lumber?
    A. It is overpriced.
    B. It's better than any lumber one could make at home.
    C. It is not up to Maurice's high standards.
    D. None of the kinds of wood available at the store are suitable for a harpsichord.
    E. The best lumber sells out too quickly to be relied on.

4. Which of the following is the best description of the role of the soundboard?
    A. It serves to muffle unwanted sounds.
    B. It prevents the harpsichord from collapsing under its own weight.
    C. It makes the player louder than she otherwise would be.
    D. It holds the sheet music so the player can read it.
    E. It is struck like a drum to produce each musical note.

5. Why does Maurice appreciate making harpsichords?
    A. It helps him to understand a lost society.
    B. He thinks it is the most beautiful of instruments.
    C. It is the instrument he plays best.
    D. He needs the money to support his farm.
    E. He craves fame and respect from museumgoers.

6. What does "commissioned" most closely mean as it is used in the third paragraph?
    A. Left with
    B. Hired Maurice to build
    C. Played
    D. Inspected
    E. Measured

Nuts & Bolts of Reading

1. Read the passage.
2. Keep reading until you've got your three T's. Usually you'll know your Theme and Thesis by the first few sentences of the **second** paragraph, but sometimes the author doesn't spit it out until much later. Hang in!
    a. Make sure you are clear on what the topic truly is [THEME]: just because they're talking about *bananas*, it doesn't mean that the topic is really *bananas*.
    b. Make sure you are clear on what the author's viewpoint is [THESIS]. Look out for the "but." Just because the author writes "most people think bananas," it doesn't mean the author thinks "bananas." In fact, he probably thinks "not bananas."
3. Once you've established what the "but" **and/or** author's point is, you will see that every body paragraph is designed to support that point.
4. Occasionally, authors will devote a body paragraph to an opposite example—something that seems to disagree with their point of view. Authors do this in order to:
    a. Seem fair—they want to create the appearance of examining all sides of an argument and of demonstrating their awareness of all sides of an argument or
    b. Strengthen their point—by raising and then ultimately rejecting opposing points of view, authors ultimately hope to make their own points of view look better.
5. Most passages make one and only one main point, and most of the questions depend on your being aware of what that point is.
6. Once you are done reading, follow this process for answering questions:
    a. Read the question,
    b. Paraphrase[10] the question so as to be sure you know what it's asking,
    c. Determine *your* answer to the question. If you don't have one, look back to the passage (especially and most definitely if the question is about a specific DETAIL). Don't flip back to the question until you've figured something out.
    d. Once you have an answer in mind:
        i. Read the answers given.
        ii. Eliminate any answers that seem wrong right off the bat.
        iii. If you find your answer during your first read-through of the answers—pick it.
        iv. If you don't find the answer you want but have one or two choices left, look closely at the remaining answers and try to find one or two words in an answer that would make it ***wrong***.
        v. If you are still left with more than one answer choice, pick the answer that seems the most limited [with words like *some*, *often*, *occasionally*, etc.] and the most like previous answers to other questions in the section. And then,
        vi. Move on! Remember, the longer you spend on a reading comprehension question the more likely you are to get the question wrong anyway, SO save time, energy and points and GTHOOT![11]

---

[10] put in your own words
[11] Get the Heck Out of There!

2nd Ed. © ibidPREP llc

NOW LET'S PRACTICE ALL THESE GREAT IDEAS ABOUT READING ON THE PASSAGE BELOW

Reading Passage One

Fog

To many people, nothing is more troublesome than a dense fog in a large town. It paralyzes traffic, it is dangerous to pedestrians, it chokes the asthmatic, and chills the weak-lunged.

On the sea, too, the fog is disagreeable and fraught with danger. In its deep, somber note, the foghorn is heard from the lighthouse tower onshore, and its roaming light struggles to catch the eye of ships sailing past.

The presence of fog has played a key role in strategic battles throughout history. Armies have concealed their escape or arrival by its haziness, but then they have had to contend with the fog during the battle as well.

Sometimes during a foggy day, the sun will be dimly seen through a thinner portion, like the moon under an eclipse. But what is fog? How is it formed?

Fog can be considered a type of low-lying cloud and is heavily influenced by nearby bodies of water, topography and wind conditions. In turn, fog has affected many human activities, such as shipping, travel, and warfare. By definition, fog reduces visibility, whereas mist is easier to see through.

Fog begins to form when water vapor condenses into tiny liquid water droplets suspended in the air. First, water vapor begins to condense on particles made of dust, ice, or salt to form clouds. These clouds become fog when a cool air mass is trapped underneath a warm air mass.

Fog normally occurs when the air is fully saturated with water (100% humidity). However, fog can also form at lower humidities, and can sometimes fail to form with a humidity of 100%. Fog can form suddenly and can dissipate just as rapidly. The sudden formation of fog is known as "flash fog." In addition, fog commonly produces precipitation in the form of drizzle or very light snow.

Fortunately, we have methods of dealing with fog, like lighthouses, fog lights on cars, foghorns, and even anti-fog glasses. Still, many lives are lost each year worldwide from accidents involving fog conditions on the highways, and civilian airports often delay flights when fog is present. As much as we have tried to address it, fog stubbornly remains a thorn in our side.

THEME—What is this passage about?

_____

_____

THESIS—What is the main point of the passage?

_____

_____

Practice

TONE—What is the tone of the piece and what type of writing is this, most probably?

_____

_____

MULTIPLE CHOICE QUESTIONS

1. Which of the following is not offered as a way fog can be dangerous?
   A. Fog can cause bad traffic accidents.
   B. Fog can make airplane travel and landings unsafe.
   C. Fog can cause ships to crash into land and sink.
   D. Fog can worsen the illnesses of those already sick.
   E. Fog can make you think things are closer than they really are.

2. What does the author suggest is necessary for fog to form?
   A. A nearby body of water
   B. Salt in the air
   C. A steep hill
   D. Humidity in the air
   E. Lots of wind

3. What role do particles of ice, dust or salt play in the fog formation process?
   A. They become absorbed by water particles.
   B. They engage in a chemical reaction with oxygen in the air.
   C. They help break apart clouds so they can reassemble as fog.
   D. They give water vapor a landing spot on which condensation can occur.
   E. They can change the shape, color, and opacity of different types of fog.

4. Why does the author mention drizzle and light snow?
   A. The author is listing different kinds of things water can do in the atmosphere.
   B. To discuss the types of precipitation that can make fog dissipate (go away).
   C. To mention some weather-related side effects of fog.
   D. The author thinks they are the most pleasant types of weather.
   E. To show that all precipitation is basically the same.

5. What can we infer about the author's attitude toward fog?
   A. The author finds it fascinating to study.
   B. The author has no opinion about it one way or another.
   C. The author thinks all military operations should try and use fog for their battles.
   D. The author dislikes fog for its hazards and gloominess.
   E. The author loves watching ships from lighthouses on the shore.

2nd Ed. © ibidPREP llc

Let's try practicing some more with the readings below. Since this is nonfiction, please find the theme, thesis and tone of the piece!

THE MOON LANDING HOAX CONSPIRACY

On July 20, 1969, the world watched on television with bated breath as Neil Armstrong appeared live from the surface of the moon. "One small step for man;" he said, "one giant leap for mankind." A few days before the landing, on July 16, many had also watched the spacecraft lift off from the NASA center on the east coast of Florida, but few could envision what it would be like to see the space landing.

In completing this mission, Armstrong and fellow astronaut Buzz Aldrin ended a decade-and-a-half-long "space race" with the Soviet Union to land a human successfully on the moon and to return him safely to earth. This accomplishment not only fulfilled a goal President John F. Kennedy proposed in 1961 but also incited the imagination, pride and excitement of all Americans.

About seven years later, however, former U.S. Navy officer Bill Kaysing publicly questioned the legitimacy of this claim. Did we really land on the moon? he asked. People had seen it with their own eyes on TV, but what did that prove? Technology had advanced so quickly; who was to say that they couldn't have faked a landing to appear superior to the Soviets during the Cold War? He thought it likely that Apollo 11 did take off, but he believed it only circled the moon before returning to earth.

Kaysing self-published *We Never Went to the Moon* in 1976, and there have been roughly 20 additional conspiracy theorists to produce literature on the subject since. Many pointed to similar elements of the televised moon landing that they thought looked suspect. For example, the American flag that the astronauts planted on the moon waved and fluttered, as though in a breeze. Since there is no air in the moon's atmosphere, theorists point to this as evidence. Other elements include missing cameras, a starless-looking sky, a lack of a dust cloud around Apollo 11, multidirectional shadows, too-clear footprints, and more.

While historians and other experts have given their refutations of these claims, these rumors persist. Take the issue of the flag: scientists have explained that the wave fluttered from residual inertia—Armstrong had just unfurled it. All such concerns have been fully accounted for, including those which deny that the spacecraft ever even left earth.

Some scholars note that these rumors began proliferating after the Richard Nixon/Watergate scandal, when American citizens were inclined to distrust official government accounts. Whatever the reason, the fact that these conspiracies still circulate show how unfounded suspicion can be put to powerful, potentially destructive use.

THEME—What is this passage about?

_____

_____

THESIS—What is the main point of the passage?

_____

_____

Practice

_____

_____

1. With which of the following statements would the author of this passage most likely agree?
    A. Bill Kaysing makes a lot of valid points that, while controversial, should be seriously considered.
    B. Most likely, the television footage of the spaceship takeoff at NASA is genuine, but the video of Armstrong on the moon is faked.
    C. The rapid technological developments of the 1960s were the main reason the Apollo 11 mission happened.
    D. Even though many writers have made a lot of noise in support of the "moon landing hoax" theory, it is unlikely that Apollo 11's moon landing was faked.
    E. The moon landing was ultimately a fairly inconsequential event, so whether or not it really happened doesn't matter.

2. Why does the author of the passage provide the details about the moving flag in paragraphs 4 and 5?
    A. To paint a picture of what the moon landing footage looks like.
    B. To give an example of a concern raised by conspiracy theorists.
    C. To show that there is air in the moon's atmosphere.
    D. To explain the level of patriotism involved in the Apollo 11 mission.
    E. To help explain why Armstrong planted it.

3. According to the passage, what was the greatest significance of the moon landing?
    A. It was televised live for anyone to see.
    B. It made Americans proud of their country.
    C. It broadcasted an image of strength to the Soviet Union.
    D. It sparked a series of conspiracy theories.
    E. There is not enough information provided to know.

4. "Legitimacy," as it is used in the third paragraph, most closely means which of the following?
    A. Legality
    B. Validity
    C. Justice
    D. Sincerity
    E. Believability

5. What was the author's main purpose for writing this piece?
    A. To argue against the idea that the moon landing was faked.
    B. To paint a picture of the moon landing for those who were not alive to see it on television.
    C. To describe a story that runs contrary to general opinion, and suggest its plausibility.
    D. To describe the United States' relationship with the Soviet Union in the 60s.
    E. To valorize Kaysing for the series of theories that he set in motion.

2nd Ed. © ibidPREP llc

6. Which of the following, if true, would most undermine the writer's thesis?
    A. The Soviet Union beat the United States in the race both to launch a satellite into space and to put the first human in space.
    B. In the past ten years, several new books raising suspicion of the moon landing have been published.
    C. Neil Armstrong agreed to do an interview with Bill Kaysing, which is included in his book.
    D. NASA experts cannot explain why the footage of Neil Armstrong on the moon does not show stars in the sky.
    E. The moon landing actually occurred on July 19, 1969.

7. Read the following sentence from the passage.

    This accomplishment not only fulfilled a goal President John F. Kennedy proposed in 1961, but also incited the imagination, pride and excitement of all Americans.

    In the sentence, the word "incited" most nearly means:
    A. Aggravated
    B. Enflamed
    C. Inspired
    D. Provoked
    E. Instigated

ANNIE BESANT—AN AUTOBIOGRAPHY

My earliest personal recollections are of a house and garden that we lived in when I was three and four years of age, situated in St. John's Wood, Northwest London. I can still recall my mother hovering around the dinner table to see that all was right for her homeward husband; my older brother and I watching for Papa. I remember the loving welcome and the game of romps that always preceded the dinner with our parents.

We were very close, and we took our family dinners seriously. On the 1st of October, 1851, I jumped up in my little cot and shouted out triumphantly, "Papa! Mama! I am four years old!" And my brother, a sage six-year-old, made a grave demand by asking at dinner for me, "May not Annie have a knife today, as she is four years old?"

It was a sore grievance during that same year, 1851, that I was judged too young to go to the Great Exhibition. I have a faint memory of my brother consolingly bringing me home one of those folding pictured strips that are sold in the streets, on which were such beautiful pictures that it only increased my longing to have gone.

But these are all far-away, dusky, trivial memories. What a pity it is that we cannot retain our impressions of the world during infancy, what the feeling was as strange shapes became familiar objects and people. If only memory would not become a mist when we strive to throw our glances backward into the darkness of our childhood, what lessons might we learn about ourselves, about all of humanity?

The next scene that stands out clearly against the background of the past is that of my father's death-bed. About the middle of August, 1852, he got stuck in the rain for a long time, and the thorough wetting resulted in a severe cold, which "settled on his chest." After a brief while, this cold turned out to be consumption, and he only had a few weeks to live. I was led to my parents' bedroom and lifted onto their bed to "say good-bye to dear Papa." It was the day before his death, and I remember being frightened at his eyes which looked so large, and his voice which sounded so strange, as he made me promise always to be "a very good girl to darling Mama, as Papa was going right away."

He died the following day, October 5th, and I do not think that my brother and I—who were staying at our grandfather's—went to the house again until the day of the funeral. With the death, my mother broke down and locked herself into her room for the night. I have heard that the love between my father and mother was a very beautiful thing, and it most certainly stamped her character for life. On the following morning her mother, at last persuading her to open the door, saw her and cried, "Good God, Emily! your hair is white!" And it was so—her hair, black, glossy and abundant, which contrasted with her large gray eyes, had turned gray in that night of agony, and in my memory my mother's face is forever framed in exquisite bands of hair as white as the unsullied snow.

In complete sentences, please use the text to answer the Three T's.

THEME—What is this passage about?

_____

_____

THESIS—What is the main point of the passage?

_____

_____

TONE—What is the tone of the piece and what type of writing is this, most probably?

_____

_____

MULTIPLE CHOICE QUESTIONS

1. The narrator of this passage could best be described as
   A. flippant
   B. miserable
   C. narrow-minded
   D. passionate
   E. sunny

2. As used in paragraph 3, "consolingly" means
   A. gravely
   B. soothingly
   C. off-handedly
   D. reassuringly
   E. mockingly

2nd Ed. © ibidPREP llc

3. In the last sentence of the 4th paragraph, the narrator suggests that
    A. if we had perfect memories, we would have a better understanding of human psychology.
    B. memories alter as time goes on.
    C. everyone has a childhood filled with pain and difficulty.
    D. thinking about the past will only result in confusion.
    E. no one can control which events they will remember and which they will forget.

4. The narrator becomes frightened of her father (5th paragraph) because
    A. she understands he is nearing death.
    B. he has asked her to make a promise she can't keep.
    C. she knows her father is mad at her.
    D. she is worried she will catch her father's illness.
    E. his physical appearance has dramatically worsened since his illness.

5. The description of the narrator's mother in the sixth paragraph suggests that
    A. the narrator cannot understand her mother's actions.
    B. her mother is mentally unstable and unfit to raise her children.
    C. her husband's death caused her such pain that she underwent a physical change.
    D. the narrator misses her mother's dark hair because they contrast nicely with her light eyes.
    E. the narrator wishes she could comfort her mother in this dark time.

Hard Passages

Breaking It Down and Putting It All Together

Some Hunter Test passages may be a bit harder than you're used to. In these cases you must really rely on good, solid methods to get through the piece:

- Read for the Three T's.
- Follow HOW TO ANSWER to the letter! and
- Break it down.

FOCUS ON THE BAGEL – NOT ON THE HOLE

WHEN YOU ARE IN THE MIDST OF CHEWING THROUGH THE DENSE PART OF A TEXT OR EVEN WHEN BREEZING THROUGH AN EASY STRETCH, BE SURE TO REMAIN CLAM! WHEN YOU COME ACROSS WORDS YOU DON'T KNOW, DO NOT LET THESE WORDS SEND YOU RUNNING. FIND A WAY TO WORK AROUND THESE WORDS. FOCUS ON WHAT YOU KNOW AND NOT WHAT YOU DON'T! UNLIKE THE VOCABULARY IN SYNONYM QUESTIONS OR SENTENCE COMPLETIONS IN OTHER TESTS, VOCABULARY IN READING COMPREHENSION CAN BE FIGURED OUT THROUGH CONTEXT OR, EVEN BETTER, THROUGH REPETITION.

MOST ESSAYS YOU WILL READ ON THE HUNTER TEST MAKE ONE POINT AND THEN REPEAT IT THROUGHOUT THE PASSAGE. SO REST ASSURED THAT IF YOU DON'T UNDERSTAND A WORD, READ ON AND ODDS ARE GOOD YOU'LL COME TO ANOTHER VERSION OF THE WORD.

E.G. THE DOCTOR REMAINED PHLEGMATIC EVEN IN THE FACE OF THE MASSIVE NUMBER OF CASUALTIES STREAMING INTO HIS WARD. HE WAS CALM AND COMPOSED DESPITE THE GRAVE TASK THAT LAY IN FRONT OF HIM. IT WAS GOING TO BE A LONG NIGHT.

BASED ON CONTEXT AND ON THE REPETITION IN THE PASSAGE, WHAT DO YOU THINK "PHLEGMATIC" MEANS?

2ⁿᵈ Ed. © ibidPREP llc

How to Eat Steak

If you eat meat [and if you don't, imagine it], then you know that when you are given a big hunk of steak, you don't just pick the whole thing up and swallow it in one bite. Even if you could do that without choking, you wouldn't enjoy it very much because you wouldn't be able to **taste** it. It's the same with difficult readings.

If you try to take a difficult, complex reading in in one quick pass, you will be able to swallow only a few random bits and not truly grasp the flavor of what you're reading at all. In order to comprehend these passages, you must break them down into smaller and smaller bites as needed.

There is no need to concern yourself about "wasting time" doing so, as you are almost guaranteed that these dense, chewy sections are the ones that test makers will come back to in the questions [in spite of all your wishful thinking that they might go away if you just ignore them]. Besides, breaking it down in this way is what you do in all reading, you just do it naturally and faster with sections that are clearer at first read. You will get faster at doing this with ALL sections, but only if you practice doing it the right way! In fact, the whole dopey chewing analogy holds for ALL READING. Break each paragraph, sentence, clause and word down as you go and as needed. If you don't understand a passage, keep breaking it down until you do. The way we break it down is to put each and every part into our own words and find workarounds for those words, phrases or clauses we cannot interpret. Keep in mind: the way you break down readings does not have to sound good or even be in good form—it just has to make sense to you!

For example:

In spite of all the professional advice to the contrary, it seems, at first blush and by simple common sense, that the best way to combat the spread of highly contagious diseases is through quarantine and by restricting travel access to and from infected regions. However, as with most received notions that seem to be the result of common sense and spontaneous judgment, the idea of broad quarantines and barring travel ultimately lacks both sense and judgment. Whew!

What was that? Well, let's break it down:

In spite of all the professional advice to the contrary,
What does this mean? *In spite of* means *regardless of,* or *without being affected by,* so…

Without being affected by all the *professional advice to the contrary*
[*to the contrary* means *in opposition to* or *against*]

Without being affected by all the professional advice against it, *it seems, at first blush and by simple common sense*,
[*at first blush and by simple common sense*—who knows what *at first blush* means? maybe, *at first sight*? not sure…move on to more context: *by simple common sense* we know means *by ordinary logic*], so

Without being affected by all the professional advice against it, it seems, at first sight
[?]

and by natural logic, *that the best way to combat*
[fight]

the spread of highly contagious diseases

[like the flu, maybe?]

is through quarantine

[what the heck is that? Oh yeah, *keeping people isolated*]

and by restricting

[*preventing* or *limiting*]

travel access to and from infected regions

[*infected regions*—is that like the parts of the body that are infected? well, you can't travel to an infected part of the body, so it probably means the countries or areas that have people infected with the disease],

Without being affected by all the professional advice against it, it seems that by common logic the best way to fight the spread of the flu is to keep people isolated and prevent travel to sick countries.

However,

[but]

as with most received notions

[no idea!]

that seem to be the result of common sense

[natural logic]

and spontaneous judgment

[*spontaneous*, not sure, but *judgment* = opinion], SO:

But as with most things that seem to be the result of ordinary logic and opinion, the idea of isolating and not letting people travel lacks both sense [doesn't make sense] and good opinion.

Put It All Together

Without being affected by all the professional advice against it, it seems that by common logic the best way to fight the spread of the flu is to keep people isolated and prevent travel to sick countries. But as with most things that seem to be the result of ordinary logic and opinion, the idea of isolating and not letting people travel doesn't make sense and is not a good opinion.

2nd Ed. © ibidPREP llc

Now try it for yourself on the tough parts of the passage below! Afterward, we break it down for you!!

Anne of Green Gables

"Oh, isn't that pretty!" the girl said happily, pointing out the buggy window.

They had driven over the crest of a hill. Below them was a long and winding pond, looking almost like a river. A bridge spanned it from its middle to its lower end, where an amber-hued belt of sand-hills shut it in from the dark blue gulf beyond. The water was a glory of many shifting hues—the most spiritual shadings of lavender and rose and ethereal green, with other colors harder to name. Above the bridge, the pond ran up into bordering groves of fir and maple and lay all darkly translucent in their wavering shadows. Here and there a wild plum leaned out from the bank like a girl tip-toeing to her own reflection. From the marsh at the head of the pond came the clear, mournfully sweet chorus of the frogs. There was a little gray house peering around an apple orchard on a slope beyond and, although it was not yet quite dark, a light was shining from one of its windows.

"That's Barry's pond," said Matthew, tightening his grip on the sorrel mare's reins.

"Oh, I don't like that name. I shall call it—let me see—the Lake of Shining Waters. Yes, that is the right name for it. I know because of the thrill. When I hit on a name that perfectly fits, it gives me a thrill. Do things ever give you a thrill?"

Matthew pondered. "Well, yes. It always kind of gives me a thrill to see them ugly white grubs that spike up in the cucumber beds. I hate the look of them."

"Oh, I don't think that can be exactly the same kind of a thrill. Do you think it can? There doesn't seem to be much connection between grubs and lakes of shining waters, does there? But why do other people call it Barry's pond anyway?"

"I reckon because Mr. Barry lives up there in that house. Orchard Slope's the name of his place. If it wasn't for that big bush behind it, you could see Green Gables from here. But we have to go over the bridge and round by the road, so it's near half a mile further."

"Does Mr. Barry have any little girls? Well, not too little—about my size?"

"He's got one about eleven. Her name is Diana."

"Oh!" she said with a long inhale of breath. "What a perfectly lovely name!"

"Well now, I dunno. There's something dreadful heathenish about it, seems to me. I'd rather Jane or Mary or some sensible name like that. But when Diana was born there was a schoolmaster boarding there and they gave him the naming of her and he called her Diana."

"I wish there had been a schoolmaster like that around when I was born. Oh, here we are at the bridge. I'm going to shut my eyes tight. I'm always afraid going over bridges. I can't help imagining that perhaps just as we get to the middle, they'll become crumpled like a jack-knife and nip us. So I shut my eyes. But I always have to open them when I think we're getting near the middle. Because, you see, if the bridge did crumple up I'd want to see it crumple. What a jolly rumble it makes! I always like the rumble part of it. Isn't it splendid there are so many things to like in this world? There we're over. Now I'll look back. Good night, dear Lake of Shining Waters. I always say good night to the things I love, just as I would to people. I think they like it. That water looks as if it was smiling at me."

When they had driven up the further hill and around a corner Matthew said: "We're pretty near home now. That's Green Gables over—"

"Oh, don't tell me," she interrupted breathlessly, catching at his partially raised arm and shutting her eyes that she might not see his gesture. "Let me guess. I'm sure I'll guess right."

1. The narrator's description of the pond in paragraph 2 suggests that it
   A. is a place where people come for religious purposes.
   B. has a beauty so stunning it seems sacred.
   C. has magical color-changing abilities.
   D. is highly unusual for reasons the narrator does not understand.
   E. is changing colors because it is slowly dying from decay.

2. The image of "a girl tip-toeing to her own reflection" is used
   A. as a metaphor for how the young girl feels about her journey.
   B. to remind us that the story is about a young girl.
   C. to bring up a memory the narrator is having.
   D. as a simile for how a wild plant appeared.
   E. as a symbol of the lake's role in the town.

3. In paragraph 5, Matthew suggests that
   A. the feeling he gets from seeing garden insects is similar to the feeling the girl gets from aptly naming something.
   B. feeling a thrill is immoral and should be discouraged.
   C. he does not understand what the girl means when she talks about naming the lake.
   D. grubs are something every person should hate.
   E. it is difficult to eradicate weeds from your garden.

4. From paragraph 11, what do we know about the schoolteacher?
   A. He is a bad influence on the town.
   B. He has cursed Diana with a bad name.
   C. He does not like the girl he named.
   D. He comes from out of town.
   E. He has different tastes from Matthew.

5. As used in the last paragraph, "crumpled" means
   A. creased
   B. furrowed
   C. exploded
   D. scrunched
   E. crushed

2nd Ed. © ibidPREP llc

6. Which word does not describe the young girl in the story?
   A. curious
   B. energetic
   C. cold
   D. imaginative
   E. talkative

BREAKING IT DOWN FOR YOU!

Answers with explanations. Now let's see if we practice what we preach!! If you've been reading for your 3 T's (theme, thesis, tone), then you are ready for these questions.

1. The narrator's description of the pond in paragraph 2 suggests that it

What kind of a question is this? The key word here is "suggests." This is an Inference question! Remember: for these questions we are looking for an idea that we can conclude is true from the text, but which the text does not explicitly state. Before we even look at the answer choices, we need to come up with the answer in our own words. So what does the description of the pond in paragraph 2 tell us? "The water was a glory of many shifting hues—the most spiritual shadings of lavender and rose and ethereal green, with other colors harder to name." The words "glory," "spiritual," and "ethereal" stand out as key and describe the pond as almost too beautiful for words. So now let's look at the answer choices to find something along those lines.

A. *is a place where people come for religious purposes*. While it's true the words "spiritual" and "religious" are often related, the passage never explicitly says anything about religious practices happening here. This answer is wrong.

B. *has a beauty so stunning it seems sacred*. This is pretty similar to what we came up with, but let's check the other answer choices just to be sure.

C. *has magical color-changing abilities*. While the lines list many different colors of the pond, it says nothing about magic or changing colors. This answer is wrong.

D. *is highly unusual for reasons the narrator does not understand*. The only thing the narrator seems unable to do in these lines are name the colors; she can understand them just fine. Wrong!

E. *is changing colors because it is slowly dying from decay*. While we know the pond changes color, we are given no indication why it is doing so, so we can't pick this choice. Therefore we were right to choose B. B is the right answer!

2. The image of "a girl tip-toeing to her own reflection" is used

What kind of question is this? This is an Analysis question. It is similar to an Inference question in that we are required to make a conclusion, but instead of looking for what is "implied" or "suggested," we are required to analyze why a line or phrase is being used. Again before we look at the answer choices, let's come up with our own answer. What it this image doing? It is describing the way a plum branch leans over the pond. Let's look at the answer choices!

A. *as a metaphor for how the young girl feels about her journey*. This answer is wrong because the young girl in the story has nothing to do with the image of the girl tip-toeing.

B. *to remind us that the story is about a young girl*. While this could possibly be true, it does not explain why the image is specifically used. Wrong.

C. *to bring up a memory the narrator is having*. There is no indication whatsoever of this. This answer is totally wrong.

D. *as a simile for how a wild plant appeared*. From the word "simile" we know we are looking for the words "like" or "as." Are either of those in the line itself? Yes! More importantly, this one seems close to our own answer. Let's keep reading, just in case.

E. *as a symbol of the lake's role in the town*. This answer has no support in the passage itself. D is the right answer.

3. *In paragraph 5, we can infer from Matthew's response that*

The word "infer" should tip us off right away—this is another Inference question. We'll just tackle it the same way we did question 1. This time, however, we need to look at the answer choices first because we don't know what kind of inference the test makers are looking for. But we know that the answer choice will have to fit with Matthew's character, beliefs or opinions.

A. *the feeling he gets from seeing garden insects is similar to him to the feeling the girl gets from aptly naming something*. While Matthew describes his feelings towards the grubs as one of hate, he also admits to getting a thrill from seeing them, which is the same word the girl uses to talk about giving something the right name. This seems correct, but let's look at the other choices, too.

B. *he believes that feeling a thrill is immoral and should be discouraged*. Matthew nowhere mentions a judgment about the idea of feeling a thrill; he only describes an instance of feeling it. This answer is wrong.

C. *he does not understand what the girl means when she talks about naming the lake*. While it does seem true that Matthew is confused by the girl, he responds with an answer that he seems to be confident in. This answer is wrong.

D. *grubs are something every person should hate*. Matthew nowhere discusses how other people should feel towards grubs. Wrong!

E. *it is difficult to eradicate weeds from your garden*. This has no basis in the passage. A is the right answer.

4. *From paragraph 11, what do we know about the schoolteacher?*

This is a Reading for Detail question. Before we read the answer questions, we know that the schoolteacher is responsible for giving a girl the name Diana, and that Matthew finds this name "heathenish." We also know that he boarded at Orchard Slope when Diana was born.

A. *He is a bad influence on the town*. This is an assumption we cannot make based on the passage. Wrong.

B. *He has cursed Diana with a bad name*. Matthew might think this to be true, but it is not an objective fact. This answer is also wrong.

C. *He does not like the girl he named*. We have no reason to think that the schoolteacher does not like Diana. This is absolutely wrong.

2nd Ed. © ibidPREP llc

D. *He comes from out of town*. This question is tempting, because we might assume that he is boarding with Mr. Barry because he is from out of town, but we cannot be absolutely sure of this based on the passage.

E. *He has different tastes from Matthew*. This is the right answer. Clearly there is something different about Matthew's belief system and the schoolteacher, because he liked the name "Diana," whereas Matthew finds it inappropriate. E is the correct answer.

5. *As used in the last paragraph, "crumpled" means*

What kind of a question is this? Obviously this is a vocab question! We've got a word here that you may know, but they are asking you what it means in this context in particular. For this problem, we should replace the word "crumpled" in the passage with one that also works. When the girl talks about the bridge crumpling, she is basically saying that it might fall apart.

A. *creased*. This doesn't really describe something that could happen to a bridge. Wrong.

B. *furrowed*. This could be substituted for the word "crumpled' in some contexts, but not this one. Next!

C. *exploded*. This is neither a synonym for crumple nor does it fit in the context. This is completely wrong.

D. *scrunched*. Getting closer, but this word doesn't quite fit. Wrong.

E. *collapsed*. This is both a synonym for "crumpled" and is something you can see happening to a bridge that would cause it to fall apart. E is the right answer.

6. *Which word does not describe the young girl in the story?*

If you've been reading for the third T—tone—you will already have a sense for the answer to this question. The young girl has been speaking for the majority of the passage! She likes to notice things, ask Matthew questions and talk about her surroundings. We can't come up with an answer before looking at the choices because we don't know which word is not like her. What we need to do instead is evaluate each answer choice by comparing it to the text. If a choice makes a claim the text does not support, that will be the right answer. It is important to treat these questions like true or false questions, so you don't forget what you're looking for. If you see four trues and one false, pick the false. And vice-versa.

A. *curious*. True; the girl never stops asking Matthew questions about the landscape they're traveling through. Next!

B. *energetic*. Also true; the high number of exclamations points she uses indicates she is full of energy.

C. *cold*. This seems likely to be the right answer. Why? Because the girl is warm in the way she relates to Matthew and her environment.

D. *imaginative*. The young girl not only names the pond they pass by, she also tells Matthew that she makes up names for objects often and gets a thrill when she finds a good one. This is true.

talkative. Clearly true! Just look at the many strings of sentences she says one after the other: "Look at the lake! Whose house is that? I'm afraid of bridges. Oh look we're almost there!" The right answer is clearly C.

"MEN OF COLOR TO ARMS!" BY FREDERICK DOUGLASS

Frederick Douglass, a free black abolitionist during the 19th century, gave this address to a crowd of African Americans, calling on all who could fight to fight in the Civil War which was raging at this time.

When first the rebel cannon shattered the walls of Sumter and drove away its starving garrison, I predicted that the war would not be fought out entirely by white men. These dreary years have confirmed that opinion. Yet, the arm of the slave is the best defense against the arm of the slaveholder. Hence with every exulting shout of victory raised by the slaveholding rebels, it is implored that the imperiled nation to unchain against her foes, her powerful black hand.

Slowly and reluctantly that appeal is beginning to be heeded. Do not stop to complain that it was not heeded sooner. This is not the time to discuss that question. Leave it to the future. When the war is over, the country is saved, peace is established, and the black man's rights are secured (as they will be) history will dispose of that and sundry other questions with an impartial hand.

Action! Action! not criticism, is the plain duty of this hour. Words are now useful only as they stimulate to blows. The purpose of speech now is only to point out when, where, and how to strike to the best advantage. There is no time to delay. From East to West, from North to South, the sky is written all over, "Now or never." Liberty won by white men would lose half its luster. "Who would be free themselves must strike the blow." "Better even die free, than to live slaves." This is the sentiment of every brave colored man amongst us.

There are weak and cowardly men in all nations. We have them amongst us. They tell you this is the "white man's war"; that you will be "no better off after than before the war"; that the army will "sacrifice you on the first opportunity." Believe them not; cowards themselves, they do not wish to have their cowardice shamed by your brave example. This is your hour and mine.

In earnest and after the best deliberation, for the first time during this war, we call you to arms. By every consideration which binds you to your enslaved fellow-countrymen, and the peace and welfare of your country; by every aspiration which you cherish for the freedom and equality of yourselves and your children; by all the ties of blood and identity which make us one with the brave black men now fighting our battles in Louisiana and in South Carolina, we urge you to fly to arms, and smite the enemy that would bury the government and your liberty in the same hopeless grave.

The day dawns; the morning star is bright upon the horizon! The iron gate of our prison stands half open. One gallant rush from the North will fling it wide open, and four millions of our brothers and sisters shall march out into liberty. The chance is now given to you to end in a day the bondage of centuries, and to rise from social degradation to common equality with all varieties of men.

The case is before you. This is our golden opportunity. Let us accept it, and forever wipe out the dark reproaches unsparingly hurled against us by our enemies. Let us win for ourselves the gratitude of our country, and the best blessings of our posterity through all time.

1. In this passage, the war
   A. Has been over for many years
   B. Has been going on for years
   C. Has just begun
   D. Was about to end
   E. Has yet to begin

2. As used in line 10, the word "sundry" means
   A. Various
   B. Frivolous
   C. Hot
   D. Racially biased
   E. Complex

3. As used in line 10, the phrase "history will dispose of that and other sundry questions" means
   A. The war will be forgotten, as well as those who cared about who won and who lost.
   B. The war's purpose changes every day, and by the end it won't matter who fought for what.
   C. Once the war is over, it won't matter why African Americans weren't called to fight earlier.
   D. Slavery will not be remembered once the war is over.
   E. When people look back at the war, the contributions and struggles of African Americans will not be seen as important.

4. "Liberty won by white men would lose half its luster" (lines 15-16) suggests that
   A. To fight in this war is to fight for freedom forever and everywhere.
   B. Freedom that slaves did not fight for won't be as meaningful.
   C. Liberty can never exist without both African Americans and Whites fighting for it.
   D. White men will not remain loyal to the cause of equality for African Americans.
   E. All of the above.

5. "Believe them not; cowards themselves, they do not wish to have their cowardice shamed by your brave example" (lines 20 and 21) suggests that
   A. Some were too timid to fight and encouraged others not to as well.
   B. African Americans fought during the early years of the war because they were all afraid.
   C. The brave would only fight if encouraged to be better than their cowardly brothers.
   D. The speaker thinks that all who don't believe in the war's cause are cowards.
   E. The speaker is himself an angry veteran of the war.

6. The phrase "to end in a day the bondage of centuries" (lines 31 - 32) suggests that the speaker believes that
   A. Slavery and the war are not connected.
   B. Having African Americans fight in the war will win freedom for all and end the war quickly.
   C. It is more important to remember the crimes of slavery than think about the good winning the war would do.
   D. Racism is the reason many are refusing to fight.
   E. The consequences of the war will not last.

7. According to the narrator, the motivations to answer his call to arms are
   A. Universal and personal
   B. Fear and pride
   C. In opposition to patriotism
   D. Too idealistic
   E. Different for each individual

8. As used in line 32, the word "degradation" means
   A. Reinvention
   B. Devotion
   C. Dissolution
   D. Humiliation
   E. Commendation

9. As used in line 36, the word "posterity" means
   A. Future generations
   B. Ancestors
   C. Successes
   D. Estate
   E. Organization

10. The tone of this piece is primarily
    A. Aspirational
    B. Confrontational
    C. Inspirational
    D. Descriptive
    E. Argumentative

A LEAGUE OF NATIONS

After World War One, the world had to face the aftermath of a conflict the likes of which it had never seen before. Countries assessed the destruction that they had endured and began the long process of making peace.

The Paris Peace Conference was held at the end of the war in 1919. There, Western leaders met to discuss the terms of surrender and craft what would be known as the Treaty of Versailles. American President Woodrow Wilson arrived at the Peace Conference with his Fourteen Points - a plan for a new world order based on sovereignty and self-determination. His final goal was The League of Nations, an international organization that would keep peace among countries and cultivate diplomacy instead of war. Wilson's goal was a global cooperative that would prevent another war from ever taking place.

Unfortunately, Wilson's European counterparts were not as hopeful. Instead of thinking of the future, they wanted retribution for the past. The leaders of Great Britain, France, and Italy had suffered more physical damage and casualties than the United States, a latecomer to the fighting which had occurred only in Europe. The European Powers wanted to reduce German land and force Germany to admit guilt and pay reparations. The only major goal of Wilson's which was accepted was the League of Nations.

However, the League of Nations was not well-received in Wilson's native country. Congress believed that the League of Nations would prevent the United States from going to war, or that the League would force it to go to war on another country's behalf. Such conditions would limit the United States' freedom of action and its ability to choose its own conduct. In the end, Congress did not approve the Treaty of Versailles and did not agree to join the League of Nations.

Without the United States as a strong backbone for the League, the organization was unable to perform as Wilson and the other leaders had planned. In addition, the punitive measures taken towards Germany in the

Treaty, including forced demilitarization and payment of reparations, left the country economically crippled and socially humiliated. Anger in Germany allowed national hatred rise and another war to boil. The League of Nations was not able to help prevent the second world war that Wilson had feared.

1. Wilson's goal during the Paris Peace Conference could best be described as
   A. The creation of a new world order in which the United States was the leader.
   B. The institution of his ideas to keep peace everlasting in Europe and the world.
   C. Cooperation with the other world leaders who also wanted peace and justice.
   D. The disillusion of the peace agreements which had failed and the institution of marital law.
   E. The maintenance of aggressions until the United States received all that it wanted.

2. Paragraph 5 of the passage suggests that
   A. It was Wilson's personal failure which led to the Second World War.
   B. The weakness of the League of Nations was the fault of the Europeans.
   C. Germany was not in the League of Nations and could begin wars as it pleased.
   D. Had Wilson's League of Nations included the United States, the Second World War would still likely have happened.
   E. The League of Nations was weak but still able to prevent any catastrophes for the majority of its existence.

3. The description of the European leaders in paragraph 3 suggests that
   A. Damage and loss from the war made the Western leaders lose sight of peace.
   B. The leaders resented Wilson for his delay in entering the war and wanted to foil his plans.
   C. The leaders were inexperienced and did not know how to put their country's interests over their personal issues.
   D. Wilson and the leaders came to the Conference all expecting to be the weakest in attendance.
   E. Germany was not invited to the conference due to long grudges held by Wilson.

4. As used in line 7, the word "sovereignty" means
   A. Mutual respect
   B. Strength
   C. Authority to self-govern
   D. Equality
   E. Peacefulness

5. Congress did not like the League of Nations because
   A. The United States was not involved in the creation of the League.
   B. The other countries in the League did not consider the United States important.
   C. They did not see the purpose of international cooperation.
   D. They wanted the freedom to start their own wars.
   E. The League of Nations would decrease the United States' independence.

6. As used in line 12, the word "retribution" means
   A. Payment
   B. Reward
   C. Respect
   D. Revenge
   E. Forgiveness

7. As used in line 23, the word "punitive" means
   A. Pardoning
   B. Disciplinary
   C. Prompt
   D. Beneficial
   E. Rigorous

8. Wilson wanted to create a League of Nations in order to
   A. Maintain a long-lasting peace after the worst war ever seen.
   B. Spread his new world order to the defeated countries of the war.
   C. Show that the United States had recovered faster from the war than the other participating nations.
   D. Keep countries peaceful so that the United States could dominate the world order.
   E. Emphasize that the United States keep soldiers in Europe to keep countries safe.

9. The tone of the entire peace could be described as
   A. Ironic
   B. Nostalgic
   C. Informative.
   D. Angry
   E. Comedic

GRAMMAR

When we teach reading, we teach the ABCs; when we teach math, we teach the 1, 2, 3s; but when we teach writing, for some reason, we do not teach nouns, verbs and adjectives, or spelling, or how to make sentences connect to each other. Instead, we teach students how to say ABSOLUTELY NOTHING over the prescribed length of an assignment [which is really the only thing most kids end up caring about when they write: how long does it have to be?] Yuck.

Imagine a world in which students are taught certain rules about the words they are meant to write with and certain rules about how to put those words together! Imagine a world in which students are taught to mine their thoughts and lay them out in an ordered fashion!! Imagine. It's easy if you try.

Below, I will give you the benefit of our brief but extremely clear grammar recipe. If you learn and follow it, not only will you do better on grammar questions, not only will you write better and with greater focus, not only will you learn to proofread your work for grammar and sense, but you will also end up having a better handle on English grammar than 92% of your fellow citizens, including the grown-ups [Stufact!].

How to Learn Grammar—It's WRITING, not SOUNDING

The thing to remember about grammar is that it is a measure of **WRITTEN** English, not **SPOKEN** English. Spoken English relies on a lot of implied meaning and, often, what *sounds* good or right. But since no one is around to explain what has just been said, **written** English needs to follow certain rules in order to be clear. As a result, what **sounds** right may be wrong, and what sounds weird or awkward may be 100% correct.

Which are correct?

- Beth is taller than her. / Beth is taller than she.
- I feel badly for you. / I feel bad for you.
- There is competition between the teams in the league. / There is competition among the teams in the league.
- Just between you and I, this test sucks. / Just between you and me, this test sucks.

If you go by how things sound on the questions above, you would probably be wrong every single time: the second option is the right one in each example! We explain below...

Before you learn the grammar of what is, for many of you, your *native* tongue [for heaven's sake!], you need to learn the basic building blocks of our grammar, the parts of speech.

Parts of Speech

Noun
- person, place, thing, idea:
  - chef, mall, bat, freedom

Proper Noun
- particular person, place, thing or idea:
  - George, Nevada, Coke, Communist

Verbs
- Action words [he **runs**, she **has**, they swam] **+**
  - Being verbs and the verb "to be" [I **am** short]

	To Be	
	Singular	Plural
1	am/was	are/were
2	are/were	are/were
3	is/was	are/were

- **Linking Verbs** are verbs that describe **how** we notice things through our senses or **how** things change from one way of being to another....
  - *appear, taste, smell, feel, look, sound, grow [when it means "become," not "get bigger"], seem, remain, become*
  - I **remained** still while the nurse removed the splinter from my foot.
  - The jester **seemed** crazy.
  - The jester's laugh **sounds** creepy.
  - I **grow** tired of your whining.

- **Verb Tenses**
  - Agreement—when we say a verb "agrees" with its subject, we mean that it has the right "number" and tense —i.e., the verb is singular or plural if the subject is singular or plural, and the verb takes place in the right time period (past, present, future, etc.)
  - The basic verb tenses are fairly straightforward. You probably already knew that the verbs in the sentences below agree with their subjects.
    The coat **hangs** in the closet.
The cats **played** with the mice.
The house of cards **shook**.

- **Parallel Structure**
  - This is one of the main concepts of grammar. Any time you have consecutive actions in a list, all the verbs must be in the same form and tense. Parallel structure also holds true for lists of nouns, adjectives or anything else—all items must be in the same form.
    - YES: After school, I like to change my clothes, eat a snack and do my homework.
    - NO: After school, I like to change my clothes, eat a snack and doing my homework.
    - YES: I like swimming, fishing and singing.
    - NO: I like swimming, fishing and to sing.

- **Passive Voice**
  - In English, we much prefer to have our subjects be the **active** partners, the nouns that are performing the verbs. We do not like passive constructions, where the subject is being acted upon, but they are not technically ungrammatical.
    - YES: John Guare wrote *Six Degrees of Separation.*
    - NO: *Six Degrees of Separation* was written by John Guare.

    - YES: The dog was wagging its tail.
    - NO: The tail was being wagged by the dog.

    When it comes to active voice, also definitely avoid having too many "ing" words [aka gerunds] lead off your sentences. Especially "being."

    - NO: Being that we were hungry, we got pizza.
    - YES: We were hungry, so we got pizza.

Adjectives
- Words that modify [describe] nouns:
  - The **blue** hat.
  - The **delicious** burger.
  - The **angry** leprechaun.

2ⁿᵈ Ed. © ibidPREP llc

Adverbs
- Words that modify verbs, adjectives AND other adverbs.
  - The boy ran **quickly.**
  - She wore a **pale** blue hat. ["pale" modifies the adjective "blue"]
  - He ate a **red** hot chili pepper. ["red" modifies the adverb "hot" which is itself an adverb modifying "chili" which is an adjective describing "pepper"—whew!]

How do you know when it's an adverb modifying an adjective and not just two adjectives strung together? If you see a comma between the modifiers, they are distinct [separate] adjectives. If there's no comma, then the first word is the adverb modifying the following word. E.g.,

  - *The still, dark night* means the night was still AND dark.
  - *The still dark night* means the night continues to be dark.

One of the reasons teachers became loath[1] to teach grammar was due to the weight of exceptions. Kids love rules/hate exceptions because they require thought. Ugh.

Luckily, there are far fewer exceptions of consequence in English grammar than there are in English spelling, which truly is bonkers and rule-resistant.

WHY WE HATE GRAMMAR

EXCEPTION #1: WHEN WE DON'T USE ADVERBS

There are times when we don't use adverbs. Pay attention to the following scenarios. **Sense** [verbs dealing with the senses] **do not** take adverbs; they take adjectives instead.

Modifying the Five Senses [Especially Important for the Essays That Ask for *Sensory* Detail]

1. ***Feel:*** [emotions vs. touch] Mary feels **bad** about your pain.

   If Mary felt "badly," that would mean that there was something wrong with her fingers and she couldn't feel things properly when she touched them. In other words, "badly" used here would be referring to/modifying her ability to touch. If you're having trouble understanding this point, try replacing "badly" with another adverb. If you say, "I feel greatly," that doesn't really make sense, does it?

2. ***Smell:*** [scent vs. smelling] I just took a shower; I smell good. / The perfumer smells excellently; he can tell what kind of cologne you are wearing in an instant.

3. ***Look:*** [appearance vs. seeing] That piece of pizza sure looks good. / Make sure you look over the contract well.

4. ***Sounds/Hear:*** That song sounds good. / I haven't been able to hear well since touring with my band.

5. ***Taste:*** The rabbit stew tastes good. / The food critic accurately tastes all the spices in the dish

---

[1] resistant to, dread

ADVERB ABUSE

SOME PEOPLE GROW UP NOT USING ADVERBS TOO OFTEN IN THEIR EVERYDAY SPEECH AND WRITING. THEY GET IN THE HABIT OF SAYING THINGS LIKE: "I DID GOOD," "HE EATS FAST," "SHE RAN SO QUICK..." SOMETIMES LATER IN LIFE [LIKE IN COLLEGE], THESE PEOPLE DISCOVER THE BEAUTY AND PURPOSE OF ADVERBS. OFTEN, LIKE A COOK WHO HAS JUST DISCOVERED SPICES, THEY THEN START SPRINKLING THEM ON EVERYTHING.

MY FAVORITE OVERUSE OF ADVERBS PERTAINS TO THE WORD "FEEL," AS IN ONE'S EMOTIONAL STATE. A LOT OF LATE ADVERB LEARNERS LOVE TO SAY, "I FEEL BADLY ABOUT THAT." I FEEL BAD THAT THEY FEEL COMPELLED TO DO THAT. PRESIDENT BILL CLINTON, WHO GREW UP IN RURAL ARKANSAS [PROBABLY NOT A HOTBED OF ADVERB USE], SAYS, "I FEEL BADLY." NO ONE HAS HAD THE TEMERITY[2] TO TELL HIM HE'S WRONG, SO PLEASE DON'T FEEL BAD [AND DEFINITELY DON'T FEEL BADLY] IF YOU MAKE THE SAME MISTAKE!

EXCEPTION #2: WHEN WE DON'T USE ADVERBS

The verb "to be" **does not** take adverbs; it takes adjectives instead. That's because the modifiers correspond to the subject, not the verb.

- I am fast [not "I am quickly"].
- He is loud.
- Those potato chips are excellent.

PRONOUNS

Pronouns are generic[3] words that take the place of specific nouns. The noun that a pronoun replaces is called its "antecedent." It is always important, as a reader, to be able to identify the antecedent of a pronoun; likewise, as a writer, it is your job to make sure your writing is free of ambiguity and that antecedents are easily identified. ("The novel's plot is tedious, as is the writing style. It could definitely use some improvement." What does "it" refer to? The novel's plot, or its writing style? Or the novel as a whole? Don't confuse your readers!)

There are many, many kinds of pronouns in the world of grammar, but the ones you most have to concern yourself with here are subject and object pronouns.

[2] nerve, chutzpah, boldness
[3] universal, all-purpose

2nd Ed. © ibidPREP llc

Subject Pronouns replace nouns that function as the subject.
Object Pronouns replace nouns that function as the object.

So what's a subject? A **subject** is the noun that performs the verb.

Examples:

The dog drove the bus. ("dog" is the subject)
Cats and dogs fight all the time. ("Cats and dogs" is the subject)
Pet ownership requires commitment. ("Pet ownership" is the subject)

So a **subject pronoun** is a pronoun that takes the place of one of these subjects. Here are the same sentences with subject pronouns.

It is a terrific movie.

They are happiest in the tropics.

They have strengths and weaknesses.

Simple enough. But what about objects. What are they? **Objects** are usually the nouns that receive an action from the subject. E.g.,

My grandmother and I went to a baseball game. (The object is "baseball game")
A player gave autographs to George and Tony. (The objects are "George and Tony")

So, with **object pronouns** taking the place of these nouns, we get:

My grandmother and I went to it.

A player gave autographs to them.

Here's a table of the subject and object pronouns for you to learn.

Subject Pronouns:		Object Pronouns:	
I	We	Me	Us
You	You	You	You
He/She/It/Who	They	Him/Her/It/Whom	Them

SPECIAL SINGULAR PRONOUNS—BE ON THE LOOKOUT!

Singular pronouns such as *everyone, no one, none* and *one* all take singular pronouns. That means if you want to write:

Everyone knows _____ must learn how to write better,

the pronoun in the blank must be *one, he, she* or *he or she*, NOT *they*. No matter how much sense *they* makes [it maintains gender neutrality for everyone and is so much less clumsy], *everyone* is singular, so the pronoun replacing it must also be singular. If you catch this in your writing, it will signal serious grammar chops!

HOW TO FIND SUBJECTS

With all this talk of subjects, how do we know how to find them? The subject of a sentence is the noun that is performing the action. Usually in English, the subject comes before its verb and is toward the beginning of the sentence.

Betty eats cake for breakfast. / **Lou** likes toad racing. / **We** are family.

Occasionally in English, however, the subject comes after its verb, and of course tests love to exploit this fact:

There are three **things** that I like. / Here are **a key and a hat** for you. / [Weird, huh?]

Sentences can contain more than one verb and so can have more than one subject [each verb gets a subject even if it's just implied: Get over here! [the subject is whoever is getting bossed around]. When there's more than one verb in a sentence, get in the habit of determining the subject for each one. As for objects, they're easy: whatever nouns aren't subjects are objects!

Pronouns are especially difficult to use when we're making comparisons. Consider which of the following two sentences is right:

I am cooler than[4] he. OR I am cooler than him.

In normal speech, most people would say, "I am cooler than him." Again, if this were the **Sounding Section,** they'd be right. However, this is GRAMMAR, and according to the rules of WRITTEN grammar, in a comparison, both nouns [things being compared] are considered **subject** nouns, so both take **subject pronouns.**

*So…*the correct answer is: *I am cooler than he!*

Here's a trick for understanding this odd rule. Because both "I" and "he" are subjects, they must both have verbs. But, you say, there's only one verb here, "am," and it definitely does not go with "he." That's true. But that's just because we cut off the second verb.

What we're *really* saying is this: *I am cooler than he [is]!*

You would never say, "I am cooler than him is," so that's why you do NOT say "I am cooler than him." Just put in that missing verb yourself, and you'll see that the subject actually sounds better than the object.

---

[4] Whenever you see the word "than" you know you have a comparison.

2ⁿᵈ Ed. © ibidPREP llc

DON'T ABUSE THE "I"

ANOTHER COMMON ERROR PEOPLE MAKE WHEN THEY START WANTING TO USE GOOD GRAMMAR IS OVERUSING "I." PEOPLE WHO GROW UP SPEAKING WITH LESS THAN PERFECT GRAMMAR OFTEN UNDERUSE "I": ME AND MOM WENT TO THE MALL, MY FRIEND AND ME ATE PIE...YOU GET THE IDEA. ONCE THESE PEOPLE FIND OUT THAT IT'S "MY MOM AND I...," "MY FRIEND AND I...," ETC., THEY START STICKING "I" IN EVERYWHERE, INCLUDING INTO PREPOSITIONAL PHRASES AND THE OBJECTS OF THE SENTENCES WHERE THEY DON'T BELONG!

YES: HE GAVE THE BALL TO MY FRIEND AND ME.
NO: HE GAVE THE BALL TO MY FRIEND AND I.

YES: THERE ARE MANY DIFFERENCES BETWEEN MY TWIN AND ME.
NO: THERE ARE MANY DIFFERENCES BETWEEN MY TWIN AND I.

Phrases

A phrase is a group of words that contains **neither** a subject **nor** a verb. Phrases provide additional information about the material in the sentence but have no overall impact on the rest of the sentence they live in.

My brother, by the way, is an idiot.

"By the way" is a phrase that tells you this is incidental[5] info about my brother. If you get rid of that phrase, you still have a fine [if troubling] sentence:

My brother is an idiot.

- NOTE: Sometimes students write in PHRASES rather than COMPLETE SENTENCES. This is when you end up writing INCOMPLETE SENTENCES. Don't do this! Remember: Each sentence must contain a SUBJECT and a VERB.

Prepositions

Prepositions are words that describe the relationship between a subject and an object. The relation generally refers to location, direction or time.

The dog is **under** the tree.

5 Less important

"Under" tells us where the dog is in relation to the tree.

The cat came **from** the house.

"From" tells us the direction in which the cat is moving.

There are many words that may be used as prepositions. Fortunately, only [only!] about 48 are in common use. The highlighted ones in the box below are words that at first do not seem like prepositions. [Learn to know them on sight.]

About	Among	Beneath	During	Into	Over	Until
Above	Around	Beside	Except	Like	Since	Up
Across	At	Between	For	Near	Through	Upon
After	Before	Beyond	From	Of	To	With
Against	Behind	By	In	Off	Toward	Within
Along	Below	Down	Inside	On	Under	Without

Prepositions always take **objects**, never subjects. So:

NEVER	*Between you and I.*
ALWAYS	*Between you and me.*

NEVER	*Math is the hardest subject for him and I.*
ALWAYS	*Math is the hardest subject for him and me.*

Another challenge many people have with prepositions is simply knowing which one to use. The most common mistake involves "among" and "between." When we're speaking casually, most of us use "between" even when we shouldn't. "Among" is correct when we're picking from three or more things; "between" can only be used with two things.

ALWAYS	*Among the players in the American League, there are many stars.*
NEVER	*Between the players in the American League, there are many stars.*

ALWAYS	*Choosing between the two of them is easy.*
NEVER	*Choosing among the two of them is easy.*

Prepositional Phrases

All prepositional phrases begin with prepositions. Prepositional phrases combine a preposition + an object of the preposition [since there are no *subjects* of the preposition]. **Since phrases do not contain either subjects or verbs, they have NO impact on the number or tense of the verbs in the sentence [subject / verb agreement].** Which of these is correct?

Each of the boys **is** tired.
OR
Each of the boys **are** tired.

Here, "of the boys" is the prepositional phrase, so it **cannot** contain the subject. In fact, to avoid getting confused, whenever you see a prepositional phrase in a sentence, put parentheses around it and <u>then</u> look for the subject. In this case, "Each (of the boys) is/are tired," the only word left that could be the subject is the word

 2nd Ed. © ibidPREP llc

"each." "Each," unlike "boys," is singular [a singular pronoun in thise case], sooo...the answer is:

Each of the boys **is** tired.

Pronouns in Prepositional Phrases

Since the nouns in prepositional phrases are never the subject of the sentence, the pronouns inside prepositional phrases are NEVER subject pronouns.

Between you and me, this test sucks.
OR
Between you and I, this test sucks.

As we know from our chart, "between" is a preposition, so "between you and ___" is a prepositional phrase, *sooooo* you have to put an OBJECT pronoun in it, *sooooo* the correct answer is:

Between you and me, this test sucks.

PARTS OF THE SENTENCE

Every sentence must contain a verb and a subject. That's it! In fact, in English sentences, the shorter the better. Some sentences may even have only one word. When the verb is a command, the subject is implied in the verb:

Stop! [It is implied that someone should stop.]

If, in your writing, you find yourself tacking together clause upon clause with lots of phrases sprinkled in among your sentence, START ANOTHER SENTENCE. They're free!

Clauses

Clauses are groups of words that contain a subject AND a verb [the opposite of phrases, which contain neither]. There are two principal types of clauses:

TYPE 1: Dependent Clause—Contains a verb and a subject [stated or implied] but cannot stand alone as a sentence; it must be joined to an independent clause. When a sentence **begins** with a dependent clause it HAS TO BE set off by a comma:

***Waking up this morning**, I heard the telephone ring.*

Immediately following the comma, the independent clause MUST start with the implied subject of the dependent clause. The subject must be in subject form, not possessive or anything else:

YES   *After seeing the movie, John did not like Jennifer Lawrence as much as he once did.*

NO   *After seeing the movie, Jennifer Lawrence was no longer John's favorite.*

YES   *While leaping a tall building in a single bound, Superman smiled at Lois.*

NO   *While leaping a tall building in a single bound, Superman's cape fluttered in the breeze as he smiled at Lois.*

Grammar

TYPE 2: Independent Clause—These can stand alone as their own sentences, but they don't have to!

The monkey laughed.

Or:

When the dog barked, the monkey laughed.

• An independent clause must immediately restate the subject of the dependent clause (or modifying phrase) linked to the front of it.

*When he hit his keeper with poop, **the monkey** laughed.*

• If two independent clauses are joined together in a sentence, they must be connected either by a **comma with a conjunction** or the mysterious **semicolon** (without a conjunction).

*The monkey laughed, **and** the zookeeper cried.*

The monkey laughed; the zookeeper cried.

Conjunctions

There are a lot of different kinds of conjunctions out there. The main ones we are interested in are called *co-ordinating conjunctions*—these are your basic conjunctions:

For, And, Nor, But, Or, Yet, So—aka FANBOYS! But remember—

• ***And, Nor, Or*** are NOT conjunctions when they are part of a list or grouping—Jack **and** Jill / beer, wine **and** sangria / neither Jack **nor** Jill / either beer **or** wine.

• ***For*** is a conjunction when it means **because.** It is not a conjunction when it's acting like a preposition.

    Conjunction: I went to the store, for the books were on sale.

    Preposition: I went to the bookstore for the book sale.

• ***Yet*** is not a conjunction when it means, "now" or "at this time."

Interrupters

What the heck is an interrupter?

    All of you, *by all means*, eat more cheese!

    Heck, we all want more cheese!

An interrupter interrupts!

2ⁿᵈ Ed. © ibidPREP llc

CLASSIFY PARTS OF SPEECH PRACTICE

Part A: Please classify each of the following as a noun, proper noun, verb, adjective, or adverb.

1. game — *noun*
2. Apples to Apples — *proper noun*
3. whale — *noun*
4. funny — *adjective*
5. play — *verb*
6. am — *verb*
7. quickly — *adjective*
8. slowly — *adjective*
9. slow — *adverb*
10. correct — *verb*
11. Thomas — *proper noun*
12. doctor — *noun*
13. Dr. McKay — *proper noun*
14. better — *adj/adj*
15. number — *noun*
16. Saturday — *proper noun*
17. November — *proper noun*
18. France — *proper noun*
19. frantically — *adjective*
20. Yo Gabba Gabba — *proper noun*

Part B: Please list the conjunctions in FANBOYS:

F — For
A — And
N — Nor
B — But
O — Or
Y — Yet
S — So

PUNCTUATION

COMMAS

At last the secrets are revealed!

Let's be honest. Besides using commas to separate items in a list, most of us have NO idea when to use them. Most students drop them into sentences whenever they feel it may have gone on too long or where they feel a breath should be taken or just 'cause! Wrong, wrong and wrong.

If you were marking a speech you were giving, you might put a comma in to remind yourself where to pause for breath. But again, reading isn't writing, and you don't need to tell your reader when to breathe. She can figure that out all by herself.

HERE IS A LIST OF WHAT COMMAS ARE FOR:

1. To separate a dependent clause at the start of a sentence from the rest of the sentence: while waking up this morning, I heard the phone ring.
2. To separate a long prepositional phrase or phrases at the start of sentence from the rest of the sentence: after a night of dancing, Cinderella needed a rest.
3. To separate items in a list of nouns, verbs, or adjectives:
   a. The hats, coats and scarves were in a pile on the bed.
   b. After school I like to change clothes, eat a snack and draw stuff.
   c. It was a cold, dark, stormy, scary, dread-filled night.

   You may also put a comma before the "and" in a list, but I prefer not to because that confuses things with number 4.
4. To separate independent clauses linked by conjunctions:
   a. I like cake, and I like soda.
   b. I like cake, but I hate pudding.
5. To set off appositive [descriptive] phrases within or at the end of sentences:
   a. My brother, the one in Boulder, likes rocks.
   b. Genie, the devil, loves grammar.
   c. There's nothing better than sleep-away camp, which is usually a bug-infested swamp of adolescent and pre-adolescent angst[6].
6. To separate out interrupters or exclamations:
   a. **However,** I disagree.
   b. There are, **nevertheless,** many things still to learn.
   c. **Holy guacamole,** Batman is in trouble!
7. To set off what a quotation:
   a. John said, "I do not want to go school today."
   b. "But you must, " answered his mother, "because an education is a wonderful thing.

---

[6] Anxiety; unease

2nd Ed. © ibidPREP llc

Here Is a List of What Commas Are <u>Not</u> For:

1. Don't add a comma before a conjunction when you are NOT adding a new subject or repeating the old one.

    Yes: I ate lunch with my friends and worked on my book all afternoon.

    No: I ate lunch with my friends, and worked on my book all afternoon.

    Yes: I ate lunch with my friend, and I worked on my book all afternoon.

2. Don't add a comma just because you've been writing for a while and haven't used one.

3. Don't add a comma where you think the reader might want to pause or catch her breath.

4. Joining two independent clauses by themselves. This is called a **comma splice** and it is wrong.

    NO: I like to eat hoagies, you like to eat subs.

    YES: I like to eat hoagies, and you like to eat subs.

    YES: I like to eat hoagies. You like to eat subs.

5. You don't have to add a comma before the "and" in a list. That's just what British people do.

    GOOD: Bobo likes to eat, run, and poop.

    BETTER: Bobo likes to eat, run and poop.

All of the commas in the following paragraph have been removed. Read through it and insert commas where they are needed based on the rules you just read.

> *Did you notice the title of this book? Did you notice what was wrong with it? Or did you think the title was **Remain Calm**? Don't be embarrassed if you did. MANY people grown-ups and kids alike make the same mistake. Why? Well the brain wants the title to make sense. Remain Calm makes sense; Remain Clam doesn't. Also most of us only glance or skim things like titles instructions or epigraphs [which is what this paragraph is]. If we do read more closely we might read too quickly or too anxiously and flip letters automatically. This is what some dyslexic people do and when we're stressed we all become a little bit dyslexic: letters switch negatives and positives flip and up becomes down. So? Why does this matter? It matters because test makers on every level are all too aware of this tendency which is especially common in young minds. They know if you feel rushed stressed or distracted that you'll be prone to miss details get things backwards or answer the question you imagine rather than the one on the page. That means it is VERY important that you find a way to quiet your mind focus on ALL the words and by all means no matter what Remain Clam!*

Done? Check your commas against the epigraph on the first page of this book!

Comma Practice
Write each sentence correctly adding commas as needed.

1. Darrin likes to eat, to drink and to fly kites.

2. The way Bobby, my brother talks you would think he's from a different country.

3. Tomorrow will be July 4, 2020.

4. My favorite date is Wednesday November 22, 1961.

5. Mr. Getz, my principal also teaches math science and gym.

6. Noah shine the light over here, so I can see you better.

7. The kids were wearing fuzzy wool hats over their big round heads.

8. Even though you saved your money, you still do not have enough for a bicycle.

9. Since you are late, we had to start without you.

10. If you don't finish the project by tomorrow, you won't get a good grade on it.

11. Before we moved to the city, we had many animals on our farm.

12. Providing that you study for the test, I am sure you will do well.

13. No, there is not enough time to play a game of Monopoly before we leave.

14. Before we leave, we need to turn off all the lights.

15. Well, if you must choose the red dress I guess that is all right with me.

16. The light fluffy lemon cake, was the hit of the party.

17. A new highway was built, so motorists can move around the city more smoothly.

18. However, we have tried to find our dog for two days.

19. Well, do you want to be a squirrel instead?

20. The last time you told me a lie, I believed you but not this time.

The Mysterious Semicolon

Semicolons are not so mysterious after all. Their sole purpose is to allow you to connect two independent clauses WITHOUT using a conjunction, so you can write:

Studatuta likes hot dogs, so he's fat.
Studatuta likes hot dogs; he's fat.

Semicolons are great for linking two VERY closely related independent clauses—such as those pertaining to my love of hot dogs and my weight!

The Mysterious Colon

Even less mysterious than the semicolon is its big, two-buttoned cousin, the colon. The colon does two closely related jobs.

1. Colons introduce lists and examples.

    These are my favorite things: dog bites, bee stings and pies.

2. Colons also provide a singular example, presenting it with a sort of ta-da! effect. Sort of like this:

    There is one thing I like best in the whole world: pizza!

APOSTROPHES

An **apostrophe** is a punctuation mark that has two main uses: to show **possession** [this belongs to...] and to make **contractions** [combine two words into one].

Contractions

We use contractions to combine two words. **Use an apostrophe to show where a letter or letters have been removed (a contraction).**

Examples:

it is	**it's**	**class of 1987**	**class of '87**
does not	**doesn't**	**who is**	**who's**
they are	**they're**	**cannot**	**can't**
were not	**weren't**	**will not**	**won't**
you are	**you're**		

Examples:

Why didn't you answer the phone?

She hasn't received her paycheck yet.

Examples:

Why didn't you answer the phone?

She hasn't received her paycheck yet.

CONTRACTION PRACTICE 1
Add apostrophes where necessary.

1. Sam isnt coming to the library with us.

2. Dont you want something to eat?

3. Weve been working on this project all month.

4. Its starting to feel like spring.

CONTRACTION PRACTICE 2
Write the contraction form of the following words.

1. She would _she'd_
2. Could not _couldn't_
3. Will not _won't_
4. He is _he's_
5. We would _we'd_
6. I have _I've_
7. You are _you're_
8. We will _we'll_
9. Should not _should'nt_
10. She is _she's_

11. It is _it's_
12. I would _I'd_
13. That will _that'll_
14. Who is _who's_
15. Did not _Did'nt_
16. They are _they're_
17. He would _he'd_
18. We are _we'ce_
19. Would not _would'nt_
20. They would _they'd_

21. I am _I'm_
22. You will _you'll_
23. That would _____
24. She will _she'll_
25. You would _you'd_
26. That is _That's_
27. What are _what'ce_
28. He will _he'll_
29. It would _it'd_
30. I will _I'll_

Possession

Use an apostrophe to indicate possession by adding ' or 's to the end of the word. But how we do this depends on if the word is singular, plural, ends in s or does not end in s!

Add **'s** to the singular form of a word (even if it ends in s)
>Jason's car
>James's cat
>The printing press's pages

Add **'s** to plural forms that do not end in s.
>The children's museum
>The geese's food

Add **'** to plural forms that end in s.
>Three friends' letters
>Two cats' toys

If something belongs to two nouns, just make the second one possessive.
>Tom and Jerry's apartment.
>Jim and Jess's cake.

Examples:

All the players' uniforms are blue.   (uniforms belonging to all the players)
The player's uniforms are blue.   (uniforms belonging to one player)
A child's ball was kicked in our yard.   (ball belonging to the child)
The men's department is on the second floor.   (department for men)

Possessive Pronouns

Possessive pronouns confuse most kids because, right after we tell them that possessive nouns do take apostrophes, we tell them that possessive pronouns don't.

Remember, a pronoun takes the place of a noun and stands in for all nouns of that type.

"He" takes the place of all males

"She" takes the place of all females

"It" takes the place of all things [including animals unless a gender has been specified]

So,

Instead of writing:

This is Jack's boomerang.

With pronouns, we write:

This is his boomerang.

Notice that "his" takes the place of "Jack's" and the word tells us that the boomerang belongs to some dude.

 2ⁿᵈ Ed. © ibidPREP llc

Also notice also the we don't write "hi's" because possessive pronouns don't take apostrophes.

Similarly, we write "hers" not "her's," "yours" not "your's," "ours" not "our's," "theirs" not "their's" and, most importantly, we write "its" not "it's"!

If I had a glass of water for every time students wrote "it's" when they meant "its," I'd have my own ocean and a lot of glasses.

The reason students write "it's" is because English grammar is frying their circuits. There is a word "it's" which is a contraction of "it is." There are apostrophes in all possessive nouns, so...it seems only logical to write:

NO: This is it's last chance to shine.

But that is WRONG, WRONG, WRONG!

Below you see what's RIGHT, RIGHT, RIGHT:

YES: This is its last chance.

YES: Its coat was shiny.

YES: The sword comes in its own case.

YES: The spaceship blew out its engines.

YES: Sugar has its benefits.

YES: It's hard to get this straight!

Possessive Pronouns and Adjectives

Pronoun	Possessive pronouns	Possessive adjectives
I/me	Mine	My
You	Yours	Your
He/him	His	His
She/her	Hers	Her
It	Its	Its
We/us	Ours	Our
You (plural)	Yours	Your
They/them	Theirs	Their

Possessive pronouns in a sentence:

The ball is mine.
Is this doll yours or his?
That red car is theirs.
He likes store-bought macaroni
      and cheese, but dislikes ours.

Possessive adjectives in a sentence:

The ball landed in my yard.
Can I go to her house?
Their pool is the biggest.
When will our car be ready?

Grammar

POSSESSION

Please put in apostrophes as needed.

1. All the boy's bicycles are gone.

2. The dancer's dress was made of silk.

3. Did the cat eat the Smith family's food off of the table?

4. Marta plays on the girls basketball team.

5. Matthew's and Marsha's toys are all over the floor.

6. The hero's arrows aimed for the villains heart.

7. The family of dragon's breathed fire on the heroes shields.

8. The heroes horse's heads were covered in flameproof armor.

9. The boys went to the girl's party and danced with her friends.

10. Some of the girl's friends danced while her other friend's played Frisbee.

11. Unfortunately, it was the girls dog's Frisbee.

12. The girl's dog chased its Frisbee, much to all her friend's fear.

POSSESSIVE PRONOUN / ADJECTIVE PRACTICE

Write the correct possessive pronoun OR possessive adjective in the blank. Look to the underlined word for help.

1. When I got in the <u>car</u>, I saw that ___its___ seatbelt was broken.

2. The house down the street is brand new, and <u>the Smiths</u> just bought it. Now the house is ___theirs___.

3. If your computer is broken, would you like to borrow ___mine___? <u>I</u> would be happy to loan it to you.

4. <u>Sandra</u> told me I could keep ___her___ sweater since it no longer fit her.

5. I remember <u>you</u> left some books around here. Are those books ___yours___?

6. <u>Peter</u> ate ___my___ sandwich while <u>I</u> ate ___his___.

7. When it got dark, <u>they</u> went back inside ___their___ house.

8. Yesterday I found <u>a bird</u> on the side of the road; ___its___ wing was broken.

9. <u>You</u> go ___your___ way and <u>we'll</u> go ___ours___.

10. Even though we fight sometimes, <u>I</u> love ___my___ brother and sister.

11. That's a great <u>basketball</u>! ___Its___ logo says "NBA" on it.

12. As soon as we got home, I went to my bedroom and <u>my sister</u> went to _hers_.

13. I need to call the <u>Johnson family and Dr. Chavez</u>. Can you look up _their_ phone numbers for me?

14. <u>My mom and I</u> went to a baseball game over the weekend; it's one of _our_ favorite activities to do together.

15. Have you been to _their_ house? <u>They</u> have a pool and a diving board!

16. After Becky made it clear that she had done all the work, <u>she</u> received the credit that was properly _hers_.

17. The <u>soccer game</u> should be canceled, but _its_ referee does not care that it's raining.

18. Do you have a favorite color? <u>I</u> know what _mine_ is.

19. When you get to the apartment building, you can ring _our_ buzzer and <u>we'll</u> let you in!

20. <u>Danny</u>, _your_ backpack is unzipped.

21. When I went to _their_ house, <u>Zach</u> showed me how to bake chocolate chip cookies.

22. If you want to use the watercolors, you need to ask <u>Mrs. Straw</u>; they are _hers_.

23. Did you know that the jacket <u>Andy</u> wears isn't actually _his_ ?

24. I wish we could use our <u>chimney</u>, but _its_ flue is broken.

QUOTATION MARKS

Quotation marks are used to indicate that words are:

- being spoken
  - "I really like clams!" said the clown.

- copied from somewhere else
  - My recipe says, "Add garlic and butter to your clams."

- being used as titles of stories, articles or poems.
  - "Death Be Not Proud" is a brilliant sonnet, but "Batter My Heart" is better.

- referring to words in order to define them or single them out
  - Some people think "disinterested" means "not interested," but it really means "impartial."

- to indicate that the words being used have different or opposite meanings from the ones intended
  - Congress is supposed to be a "working" part of government.

For a lot of us, quotations marks can be tricky to use. Mostly because there is often a lot of punctuation and capitalization to keep straight. Let us help you keep things straight!

Spoken Quotes

> Bill's mom barged into his room and said, "Clean up this pigsty!"

As is often the case with grammar, more than just quotation marks are involved here.

Grammar

Capitalization In Quotes

Whatever is between the quotation marks is what Bill's mom said; everything else is what the narrator says. Because what Bill's mom says begins a new sentence, the first word in her quote is capitalized.

*Bill's mom barged into his room and said, "**C**lean up this pigsty!"*

CAPITALIZATION

Practice: Correct the capitalization errors in the following sentences.

1. i like to go to mcdonald's on tuesdays after Soccer Practice.

   I like Mcdonalds Tuesday Soccer practile

2. meredith says it is Silly for me to go to mcdonald's after Soccer because Fast Food is not healthy.

   Meredith Silly   mcdonald soccer fast food

3. my Mom said after i finished my homework i could watch spongebob.

   My mom I   I   Sponge bob

4. at Soccer practice, I hurt my Ankle, so i am going to see the Doctor on wednesday Morning.

   At soller   ankle I   doctor wednesday morning

5. I go to sunshine elementary school and my teacher's name is Mr. oliver.

   Sunshine Elementary school   Oliver

6. my favorite Book is the star-bellied Sneeches by doctor Seuss.

   My   book starbellied   Doctor

7. one day I want to go to africa and see a real Tiger.

   one   Africa   tiger

8. for dinner last night i ate Pizza from domino's.

   For   I pizza Dominos

9. this weekend I need to study for my Spelling Test before I play Video Games.

   This   spelling test   video games

10. i made my Favorite stuffed animal at build a bear, and I named her daisy.

   I   favorite   BuildaBear   Daisy

2ⁿᵈ Ed. © ibidPREP llc

Commas In Quotes

Commas ALWAYS come after the last word the narrator said and before the quotation marks. Like so:

> *Bill's mom barged into his room and said,* *"Clean up this pigsty!"*

> *So I shouted back,* *"Well, I don't remember asking you to come in my room!"*

And so on. It doesn't matter what word comes before the first quotation mark; it is always followed by a comma.

Punctuation in Quotes

At the end of the quotes, we often have another punctuation mark. In the examples above, we have periods and exclamation points. If the punctuation is in the original quote, it always comes inside the quotation marks.

When We Don't Capitalize

If a sentence starts with a quotation, do NOT capitalize the first word **after** the quotation.

> *"I don't care. You must clean it up before you go out to play,"* **m**y mom said, angrier than ever.

Or:

> *"Fine, ruin my life, why don't you?"* **s**obbed her sulky son.

Don't let the question mark throw you: "sobbed" is still part of the sentence and therefore **not** capitalized.

But:

> *"Oh, it's hardly as bad as that." My mom examined the mess on my dresser and laughed at how thick the dust was.*

My is capitalized in this sentence because it has begun a new sentence that is separate from what has been said, and we *always* capitalize the beginnings of those. So, unless the first word after the quotation is a proper noun or the beginning of a new sentence, **DO NOT** capitalize it.

This same rule holds for a quote that has been broken up mid-statement:

> *"Oh, come on," I said, "this will take all afternoon."*

We do **not** capitalize *this* because it is a continuation of the quoted sentence that started with *Oh, come on*.

When you're trying to figure out whether or not to capitalize something, just ask yourself two questions:

- Is it the start of a new sentence [either the narrator's or the speaker's]?
- Is it a proper noun?

Unless the answer to one of those is "yes," don't capitalize it!

USAGE

Usage is all about how words are used or misused.

Run-on Sentences

If there's one problem all young writers seem to have, it's knowing when to stop a sentence. When you let them go on for too long, you get what's called a run-on sentence. Like this:

> *I really want to do well on this exam because then I'll be able to go to the school I like best, and after that I'll be able to go to a good college and study biology in order to become a doctor, and I've wanted to be a doctor since I was a kid and had to go to the hospital to get my appendix removed.*

That's a long sentence! Not all long sentences are run-on sentences, but this one sure is. How can you tell? Well, a good rule of thumb to remember is that a sentence should not have more than two independent clauses. E.g.,

NO: *On Sunday I went shopping, but before that I went to the park, and, while there, I fell and skinned my knee.*

YES: *On Sunday I went shopping, but before that I went to the park. While there, I fell and skinned my knee.*

Another thing about run-on sentences is that they are usually about a lot of different things. A good sentence expresses one idea, and at most two. The example sentence I gave is about so many ideas! It's about wanting to do well on the exam, the school the speaker wants to go to, going to college, studying biology and so much more! Don't do this!

Those of you who like to read are probably objecting right now because some of your favorite writers use run-on sentences. Roald Dahl, for one, uses them all the time to great comic effect. But that doesn't matter because you're not writing fiction! When you are writing an essay or answering grammar questions on the Hunter Test, you are doing FORMAL writing! Formal writing means you have to follow all the rules. All of them!

And since periods are free, why not start a new sentence if you're in doubt? Just do it!

Confusing Words

English is a mutt language; it is formed from a number of different languages, so not everything makes sense. Sometimes words that seem like they should be related to one another are not at all. Worse, words that seem like they should be spelled one way are really spelled another way—or are actually different words if spelled the other way! Therefore, it is very important to be aware of the confusing words and try to keep them straight!!

Unfortunately, there is no magic bullet when it comes to spelling. There is no trick we can tell you that will show you how to spell every word. Even professional writers have trouble with spelling, so don't feel bad if you struggle with it.

However, there are certain words that you absolutely must know how to spell by heart. Why? Because if you get them wrong you will spell a *different* word and change the meaning of your sentence. That's a whole additional level of spelling something wrong! Below are some of the trickier words.

2ⁿᵈ Ed. © ibidPREP llc

HOMOPHONES, HOMOGRAPHS AND COMPOUND WORDS

Homophones

As if writing weren't hard enough already, now you've got to be on the lookout for something new: **homophones**! Homophones are words that *sound* the same but are spelled in different ways and mean different things.

You probably already know a few of them. The two most common sets of homophones are made up of three words that sound the same. They are *there*, *their* and *they're* and *to*, *too*, and *two*. Here's how you use them:

There/they're/their:

There: this one is talking about a place. *Please take this book to the table over* ***there.***

Their: this one shows that people own something. *The family took* ***their*** *dog to the park to play.*

They're: this one is a contraction that means "they are." If you can substitute "they are" and the sentence still makes sense, you need to use *they're*: *Many schools are in my hometown, but* ***they're*** *not all very good.*

To/too/two:

To: this one talks about direction or is used with verbs: *It is important* ***to*** *do your homework before you go* ***to*** *the park.*

Too: this one means *also*, or it means excessively: ***Too*** *many people are in the stadium for me to enter,* ***too.***

Two: this one is simply the number 2. It's really simple: *There are* ***two*** *kinds of people: those who understand grammar and those who don't.*

These two sets of homophones are the most common, but there are many, many more. Unfortunately, there is no trick for knowing which one to use in a given situation; you just have to learn them by heart! Here are a few more common ones that you should know.

Which/witch: A *witch* is a person who casts spells on you; use *which* for everything else! (*Which* book did you read? The book, *which* is 300 pages long, is on fire.)

Rose/rows: A *rose* is a flower and the past tense of rise (I *rose* from my chair); *rows* are the lines of seats at the movie theater.

Right/write: *Right* means to be correct, and it is also a direction (turn *right* up ahead); *write* is what you do with your pencil in class.

It's/its: *It's* is a contraction that means "it is," so if you can substitute "it is," you know you need to use *it's*. On the other hand, *its* is a word that shows possession: a dog licks *its* tail. This pair is a big one, so make sure you get it straight!

Your/you're: *Your* is used to show that you own something: you clean *your* room. *You're* is a contraction that means "you are," so you have to be able to substitute "you are" in order to use this one: *You're* going to get in trouble if you do that.

Our/Are: These aren't strictly homophones, but kids (and grown-ups) still get them confused. *Our* is another word that shows ownership, and it means "belongs to us": *Our* house is in a nice part of town. *Are* is a verb that means "to be": Those men *are* all over six feet tall.

Weather/whether: These are important ones to get right. *Weather* refers to what goes on outside—rain, wind, the sun, etc. *Whether* is the word we use to signal that there's a choice: I don't know *whether* or not I'll go to the beach today. It depends on the *weather*.

Addition/edition: *Addition*, with an "a," is what you do in math class; that's why it has "add" in it. *Edition* with an "e," is a version of something: first *edition* copies of the book are quite rare and therefore worth a lot of money.

Flower/flour: *Flower*, with a "w," is something you pick from a plant to give to your valentine; *flour*, with a "u," is what you bake a cake with.

Soar/sore: *Soar*, with an "a," is what an eagle does when it flies above you. *Sore*, with an "e," is how you might feel after an injury playing sports.

Then/than: *Then* is used to talk about time: I went to the mall, and *then* I went home. *Than* is the word we use to compare things: My brother is much taller *than* I am.

Whole/hole: *Whole* is used to talk about the entire something: I can't believe I ate the *whole* thing. *Hole* is what we use to talk about a big gap: the dog was walking along and suddenly fell in a big *hole* in the construction site.

Common Homophone Pairs and Triples

are	our	
be	bee	
bare	bear	
brake	break	
buy	by	bye
cent	scent	sent
coarse	course	
dear	deer	
die	dye	
eye	I	
for	fore	four
hair	hare	
heal	heel	he'll
hear	here	
it's	its	
in	inn	
knot	not	

know	no	
mail	male	
marry	Mary	merry
meat	meet	
oar	or	
one	won	
pair	pear	
peace	piece	
pairs	pears	
pedal	petal	
poor	pour	
sail	sale	
sea	see	
seam	seem	
sew	so	sow
some	sum	
son	sun	

steal	steel	
tail	tale	
way	weigh	
weak	week	
wear	where	

2ⁿᵈ Ed. © ibidPREP llc

<u>HOMOPHONE PRACTICE—1</u>
Choose the right homophones in each sentence.

1. (Which)/witch woman was accused of being a which/(witch?)

2. In New York City, (there)/their/they're are many museums that are world-famous for the quality of there/(their)/they're collections. There/Their/(They're) an important part of New York's international appeal.

3. To/(Too)/Two many people these days struggle when they try (to)/too/two choose among their homophones. But hey, if there are only to/too/(two) choices, at least the odds of getting it right are pretty good.

4. If it's important to you that you right/(write) well, you'll have to develop the (right)/write editing habits.

5. (It's)/Its always funny to watch a dog chase it's/(its) tail.

6. Do you know weather/(whether) or not the (weather)/whether is suitable for a ski trip?

<u>HOMOPHONE PRACTICE—2</u>
Fill in the blank with the correct homophone. Choose your words from the table and explanations on the previous page.

1. I have __two__ (2) sisters but only __one__ (1) brother.

2. The bottom of my shoe, its __sole__, is about to come off.

3. Do you know __whether__ or not we have a test in math on Friday?

4. I hope __it's__ okay that I borrowed your pen!

5. I do not believe that __I'm__ going to the concert! My parents would never let me.

6. This restaurant is supposed to be great. Have you come __here__ before?

7. You can come to __my__ house if you want. My parents can make us dinner.

8. I have seven books in my bag. That's two more __then__ you have in yours.

9. Put the __brake__ to the metal, drive faster!

10. I have way more Oreos than I can eat. Please, have __some__!

11. I want to __dye__ my hair pink next year.

12. I hear that Bosc __pears__ are ripe this season. We should go order a dozen from Harry & David.

Homographs

Now for another confusing set of words: **homographs**. Homographs are words that are spelled the same (though sometimes pronounced differently in different situations) and have different meanings. Huh? Here's an example.

*I **live** in a big house on Montague Street.*
*I went downtown to see my favorite band **live** in concert.*

Live is spelled the same way in these two sentences, but it is pronounced in two different ways and means two different things. In the first sentence, *live* means where you and your family spend all your time, but in the second *live* means that the music was not a recording.

There are many homographs in English, but the only way you can learn them is by hearing people speak and being a careful reader. Just be on the lookout for them.

Compound Words

The final kind of word to look out for is the **compound word**. As you might guess, a compound word is a word that is made up of two other words stuck together. *Lighthouse*, *doorknob* and *shoelace* are common compound words you probably already know.

However, there are some compound words that are not so straightforward (see? Another compound word). Here are two of them that might be confusing.

Someone. This is a compound word. It is NOT two words. *Someone* is calling me on the phone. I need *someone* to help me with this.

Sometimes. This is also a compound word. It is NOT two words. *Sometimes*, I feel like winter will last forever. I get to go visit my family in California, but only *sometimes*.

Here are some more:

A lot NOT Alot
　　"A lot" means "very much."—Thanks a lot, Goober!
　　"Alot," is not a word. Don't use it. EVER.

All together v. Altogether
　　"All together" means "as a group."—We succeed or fail all together.
　　"Altogether" means "completely" or "entirely."—I find lumpy oatmeal altogether revolting.

Every day v. Everyday
　　"Everyday" means "ordinary" or "usual."—These are my everyday kicks.
　　"Every day" means a "period of time."—I like to eat food every day.

All right v. Alright
　　They both mean the same thing: "okay," "satisfactory," "certainty," or "safe."—
　　Everything is all right, and that's alright by me!

Some Time v. Sometime
　　"Some time" means "a considerable period of time." –For some time, the world has been turning.
　　"Sometime" means "a vague time in the future."—I'll call you sometime.

　　　　2ⁿᵈ Ed. © ibidPREP llc

Cannot NOT Can Not

"Cannot" means "unable."

"Can not" means "this is not a can."

COMPOUND WORD QUESTIONS

Choose the right word to fit the sentence.

1. A lot/Alot of people like ice cream.

2. Some people would eat it every day/everyday.

3. Celery can not/cannot make people fat.

4. Altogether/All together, the team must decide if the sacrifice is worth the risk.

5. Booboo went some time/sometime without blinking his eyes.

6. Everyday/every day thoughts usually include imagining sometime/some time when everything will be perfect.

Now let's put How to Write together with our Grammar...

Chapter Four

The Essay

Writing essays is difficult for many students. Even students who love to read may find writing difficult and dread essay assignments. Some students have a hard time answering specific questions, providing specific examples, organizing their work or proofreading their work for grammar and sense. Some students feel like they've said everything needed in four lines while their teacher wants a full page; other students go on and on and run out of time without completing their essay or making a point! Worst of all for some of you: you've been given a bunch of rules about writing and NOT ONE is helpful!

Well, take heart, because you are not alone, and we are going to show you how the essay can be much easier AND be a great way to communicate ACTUAL thoughts!! If you're willing to think, that is...

THE HUNTER ESSAY

The Hunter essay is not like the essays you're probably used to writing in school. In school, teachers usually tell you to write an essay about a book or a reading. They ask you what it's about. They ask you why a character decided to do something or why something happened. Then they ask you to prove your answer by using specific details from a specific text [book, story, article, etc.].

The Hunter essay, on the other hand, is not usually about a specific text. There is not one source you need to refer to in your essay. You're usually free to choose whatever sources you like for your examples. Hooray! Er, wait, what? How do you know what to write about?!

The best way to approach the Hunter essay and any other open-ended essay is the same way you should approach every other type of essay question:

- **Think of an answer to every part of the question.**
- **Come up with examples to support your point or story.**
- **Organize your thoughts into clear parts of an essay broken up into the appropriate paragraphs.**

Answer the Question—All of It

Most students are really good kids. They try hard to do what is asked of them and often feel uncomfortable veering from instructions. However, there are times when we are asked questions or confronted with essay topics that are unclear or open-ended or whose answer, if we are honest with ourselves, we just have no idea about. Oftentimes, the Hunter essay questions are like that.

The Hunter Test prefers to give you questions that have no right answer to see your imagination, creativity and thoughtfulness at work. Questions like "What does it mean to be fair?" "Are new things better than old things?" or "What would your perfect future look like?" The thing to realize, however, is that no other kid answering these questions knows the right answer, nor do the teachers who give you the test. How do I know that none of them knows the answer? Because there is none!

So if there's no right answer, what on earth could the test possibly be looking for from you? How could you be graded without right answers? The trick is to realize that they don't really care which side of a question you take. You can argue that new things are better than old things, or you can argue that old things are better than new things. What matters is that you pick **one** side and then provide a good reason for picking your answer.

NO: *Being fair means treating people fairly because you don't want to be treated unfairly.*
NO: *Being fair means that you don't break rules because that isn't right.*
YES: *Being fair means playing by the rules, so that people do not take advantage of each other.*

No matter how you answer, your job is just to pick a side and make a point! Do it as quickly as possible, since there's no reason to prefer one side to the other! Then make sure you've come up with an answer or dealt with every part of the question. The questions on the Hunter Test often have more than one part to them. It is **VERY** important that you address all parts of the question in your essay.

"What does it mean to be fair?"
- What does being fair mean?
- How is fairness important to you?
- Have you ever been treated unfairly or been unfair to others?

If you have trouble coming up with an answer to any part of your question and finding a reason for it, just start thinking about examples relating to your topic and see what they tell you. OR:

Make Like a Politician—Make the Question Your Own

Politicians are famous for hearing one question and then changing the question enough that they can give an answer to a question they are more comfortable with. That means that you're going to answer the question on your own terms—just like a politician. You are allowed to change a question as long as you redefine the terms. E.g., if the essay asks about giving versus receiving, and you want to talk about working, then you may say something like this to shift the conversation:

If by giving you mean contributing to the world by working, then "yes," it is better to give than to receive.

Or, to return to the question about fairness, if softball is the thing you care most about in the whole world, use softball to talk about how to be fair. Just as there's no right answer to these questions, there's no wrong kind of evidence to use (so long as you can make it apply to the question!)

So how would we build an argument about fairness? First we come up with a **thesis**—a thesis answers the question but more importantly provides a ***reason*** for your answer. A good thesis could be a **one-sentence answer** to the question. My thesis might be: *Being fair means following all the agreed-upon rules for whatever you're doing*.

This thesis answers the question, and it is something that I can **build an argument** for. Here's an example of a paragraph I might write:

> ***Being fair means following all the agreed-upon rules for whatever you're doing, so that people do not take advantage of one another. Look at softball, or any other sport. Two teams compete in order to win, but there are always people on the field who aren't playing: umpires. Why? Because in order for sports to work, someone has to make sure that everyone is following all the rules. Otherwise, one team might win, but nobody would think they won fairly and it wouldn't really count. Additionally, each team must know the rules beforehand and agree that they are the right ones to play by. Otherwise the game would fall to pieces.***

This paragraph shows how we use a specific example—softball—to make a less specific claim about fairness: *fairness means people are following the rules*. When faced with one of these ambiguous questions, we want all of our paragraphs to make some point about our thesis. Except for our conclusion!

2nd Ed. © ibidPREP llc

Why except the conclusion? Because that's where we wrap it all up! In our conclusions we restate the thesis, summarize the argument we made and explain why our answer is a good one. And that's it! Remember: if you do it well, your reader will be convinced of what you argued!

TYPES OF PROMPTS

Imagination Prompt

Half the time, the Hunter Test won't ask you to make any argument at all. Instead, they'll ask you to imagine a story and tell them that story as well as you can. Here's an example of such a prompt:

You are in your school's library. You are so wrapped up in your book that you don't hear the librarian announce that the library is closing for the day. Locked in the library, you find that at night the books come alive and you can go in and out of each one.

Write an essay imagining a journey from one book to another [choose two or three books from your own reading]. Tell us about your journey and how one book leads to the next in your travels.

You must write an essay in which you:
- *Name two or three books you have read.*
- *Use sensory detail to make the settings of your books seem real and come alive.*
- *Convey what your journey through these books means to you.*

Obviously you can't study for something like this. I'm willing to bet you've never been locked in a library over-night, and I'm positively certain you've never wandered from Narnia to Hogwarts in a single evening. But you know what? That's OK! Neither has anyone else taking the test! So how are we going to handle this question?

First, we're going to identify this as an **open-ended** essay question. This means that this question has no right answer, but it *does* require you to use your imagination. (We told you you'd have to think!) This kind of question will also require you to tell a story. And what makes a story good? The reader can picture everything. And how do we help the reader picture the story we tell? Using **sensory details**.

Sensory Details

To get our sensory details, we're going to do nothing first. Just think. Use your **imagination**. (You are allowed to think!) Think back to the books you've read in your life. Which ones did you really like? Which two presented **worlds** you really wanted to enter? Remember, there's no right answer here. You could go 20,000 leagues beneath the surface of the ocean, you can go to Pluto, and you can go hang out with dinosaurs. Doesn't matter. Just pick two.

Now start thinking about what those worlds are like. As the prompt tells us, we want to describe these worlds with **sensory details**. What are those? Details that appeal to the *five* senses. Did you even know that you had five senses? They are TOUCH, SMELL, TASTE, SOUND and SIGHT.

Here are two example paragraphs about *Jurassic Park*, one of the books I would like to enter. One of the paragraphs is full of sensory details and one of them isn't. Try to see which is which.

> ***I walked into Jurassic Park in the middle of the day. The sun was high. Cold-blooded dinosaurs were walking around eating leaves. Some of them walked on four legs but others walked on two. I ate a piece of***

fruit that I found on the ground, and then I drank some water out of a creek. There weren't any other people around, though, and I got lonely without anyone to talk to. So I walked away and decided to visit London, because that's where James Bond lives.

Here's a second paragraph:

> *I walked through the brown, squishy mud into Jurassic Park and coughed on the air because it smelled like a hot, wet towel. The sun, directly overhead in the bright blue sky, was a hard fist that made my skin itch and ache. Enormous dinosaurs with scaly green skin reflecting the sun stomped by, shaking the ground and hurting my ears with their evil roars. They shook a smelly purple fruit covered in white hairs loose from a tall tree. I tried it, but it was too bitter for me, and I had to wash out my mouth with green creek water. This was too scary for me, and I needed help. But there was no one! So I ran away from Jurassic Park to London: there, I knew, James Bond would protect me.*

Which one is full of sensory details? The second one! We learn what Jurassic Park tastes like, feels like, looks like, sounds like and smells like. The cool thing here is that because nobody has ever been to Jurassic Park (it's not real, after all), you can describe it any old way you want. You can decide that it actually feels really cold. You can decide that it's comfortable and all the dinosaurs want to invite you to a birthday party. It does NOT matter. All that matters is that you describe it. Where else in school can you write about dinosaurs and James Bond?

Memory Prompts

The techniques we use for the **open-ended**, imagination questions also help with prompts about your **memory**. Consider this one:

Living in New York City, we all take journeys, both big and small. Some occur daily, some happen once a year, and others take place only on specific occasions.

Write an essay or tell a true story about a journey you have taken, or take every day, in our city. It can be the short walk to the store or to school; a medium-length journey to a hospital, a place of worship or of entertainment; or a longer trip across boroughs to visit a relative or friend. These are just some examples of New York City journeys.

Your task is to create a portrait of New York City as it is visible on your trip. Use sensory detail to describe this slice of the city that you know personally and reveal what it means to you.

You must write an essay or tell a true story in which you:
- *Name and describe real places you are familiar with.*
- *Use sensory details to create a vivid picture of the city as you know it.*
- *Convey what your New York journey meant to you.*

Like the trip through the books, this one is a journey. So we start at the beginning again by **setting the scene**: where are you leaving from? Where are you going? Why? How do you feel about it?

Then, once you've left, you describe the sensory details of the trip. What does your part of New York sound like? What does it smell like? Is it hot or cold? Is it raining? Just as with the trip through the books, your job is to make what you describe as *vivid* as possible. ("Vivid" means intensely detailed.)

Except this one is different in that you probably already *have* taken a trip through New York. So now our job is to figure out which trip of yours to tell about.

2nd Ed. © ibidPREP llc

We know that they really want for you to be able to give sensory details, so that makes it easier to decide: pick a trip that you remember really, really well. It could be a trip that you took once but was incredibly memorable, or it could be a trip you take all the time. Either way, pick one of the trips that you can describe really well.

That will leave you with some choices, so how can you choose among them? You have to pick the one that means something to you. So don't tell about a super-boring trip to the grocery store! Instead, trips that mean something to you involve something important. You could be going to the store to get the new *Call of Duty* game that you've been wanting for six months. Or you could be taking a taxi to the hospital to meet your new baby brother. Or you could be leaving your apartment for the last time as you move to another part of town. These are all trips that can be both VIVID and MEANINGFUL. Here's an example:

My aunt and I were in the backseat of a taxi. We were heading downtown along the river, and the driver, a small man whose teeth were stained a dark color, was trying to weave his way through the impatient traffic. My aunt was biting her nails, which is something I'd never seen her do before. Usually she is so flawlessly composed, so calm. But as we pulled up in front of the hospital, she'd opened the door before the car had fully stopped. Her sister—my mom—was inside the hospital giving birth to my first brother.

In terms of how we write, we now proceed the same way we did with the **open-ended** questions. We tell the story as vividly as we can, and then we talk about its **meaning**. For this question, clearly, we'd conclude by writing how important it was to have a new brother.

Obviously, what something means to you is meant to be personal—it has to be, by definition. But this doesn't mean that you can say that from getting *Call of Duty* you learned that you're meant to be a chef when you grow up. That wouldn't make any sense. So just because you have some freedom here—and you do—doesn't mean you get to throw logic out the window!

ORGANIZATION

So you know what sensory details are. Now what? How are we going to **ORGANIZE** this essay? Well this one is pretty easy to organize because they tell you that they want you to describe a journey. If you were going to describe your summer vacation to Paris, where would you start? Would you start with the plane ride home? With some macaroons you ate on your third day? No. You'd probably start at the beginning. **Going in time order [either from beginning to end or from the end to the beginning] is always a great way to structure your writing!**

How do we begin? Realizing that you're locked up in the library and all the books are coming to life! So we start by **setting the scene**. We do this using sensory details, too, and we want to use them to help the reader understand the beginning of what's important. A good place to start is just before things start to get weird. Like this:

I was sitting in an armchair in the corner reading a novel when suddenly the lights went out with a loud noise. The library wasn't totally dark, but there sure wasn't enough light to read. I looked around to see who had turned them off but found nobody. I called out and no one answered. I realized I was all alone in the library. When I tried to run outside, I found the doors were locked. Just as I was about to panic, I heard a small voice behind me. It was a man's voice. "Sir?" I cried out. And then I almost fainted: it was a small man standing on top of a book by Charles Dickens.

This is an introductory paragraph to our story of our journey through the books. Now that the reader knows the situation, we can begin talking about going to see Jurassic Park and London.

Of course you won't get this prompt—it's already been given! But being ready to give **sensory details** and to

set the scene are useful for prompts that require imagination.

MEANING

You've come so far, now you just have to figure out how to get out. How are you going to wrap it all up? It's the end of your journey, so let's reach some conclusions. Did you like where you went? Did you learn anything about yourself? (Yes, you did, and you should tell the reader what.) This is the paragraph where you add meaning to what you've written.

What is **meaning**? This is the hardest part of the essay for most people, but fear not! Here is an example of a paragraph that show the kind of meaning they're looking for.

> *After my trips to Jurassic Park and London, I was so relieved to find that the library had opened. Even though I liked seeing all those dinosaurs, I realized that I could never be happy living without lots of other people around. So I actually liked London better, even though it was super rainy, and I think I would be happy living over there in England. They speak my language, they have really beautiful buildings, and I liked how the Thames River went through the center of the city, unlike the Hudson. Even so, I was glad to be back home in New York, and as soon as I got to my apartment, I had a big snack and went to sleep on the couch. I dreamed of dinosaurs.*

This paragraph contains meaning because it shows the narrator—me—making sense of the experience. For example, I learned that I don't actually want to be around dinosaurs and that I'm happiest being around other people. So I'm now *wiser* about who I am. Further, I've got some new idea about how I want to live my life: perhaps I will move to London. Any sort of new plan for the future is a form of finding meaning.

So, **meaning** is basically where we find the moral of our own story.

EXAMPLES

Keep It Real

Once you've figured out your answer to the question and your reason for that answer, concentrate on the theme or topic of your essay. Then cast about your mind for anything that has to do with the topic. It is not important whether it seems like a positive or negative example—just be **specific.** Choose proper nouns, people, places, events over generic nouns. If you are thinking of bullies don't write about *bullies*; write about *Draco Malfoy*. SO:

YES: *In my dream I was throwing a football like Peyton Manning.*
NO: *In my dream I was throwing like a great quarterback.*

I Can't Think of Any Examples!

Even when a Hunter essay is personal, students can have a tough time thinking of examples to support their point. There is often more than one issue at play here, so let's take them one at a time:

1. **You don't know much of the conventional stuff that you really need to know about**—OK, so you've been really busy watching cartoons for most of your young life, and your grasp on current events, past events, art and literature [all the classy stuff] is a bit weak. Well, that's not really great for you as a well-rounded person, but it's not a death sentence on the essay either.

   • **Don't worry about being classy.** Some of the brightest writers I've known have spent a good deal of time making brilliant points using Bugs Bunny, SpongeBob and Facebook to prove them. Contrary to what students have often been told, it doesn't necessarily help your cause to write only about Shakespeare or Martin Luther King, Jr., especially if you don't really know how to connect them to your point.

2. **You think everything you think of is wrong or dumb.** This is where being a kid, or a human being, can be a bit of a drag. Your self-consciousness makes you believe that if you think of it, it can't possibly be valid or interesting or right. I can't tell you how many times students have said to me, "I can't think of any examples." Then we talk about the topic a bit, and I mention a possible example or two, and they say, "Oh, I thought of that, but I didn't think it was good enough..." *Please* save the self-consciousness for your teen years [but please get over that quickly too!] and just go with the first examples that pop into your mind. As you start to write about your example, you may even point out its shortcomings as an example before your reader thinks to and then try to turn that shortcoming into further proof of your point. That's what a good lawyer does. She never allows anything to keep her from making her point.

   Of course, Draco Malfoy was not always a bully or a bad kid. Some of the reasons he acted the way he did was because his father, Lucius Malfoy, was so mean to him. However, Harry Potter was treated poorly by his aunt and uncle, and he never let that turn him into a bully or a mean person.

3. **Oh, but I can't say that!** It happens all the time. A student has an honest-to-god opinion and some honest-to-god examples to back it up. When I notice this, I'm eager to see his essay for the topic because I assume it's all teed up for him. Then I read the essay, and it has nothing to do with anything I thought he would have written about. When I ask why he didn't write about what he really thinks, he tells me: "Oh, I couldn't write about that. It's too controversial." Some of my students think every essay reader is a narrow-minded, 80-year-old grouch who dislikes anything progressive, or edgy, or retro or...interesting. Please, give the essay readers some credit here. They may not be the stuff of the next editorial board of the *New Yorker,* but they're not Archie Bunker[1] either. Your readers don't have to be in agreement with what you've said AS LONG AS YOU SAY IT WELL.

YES: *George W. Bush faced many challenges as president, and many believe that he might not have been entirely up to all of them.*
NO: *George W. Bush is the worst president ever. He ruined this country.*

YES: *Many feel that President Obama's tendency to act only after considering things for a long time meant that he was not always a strong leader.*
NO: *Obama is the worst president ever. He ruined this country.*

---

[1] look him up

Examples—Practice

In the exercise below, determine the theme of the question. Then list five examples that pertain to the theme regardless of the point the examples seem to be trying to make about that theme. Let your mind wander...

Question 1: Is it better to give than to receive?
THEME: *Giving*
EXAMPLES:
1. Getting presents for Xmas
2. Giving to charity
3. Frodo in *Lord of the Rings*
4. Scholarships
5. Scrooge in *A Christmas Carol*

Question 2: Do we learn better by doing or by being shown how to do things?
THEME: *Learning*
EXAMPLES:

testing your ideas

playing an instrement

making a recipe for cooking

learning to eat

Question 3: Tell us about your perfect summer day.
THEME: going to a lake
EXAMPLES:

Swimming

boating

eating food outside

tubing

HOW TO WRITE THE ESSAY

Now that we've tackled the topic, come up with an answer and planned it, let's write.

The Bare Bones

Everything you write should have a beginning, a middle and an end—from the shortest sentence to the longest essay. It all starts with the sentence.

2ⁿᵈ Ed. © ibidPREP llc

BAD RULES

MOST STUDENTS WE WORK WITH RECALL VERY FEW WRITING GUIDELINES, AND THE ONES THEY DO RECALL ARE OFTEN WRONG, UNIMPORTANT OR MISGUIDED.

DON'T USE "I"—IT'S NOT GREAT TO START EVERY SENTENCE WITH THE PRONOUN "I," BUT IF YOU USE "I" SPARINGLY AND CORRECTLY, THEN IT'S NOT REALLY A PROBLEM. [REMEMBER THAT I TOLD YOU THIS.]

NEVER START A SENTENCE WITH "BECAUSE"—THIS ONE MAKES NO SENSE. AGAIN, JUST DON'T USE IT AT THE BEGINNING OF EVERY SENTENCE.

LENGTH MATTERS—MOST STUDENTS SPEND MORE TIME WORRYING ABOUT HOW LONG THEIR ESSAYS ARE THAN ACTUALLY WRITING THEM. LONGER ESSAYS ARE NOT BETTER, NOR ARE SHORT ESSAYS NECESSARILY BAD OR GOOD. YOUR ONE AND ONLY JOB IN AN ESSAY IS TO ANSWER THE QUESTION IN FRONT OF YOU COMPLETELY, MAKE ONE POINT, AND SUPPORT IT WITH EXAMPLES IN A CLEAR, WELL-REASONED AND STRUCTURED ESSAY.

Sentences

Every sentence must contain a verb and a subject. That's it!

I ran home.

In fact, with English sentences, the shorter the better. Some sentences may even have only one word. When the verb is a command, the subject is implied in the verb:

Stop! [It is implied that someone, YOU, should stop.]

If, in your writing, you find yourself sticking together clause upon clause with lots of phrases sprinkled in your sentence, START ANOTHER SENTENCE. They're free!

NO: *I ran home, and then I got a drink of water because I was thirsty from running but the water was warm, so I spit it out!*
YES: *I ran home. When I got home, I got a drink of water. Unfortunately, the water was warm, so I spit it out!*

PARAGRAPHS

Paragraphs—the Beginning

We will deal with the essay later, but the first brick in the wall of the essay is the paragraph. The beginning of the paragraph may be called the TOPIC SENTENCE. This sentence usually connects to the previous paragraph (unless it's the first sentence of the first paragraph) and advances the essay (or story) to its next step. Here's an example:

Just as cotton was king in the South, manufacturing ruled the North.

After the TOPIC SENTENCE of a paragraph, the next sentence generally begins to explain the point of the TOPIC SENTENCE—we'll call it the POINT SENTENCE.

The Northern states did not have the best land for large-scale farming, but they did have many of the features needed to become strong manufacturing centers.

See? This second sentence explains and elaborates the TOPIC SENTENCE.

Paragraphs—The Middle

Now we're off to the races! Everything from here to the END of the paragraph is meant to provide specific examples to support the POINT SENTENCE.

Many of the Northern states had excellent harbors like New York and Boston harbors, which made it easier to sell their products. The Northern states also had larger city populations in which to find workers, such as those in New York, Boston and Philadelphia. Another common feature of the people of the Northern states was a strong belief in the value of work that came in part from their Puritan ancestors.

Paragraphs—The End

The thing to remember about all endings: conclusions conclude. The CONCLUDING SENTENCE should do what all endings do—wrap things up and leave us pointed toward the future.

All of these things made the North a strong manufacturing power and helped lead to the conflict of the Civil War.

All Together

Just as cotton was king in the South, manufacturing ruled the North. The Northern states did not have the best land for large-scale farming, but they did have many of the features needed to become strong manufacturing centers. Many of the Northern states had excellent harbors like New York and Boston harbors, which made it easier to sell their products. The Northern states also had larger city populations in which to find workers, such as those in New York, Boston and Philadelphia. Another common feature of the people of the Northern states was a deep belief in the value of work that came in part from their Puritan ancestors. All of these things made the North a strong manufacturing power and helped lead to the conflicts of the Civil War.

How to Edit [the soul of writing!]

Many students look at writing essays the way most people would look at swimming through a lake of acid without goggles; the sooner they can get to the other side, the better.

Here's the problem, though. Writing an essay is actually more like cooking a delicious meal, which you are going to serve up to a panel of judges (readers) who will taste it and say things like "I loved the presentation!" and "It's so interesting what you did with the quail egg here!" You get the idea. So, think about it. Would you serve up a dish to that panel without first tasting it yourself? We hope not! So remember, on the essay, save a little time to TASTE YOUR ESSAY. What are you looking for?

First, do your paragraphs and sentences have clear beginnings, middles and ends?

2nd Ed. © ibidPREP llc

Do your ideas build upon and flow into each other?

Are you repeating yourself and being repetitive and redundant, like this sentence?

BUILD AND FOLLOW

As the cars of a train go, so do your ideas. Each must **follow** the one before it. (See below.)

It does not **crash** into the idea ahead of it, nor does it **disconnect** from the one before it. (See below.)

Think of your sentences as being made of two parts, a first idea and a second idea. As you write, the second idea of your previous sentence becomes the first idea of the next sentence, and so on. This way, like the cars of a train, your ideas build upon and follow each other. By connecting sentences in this way, you ensure that you are not confusing (or boring) your reader (or accidentally hitting them with your crashing essay train).

Here's how this might work:

- The **man** went to the **store.**
  - The **store** was **crowded.**
    - **Crowds** had formed because a **storm** was coming.
      - **The storm was going to be bad.**
        - **Because it was going to be so bad, everyone went to the store to stock up.**
          - **Try writing something this way, and then go read one of the proofreading paragraphs (p. 110). It helps!**

Segues

Nope, not those weird people-mover things you see all over Washington, D.C., and other touristy towns. We mean the **words that connect** your ideas. Don't just start your sentences with "One example is..." and "Another example is..." [although that's better than just starting to talk about things out of the blue].

NO: *Idea 1: One example of an evil animal is the American housecat.*
           Idea 2: Another example of an evil animal is the Canadian mongoose.

YES: *Idea 1: American housecats are widely considered to be evil. Like the housecat, Canadian mongooses are known to eat their owners' pet goldfish.*

Some Useful Segues...

Because	Therefore	Although	While	Similarly	Furthermore
Thus	As a result	However	First of all	Consequently	Alternatively

Stop Repeating Yourself, Stop Saying the Same Things Over and Over, & Don't Be So Repetitive and Redundant

What makes English such a fabulous language in which to communicate [and American English especially] is that it favors conciseness[2] and clarity. You can get to the point really quickly. When you reread your work, watch for any sentences that do not move your argument forward at all. You want each sentence or idea to move forward from the previous one, even if that progress is only a centimeter or so.

ZERO SENTENCES

ZERO SENTENCES ARE THOSE BAD SENTENCES MANY STUDENTS ARE SO FOND OF; THEY SIMPLY RESTATE THE PREVIOUS SENTENCE. STUDENTS USUALLY RESORT TO **ZERO SENTENCES** IN ORDER TO FILL SPACE OR BECAUSE THEY CAN'T THINK OF ANYTHING ELSE TO SAY. IF YOU ARE REPEATING YOURSELF TO FILL SPACE, STOP IT—YOUR READERS AREN'T IDIOTS; THEY WILL NOTICE. IF YOU ARE REPEATING YOURSELF BECAUSE YOU CAN'T THINK OF WHAT TO SAY NEXT, LOOK TO THE END OF YOUR LAST SENTENCE. FOR EXAMPLE:

A. [SENTENCE 1] ALL CATS ARE EVIL.

B. [SENTENCE 2 – ZERO SENTENCE – BAD] THE AMERICAN HOUSECAT IS EVIL.

C. [SENTENCE 2 – POINT SENTENCE – GOOD] PERHAPS THE MOST EVIL MEMBER OF THE FELINE FAMILY IS THE AMERICAN HOUSECAT.

[2] succinctness, getting to the point, shortness, brevity

2ⁿᵈ Ed. © ibidPREP llc

Essay Structure Summary

Please remember to try to keep things simple. Don't worry so much about the number of paragraphs or the number of sentences in your paragraph as about having a strong introduction, body and conclusion.

Here's basically what they all should contain.

Intro:

Just as it is important to make a good impression when you are introducing yourself to someone, it is very important to start your essays with a strong introduction. Please try to be clear and direct and make your points efficiently in your intro. Here's what is good to include:

- State your opinion on the topic:
  - *My elementary school dance was one of the most special events of my life.*
- Tell us why you have that opinion:
  - The dance was so special because of my friends.
- Specify:
  - I got to spend time with old friends, especially my best friend.
  - I was also happy to make new friends

Body:

Discuss each specific in its own paragraph [or combine as needed].

1. My old friends [made me happy at the dance because...]
2. My best friend [made me happy at the dance because...]
3. My new friends [made me happy at the dance because...]

Conclusion:

Conclusions Conclude

No matter what you read or write on these tests, the last paragraph or lines are going to act like last lines and paragraphs. They are going to wrap up, however slightly, what has just been said, and draw a conclusion, however simple, from what came before. Once you have done that, you may point to the future.

Meeting new friends makes the dance special. Old and new friends alike come together for that great night. I look forward to the future evenings full of dancing and friends.

The Over-Read

The most important part of writing is re-writing. The first time we put down our thoughts, we are trying to get our ideas on paper as directly as possible and connect our examples while they're fresh in our minds. But, the second (and third, fourth, fifth...) times we go over our words, we are shaping and honing our message to be clear, concise and engaging to our readers. If you can communicate this way, you are writing!

So, once you have finished writing your piece, make sure you have left yourself a few minutes in which to read it over. When you read it over, you are no longer the writer of the piece; you are an **editor**, and you are reading for:

- **BEGINNINGS**, **MIDDLES** AND **ENDS**.
- **BUILD** & **FLOW** OF IDEAS.
- **SPELLING** AND **GRAMMAR**.The next chapter will help you tidy up your grammar.

It's very important that you don't just hand it in before the last period is dry. Would you eat in a restaurant in which the chef didn't taste her own food? Then why would you expect someone to read your stuff if you won't read it first?

Proofreading

Test your new grammar and reading-over skills here! Mark each paragraph with your pencil to make it right!

Proofread the readings below and correct any errors.

Reading 1
The little old lady lived by the river. She had many friends among the animals in the woods. They came to her house every morning and every morning she fed them. One day the animals came to the little old lady's house, but she wasn't there. The bird tapped on the window pane, but no one answered. the deer knocked on her door with their hoof , but still she did not answer. What had happened to the old lady. All the animals were deep concerned.

Reading 2
Goober is my worst student. She wears too sock. Goober's brain is filled with too many things Some of the things in Goober's brain is: dust bunnies, pillows, candles, and smelly socks. I also think that Goober is too big to fit in my office.

Reading 3
When I was born they broke the mold. There is no one like me in the whole world. I am seven feet tall and so handsome your eye would weep if you could Look at me. I like to ride wild pigs and arm wrestle polar bears. My favorite sport is professional metal eating; there are very few people in The world who do it. There is only one person in the world of whom I am afraid: Goober. She is biggest and meanest than I.

Reading 4
There are so many fun subject in school. It is so hard to pick a favorite subject. However, overall my absolute favorite subject is reading.

Why is reading my favorite subject? Well, that is because one, it is fun to do. Two, what do I do when I am sad, read! Someone should write a song about that. And lastly, three, I love to get wrapped up in a good story.

2ⁿᵈ Ed. © ibidPREP llc

It is fun for your mom and dad to read to you once in a while. Also, at school we have litaracher groups (book clubs). However, there is homework. Our teacher reads to us too, but after that we discuss it.

Reading in the ELA in my opinion doesn't count as real reading. Neither do practice tests. That is because they have questions about them. Also, there aren't chapters or polt twists, and worst of all, no cliff-hangers! Information book sort of count as real books. Also, in my opinion, picture books don't really count as real books. Biographys such as the Who Was… books do count as real books. They may picuters but it's ok. *has Pictures*

In conclusion, reading is my favorite subject. It is fun for the hole family (and class). *Whole*

PRACTICE ESSAYS

Now that you've thought about all the different parts of writing, please try the essays below.

Be sure to:

- **Think of an answer to every part of the question.**
- **Come up with examples to support your point or story.**
- **Organize your thoughts into clear parts of an essay broken up into the appropriate paragraphs.**

Here's a sample essay to go with a prompt you saw earlier.

Prompt:

You are in your school's library. You are so wrapped up in your book that you don't hear the librarian announce that the library is closing for the day. Locked in the library, you find that at night the books come alive and you can go in and out of each one.

Write an essay imagining a journey from one book to another [choose two or three books from your own reading]. Tell us about your journey and how one book leads to the next in your travels.

You must write an essay in which you:
- Name two or three books you have read.
- Use sensory detail to make the settings of your book seem real and come alive.
- Convey what your journey through these books means to you.

Silence

Science

Sample Essay:

I was sitting in an armchair in the corner of the library reading a novel when suddenly the lights went out with a loud noise. The library wasn't totally dark, but there sure wasn't enough light to read. I looked around to see who had switched the lights off but found nobody. I called out and no one answered. I realized I was all alone in the library. When I tried to run outside, I found the doors were locked. Just as I was about to panic, I heard a small voice behind me. It was a man's voice. "Sir?" I cried out. And then I almost fainted: it was a small man standing on top of a book by Charles Dickens.

"What book are you from?" he barked. "I don't recognize you!"

"I'm not from any book," I stammered. "I'm from my apartment."

"Humbug! I'm from <u>A Christmas Carol</u>," he sneered. "It's a really good book. At night here, we all come alive, even the bad books like—"

He was interrupted by a huge roar. It was coming from a small white paperback nearby. I walked over, picked it up to see what was roaring and suddenly found myself in a lush jungle: <u>Jurassic Park</u>! A T-Rex was running the other way, leaving me all alone on the edge of a swamp.

I walked through the brown, squishy mud into Jurassic Park and coughed on the air because it smelled like a hot, wet towel. The sun, directly overhead in the bright blue sky, was a hard fist that made my skin itch and ache. Enormous dinosaurs with scaly green skin reflecting the sun stomped by, shaking the ground and hurting my ears with their evil roars. They shook a smelly purple fruit covered in white hairs loose from a tall tree. I tried it, but it was too bitter for me, and I had to wash out my mouth with green creek water. This was too scary for me, and I needed help. But there was no one! So I ran away from Jurassic Park and jumped inside a large brown hardcover: there I knew, in London, James Bond would protect me.

I found myself, dripping with rain, standing in the plaza before the beautiful, looming entrance of England's National Gallery. A sleek black Mercedes pulled up in front of me, and a trim elderly lady stepped out from the back, hiding underneath a huge umbrella. She came up next to me and muttered, "Stay cool. Don't look at those Russian guys over there." Suddenly a bunch of men in black coats, shouting in some weird language full of consonants, pulled out big guns and started running up the steps of the museum. Then they scrambled: James Bond was in front of the main door, gun drawn, ready to take them out one by one. "No one steals my country's art! Come on, M!" And then the trim elderly lady beside me pulled out a tiny pistol and aimed at the Russian who seemed to be in charge. He froze, looked around and then fell to his knees, crying like a little child. It was so thrilling to meet the British Special Intelligence agents, but I left the book because James Bond and M had to take the criminals to headquarters.

After my trips to London and Jurassic Park, I was so relieved to find that the library had opened. Even though I liked seeing all those dinosaurs, I realized that I could never be happy living without lots of other people around. So I actually liked London better, even though it was super rainy, and I think I would be happy living over there in England. They speak my language, they have really beautiful buildings, and I liked how tough their secret agents are. Even so, I was glad to be back home in New York, and as soon as I got to my apartment, I had a big snack and went to sleep on the couch. I dreamed of dinosaurs.

2ⁿᵈ Ed. © ibidPREP llc

Imagine you get to invite a fictional character to your birthday party. The character can be anyone from a book, movie, TV show, video game, etc.

Write an essay in which you explain why you choose whom you invite and how their presence would affect your birthday party.

You must write an essay in which you:
- Name whom you would invite to your birthday party.
- Use sensory detail to make your party come alive.
- Convey what meeting the person you invite means to you.

PLANNING SPACE

— masterhand
— Pit
— dockPit
— kirby
— link (what verison?)
— inkling
— hat kid

There is a common saying: *"If something's not broken, don't try to fix it."*

Write an essay in which you explain whether or not you agree that it is best to wait until things break to improve them.

You must write an essay in which you:
- Make an argument for or against the saying.
- Use examples to help make your argument.
- Relate the saying to your own experience.

PLANNING SPACE

2nd Ed. © ibidPREP llc

All of us have possessions that are very special to us but might be insignificant to someone else. A teddy bear, for example, or the boarding pass for the first flight you ever took.

What is one of your most prized possessions?

You must write an essay in which you:
- Tell how you came to own your valuable possession.
- Use sensory details to make your possession vivid.
- Explain why your possession means so much to you.

PLANNING SPACE

Imagine you have a time machine that can instantly take you anywhere—at any time period.

Which two times and places would you visit and why?

You must write an essay in which you:

- Tell which two places you would visit.
- Use sensory details to make your destinations come alive.
- Explain why these times would mean so much to you.

PLANNING SPACE

—Future
—past

2400 BCE

American Rivoultion

(but i will use Futuristic wepons from 2400 BCE)

intro
—where i get the time machine
—I will go to the Future with from present day which will be world-wide.
—I will get wepons and wreck the british in the American Revoultion, Ending I go back and realize was what I did ...

2nd Ed. © ibidPREP llc

I was walking around my school and was going to my theator class when I saw a costudian [custodian] room open. Seeing this I looked and saw a 20 dollar bill just inside. When I walked inside to take the money I saw a time machine! I looked around set the dials and was off!

I had set the dials to the year 2957 so I found my self in New york 2957. my school was now a soccer field and the time machine was in a tree. I walked to a near by Pawn shop and asked how much for a 2018 $20 dollar bill? She said "let me see!" I showed it to her and she said "wow, 295...." "dollars?" I asked she said "no, 295 billion" I looked at her eyes wide

She said "this more the 900 year old" have a creditcard kid" I said "here is one let me load the money on it" having some mony I went to a nearby wepon shop and bought some wepons. then I went to the time macnie and went to the american revoultion!

I got to a fort near boston and asked a genral if I could join the patriots. he said yes, whats your name" Thinking I said Dean, Abecham Dean, he said ok dean, I need you to go to concord and stop the British from getting here. I got on a motor bike disguised as a horse, a wepon I bonght, and went to battle. In battle I used a coil gun to shoot down

2nd Ed. © ibidPREP llc

People say, "You can't teach an old dog new tricks."

Do you agree that it is harder to learn things as you get older?

You must write an essay in which you:
- Make an argument for or against the saying.
- Use examples to help make your argument.
- Relate the saying to your own experience.

PLANNING SPACE

2nd Ed. © ibidPREP llc

HOW TO AVOID EXAMICIDE

PART II—TIME & STUDENT MIND

1. TIME IS AN ILLUSION—REALLY

Students are fascinating creatures. They are a hybrid blend of child and adult, and you seldom know which you're going to get when—except when it comes to matters of time. When it comes to matters of time, students are infants. Even after working with thousands of students, I have yet to come across a teenager who had an accurate sense of time when it came to tests. Most students are freaked out about time from the start, so they rush—really, really psychotically and brutally rush. I have seen some kids so spooked about time they won't even take the time to work out 2 + 2 or read through to the end of a simple sentence.

Often kids have received these notions of time through their parents, who have told them, "You read too slowly." BAD PARENT! Most students who think they read too slowly actually read too quickly and don't have any idea what the heck it is they just supposedly read. So, when they get to the questions they have NO IDEA how to answer them, and that is where they lose time and points! All because of NOT, NOT, NOT reading slowly and carefully.

It's the same for math. Oftentimes, I show students the proper way to answer a math question only to hear them say afterward, "But I couldn't do that on the test, that would take me forever." To which I answer, "You're right. Let's just go back to getting it wrong quickly."

2nd Ed. © ibidPREP llc

HOW TO AVOID EXAMICIDE

2. INDECISION IS THE ULTIMATE TIME SUCK

While it is true that time is an illusion and that attempting to save time results in loss of time or points and usually both [rushing wastes time], still it is possible to save time [life is a paradox[22]—get over it]. Students waste more time resisting doing the thing than doing the thing itself would take. When students give me the "Oh, I knew how to do it, but it would have taken too much time" line, that is when I feel myself growing older and when that small vein on my temple begins to throb. DO NOT MAKE DECISIONS BASED ON HOW LONG YOU THINK SOMETHING IS GOING TO TAKE. IF YOU HAVE ANY IDEA HOW TO SOLVE A PROBLEM, START DOING IT. JUST GETTING GOING WILL SAVE YOU ALL THE TIME YOU'LL NEED TO SOLVE IT. TRUST ME ON THIS. REALLY!

3. YOU CAN GET FASTER AT GOING SLOWER—THE SLOWER YOU GO THE FASTER YOU GO

This is another one of those time paradoxes that I spend an inordinate amount of time trying to prove to my students. First, I need to slow my students down enough for them to do the thing the right way. Then I really, really have to convince them to write everything out and not skip steps. Once they get used to not rushing and being thorough, they're amazed: most problems take no time at all!

It is like learning to play a piece of music. You don't begin at full speed. First you learn the notes and the phrasing and then, as you become familiar with playing the song, you get up to speed. If you try to play a piece quickly from the outset, you'll never learn it properly. If you rush through every math problem and every reading passage, you will never learn how to read or do the math properly. Once you know how to do a thing right, you will begin to go quickly naturally and it will never feel rushed. It will feel smooth, efficient and right. As Goethe[23] said, "Never rush; never rest."

[22] something that seems to be a contradiction but is still true
[23] old, dead German writer, thinker, colorist

SEE NEXT EXAMICIDE ON PAGE 255!

CHAPTER FIVE

MATH

OVERVIEW/INTRO

The Math Section is a test of basics. Good command of arithmetic, essential number concepts, simple algebra and geometry should pretty much cover everything you'll need to know from here on out. To that end, it GREATLY behooves[1] you to get good at dopey things like your times tables, how to solve for unknown numbers and knowing the area of a triangle. Trust me, no matter how dopey you think it may be to study how to reduce fractions or do long division, being able to do these things well and without hesitation will help you score big-time throughout all your future math tests. Plus, it's a lot dopier NOT knowing how to do these things!

Beyond learning the basics inside and out, success on this test comes down to knowing how to do the math. That means knowing:

How to Read—A lot of these math questions are MUCH easier than they seem, OR they are not readily transparent at all; in other words, most students have NO IDEA what the questions are asking. I will teach you what the odd wording means and how to translate this *Math Speak* into actual, solvable math.

How to Answer—Once you've figured out what the question is asking for, figure out how you are going to set about solving it. Make a plan and follow through.

How to Execute—Once you know your basics, understand the question and have an approach to answering the question, then it is absolutely vital that you do the work necessary to follow through on your plan and get an actual answer! It is not enough to think and/or imagine how to answer a question—you must set out to answer it in an organized and thorough fashion. Writing everything out to its natural conclusion without trying TO DO MATH IN YOUR HEAD is a great start.

READING WITH 13 LETTERS

IT'S HARD TO UNDERSTAND WHY MATH IS TAUGHT THE WAY IT IS TO MOST STUDENTS. THERE IS THIS MYTH THAT EITHER YOU'RE A "MATH" PERSON OR ELSE YOU'RE OUT OF LUCK. TEACHERS TRY TO TEACH YOU A LITTLE ARITHMETIC, SOME FRACTIONS MAYBE, AND IF YOU DON'T GET IT RIGHT AWAY, THEY HAND YOU A CALCULATOR AND OFF YOU GO TO ALGEBRA, GEOMETRY AND TRIG.

GUESS WHAT? IF YOU'RE NOT COMFORTABLE WITH ARITHMETIC AND BASIC NUMBER RULES, THEN LEARNING ALGEBRA, GEOMETRY AND TRIG IS GOING TO BE A NIGHTMARE, AND YOU WILL NEVER BECOME A "MATH" PERSON, JUST ANOTHER CONFUSED MATH PERSON. FOR MATH TEACHERS TO MOVE STUDENTS ON TO ALGEBRA, GEOMETRY AND TRIG WITHOUT HAVING TAUGHT ARITHMETIC PROPERLY IS A LITTLE LIKE ENGLISH TEACHERS TEACHING STUDENTS HALF THE ALPHABET AND THEN SENDING THEM OFF TO READ.

THE RESULTS WOULD LOOK SOMETHING LIKE THIS:

I*'* A *E** *I*** *A* *O *** *O *EACH *A*H, AND *H* ** *A** **UDEN** A*E *E**IBLE IN *A** *HO DO** * HA*E *O BE.

TRANSLATION: IT'S A VERY SILLY WAY TO TRY TO TEACH MATH, AND WHY SO MANY STUDENTS ARE TERRIBLE IN MATH WHO DON'T HAVE TO BE.

---

[1] befits, serves well,

HOW TO DO
THE MATH

One thing many students want when they come to us is a sure fire method to conquer ALL the math. That is not possible. Try as you might, and in spite of whatever claims other tutors and companies may make, at certain times you're just going to have to THINK FOR YOURSELF. As with reading comprehension, learning how to process **every** word and not just letting them slide by is going to be the biggest key.

MENTAL MATH IS MENTAL

MOST EVERY STUDENT MISINTERPRETS MENTAL MATH AS ABOUT BEING ABLE TO DO MATH IN YOUR HEAD. THAT'S MENTAL. KNOWING CERTAIN MATH FACTS AND PATTERNS BY HEART [AND HEAD] IS ONE THING AND VERY HELPFUL [$4^2=16$], BUT DOING MATH OPERATIONS IN YOUR HEAD IS WORSE THAN USELESS—IT'S DESTRUCTIVE. IT LEADS TO CARELESS, RIDICULOUS ERRORS AND WASTED TIME. I CAN'T TELL YOU HOW MANY TIMES I'VE SAT AND WATCHED STUDENTS STARE OFF INTO THE AIR TRYING TO FIGURE OUT 8×18 INSTEAD OF JUST GRABBING A PENCIL AND GETTING TO WORK. YES, THERE ARE WAYS TO DO LARGER MULTIPLICATION PROBLEMS IN YOUR HEAD IF YOU KNOW CERTAIN PATTERNS AND RELATIONSHIPS, BUT LET'S SAVE THAT FOR CLASS OR WHEN YOU'RE TRAPPED ON A LIFEBOAT WITHOUT PAPER OR PENCIL AND YOUR HANDS ARE TIED BEHIND YOUR BACK.

WHEN YOU SEE PICTURES OF ALBERT EINSTEIN SOLVING THE THEORY OF RELATIVITY, IS HE STANDING IN FRONT OF A BLANK BLACKBOARD?

How to Read **MATH** Questions

1. Remain Clam!
2. Break It Down.
3. Reread the Last Part of the Question.

First, **REMAIN CLAM!** Nothing on Your Test Is Impossible!!

You open to the first question of the math section, you start to read the question, and you have **NO IDEA** what they're asking! This is definitely a good time to *Remain Clam!*

Remind yourself that you are never going to be asked to solve an impossible question. It will only ever *seem* impossible or nonsensical.

How to Do the Math

In other words, in spite of what you may think, these tests are never going to ask you anything that is impossible. It may *sound* like the question is asking,

Q. If there are 400 miles to Spooneggyville and Ansel is carrying Ponto Juice Boxes at 58 kilos per pound, what is the velocitude of the Mushroom Charger to the 5th power?

Trust me, if you chill out and read the questions clause by clause, you're going to realize that they are really just asking you,

Q. If there are 400 miles to Spooneggyville and Ansel is traveling 50mph, how long will the trip take him if he makes a one-hour stop for lunch and takes a 10 minute break at a rest stop?

It is still a long, multi-step question, but each step makes sense and can be worked out using step two:

BREAK IT DOWN

Now that the words don't throw you, let's make sure the phrasing doesn't. Here's something radical to try. DO NOT read the whole question first [this does NOT mean "do not read the whole problem ever"]. For most word problems you would be better off rubbing the test on your face than reading the whole question first. Reading the whole question first, besides wasting time, might also cause you to believe some mistaken notions, latch onto some misleading directions or just plain get confused and dispirited. Instead of reading the whole question, getting to the end and saying, "HUH?", and then starting all over [a COLOSSAL waste of time and confidence], break every question down clause by clause [basically just stop at each comma or period]. Breaking it down in this way means that as you get to the end of each clause or sentence, stop and take stock of what you're being given and start setting up whatever equations you can.

If there are 400 miles to Spooneggyville and Ansel is traveling 50mph,

$$\text{Distance} = 400 \text{ miles}$$
$$\text{Rate} = 50\text{mph}$$

Then if I remember Distance = Rate × Time, I know:

$$400 = 50 \times \text{time} \textbf{ so } \text{Time} = 8 \text{ hours}$$

NOW WE CAN CONTINUE BREAKING IT DOWN: how long will the trip take him if he makes a one-hour stop for lunch and takes a ten-minute break at a rest stop?

We already know that the trip is going to take 8 hours of driving, so now we add in the new information:

$$8 \text{ hours} + 1 \text{ hour} + 10 \text{ minutes} =$$

Be *careful* here: you may only add units of the **same** measure to each other, so either change minutes to hours or hours to minutes, and then add!

$$480 \text{ minutes} + 60 \text{ minutes} + 10 \text{ minutes} = 550 \text{ minutes}$$

2nd Ed. © ibidPREP llc

Therefore, it took Ansel 550 minutes to get to Spooneggyville!

If you set up as you go, more often than not you will have the information you're solving for before you get to the end anyway! There are only so many things you can be asked in any case.

Try reading this sentence all at once:

> *The man from Sheboygan had four daughters, each of whom had three sons, who each had one daughter and two sons who each also had two sons. How many sons did the man from Sheboygan have?*

If you read it all at once, chances are you're thinking, "Boy, that's a lot of sons, I better get my calculator, but wait, do they mean....oh never mind." However, if you stopped reading at the first comma, you would see it's really a very easy question: the man from Sheboygan had only daughters!

THIRD—REREAD THE LAST PART OF THE QUESTION [THE PART THAT TELLS YOU WHAT THE QUESTION IS TRULY ASKING FOR]

Here's a great test maker's ploy: they lay out some humongously long word problem or some multi-step geo + algebra problem for you to solve, you put your head down, get to work, and darn if you don't solve it! You get down to the last line of the problem and determine that, say, *x* = 2. You're excited and hurrying [as always], so you look right to the multiple choice answers and, sitting there waiting for you, is (B)! You pick it and move on. Unfortunately, you're wrong.

Upon rereading the LAST CLAUSE of the question, which you may never have read or have forgotten while you were busy solving the long problem, you discover that the last phrase is not asking for what *x equals* but what **2x equals**, or if there was a **y** somewhere in the problem, the equation may have been set up as **x = 2**, but then they go ahead and ask for **y**.

ALWAYS BOTHER

"SHOULD I WRITE OUT MY ANSWER?" "DO I REALLY HAVE TO FILL IN ALL THE INFO ON THE DIAGRAM?" "SHOULD I WRITE OUT ALL THE FACTORS?" "DO I HAVE TO READ THE WHOLE THING?"

YES.

HOW TO ANSWER

Come Up with an Approach [See Also HOW TO SOLVE Later]

Once you've correctly read and broken down your question, you will be able to choose from several ways to solve the problem before you. Once you decide on an approach, it is up to you to execute that approach. If you execute that approach correctly and commit to following it through and it doesn't work, check your work [by redoing everything, not just running your eyes over what you've already done], and if you're still wrong, COME UP WITH ANOTHER APPROACH!

In Math, Close Is Wrong. Really, Really Wrong.

A lot of times while doing a problem, a student makes a careless error or misunderstands something and ends up with an answer that is not among the answer choices. Correct procedure here would be to start again and redo the problem—preferably in a new way, if possible. Normal procedure for most is to panic and start picking through the answers for something "close."

One of the beautiful things about math is its clarity and simplicity. In the arts, as in life, it is often hard to know when something is right. Or complete. In math there are right answers, which means of course there are wrong answers [boohoo, kid]. However, if you've had dealings in life or in the arts, you don't worry so much about being wrong, but you might take great joy, comfort and relief in once in a while being right. Since there are right answers, you can take joy, comfort and relief in knowing there are no gray areas. If you get .5 for an answer and .5 is not an answer choice, it's because .5 is wrong. Not because you were supposed to pick .55, which is close. Or .3 when you get $\frac{1}{3}$ for an answer. Or –8 when you got 8. No, instead of freaking out in these moments, embrace the clarity and joy of knowing that at the very least you know one answer it isn't.

The Answers Are in Your Pencil

I can't tell you how often I have asked kids questions only to watch them stare up at the ceiling. Often kids try to do math that way, as if there were some sort of invisible LED screen hovering in the air. Or they'll roll their eyes into the backs of their heads and try to recall something from a passage they've just read. Of course if they just looked down at their tests and reread the passage in front of them, they'd have a far better chance of getting the right answer. Sometimes, even when students are writing things out in the math, they'll stop when it comes to doing a simple calculation and look up in the air instead of scribbling it out on the side. Dunno why. You do not score extra points for doing math in your head. You'll just waste time, energy and probably points. Don't do this. Use your paper. Use your text. Use your pencil. The answer is in it.

OH, SO I CAN JUST...?

NO!

If a tiny voice starts chirping up while you're reading a problem and says, "Oh, I can just add this!" or "Oh, I just have to pick the biggest number," etc., IGNORE IT. Most of the time, you can't JUST do anything.* That's sort of the point of the questions.

*The only possible time you might be able to "just" add or multiply [for example] is when the problem looks really hard and you would never think, "Oh, so I can just..."

2nd Ed. © ibidPREP llc

THE RAKES—MATH EDITION!

Careless Errors

Careless errors are a fact of our mathematical lives. You have to be very precise to avoid them, and still it's so easy to stumble into one or two. However, there are several ways to, at the very least, reduce them:

1. ***Slow down.***

2. As we've said before and will continue to say: read the question clause by clause, translating each part of the question from *words to math* as you go. If there's a diagram, fill in the diagram with all you know about it as you go.

3. **FINISH YOUR DARN PROBLEMS**[1] Even though the math questions are multiple choice, pretend they're not. Be sure to get into the habit of **<u>finishing</u>** solving your equation all the way down to *x = ANSWER*. Why? Most students work toward an answer and when it looks like they're getting close, they cheat and peek and look at the multiple choice selections. If you do this, you might:

   a. be in the midst of making a careless error and not get the right answer for *x*;

   b. not see your answer immediately, freak out and end up doing something dopey like picking the "close" answer;

   c. get the right answer for *x*, but not realize that they really want you to solve for *2x* or *y* or something else entirely. To be able to give them the right answer, you must complete your equation all the way, and then...

4. **<u>Reread the last part of the question</u>** to make sure you **answer the question the test is asking.** As discussed above, so often kids decide what a question is asking without really reading the question. When they invariably get those questions wrong, they are shocked and hard-pressed to figure out why. When we review it, they rework the problem step by step for me and prove that they are right. I agree and tell them, "Yes, you are right: **<u>for your problem.</u>**" Then I point out to them that the problem they were meant to answer was entirely different from what they imagined and executed.

5. **Know your and everyone else's RAKES.** When there is a question involving, for example:

   a. parentheses, you must remember to **distribute**;

   b. when there are numerators and denominators, remember *everybody* flips them;

6. If you go through all these steps and the answer still isn't there, you are still not allowed to FREAK OUT. ***Reread*** the question: Chances are VERY good that you've misread one teeny-weeny, tiny-whiny portion of the question. Clear your mind. See the problem anew, and you'll find the glitch. Then fixing it will be a breeze. If you don't find your flaw, look at the answers, get rid of any that make absolutely no sense [if possible], and then GUESS AND GO ON!

---

[1] I am at a loss to express just how vital this point is or how many thousands of points students lose each year because they don't follow through on their problems.

OMG– IT'S NOT THERE!!

IT HAPPENS TO ALL OF US. OK, MAINLY JUST TO YOU, BUT IT HAPPENS. YOU WORK HARD ON A PROBLEM, YOU SET IT UP, DO IT OUT AND SOLVE THE THING. THEN YOU STROLL OVER TO THE ANSWER CHOICES, AND IT'S NOT THERE!!!!

THE FIRST THING TO DO IS NOT FREAK OUT! NUMBERS ARE LIKE WORDS IN THAT MOST HAVE MANY EXACT SYNONYMS. 1 IS THE SAME AS: 1.00, $\frac{9}{9}$, ETC, SO IF THE YOU DON'T SEE THE NUMBER YOU GOT AMONG THE ANSWER CHOICES, DON'T WORRY; IT MIGHT ACTUALLY BE THERE, IT JUST MAY LOOK DIFFERENT FROM WHAT YOU HAVE. IF YOUR SOLUTION IS $\frac{3}{2}$, THEN IT WOULD BE COMPLETELY FINE FOR YOU TO PICK 1.5. JUST DON'T PANIC AND PICK $\frac{2}{3}$!

THIS IS WHERE KNOWING FRACTIONAL AND DECIMAL EQUIVALENTS AND FRACTIONS AND TRANSLATING MIXED NUMBERS COMES IN REALLY HANDY.

WRITE IT RIGHT:

GIVE YOURSELF ROOM. DON'T WRITE OVER TEXT OR TRAIL OFF THE END OF YOUR PAP

Among the many things I have learned from my students over the years:

1. Chances are, the straighter you write, the straighter and more organized your thoughts. I'll go one step further:
    a. Writing out steps of equations clearly and in a direct line helps you think better and more clearly. When you're solving for x as you move down the page, keep your equal signs aligned vertically. If you start solving for x with x on the right side of the equal sign, FINISH with it on the right side of the equal sign. Often kids just for the hell of it switch it to the left and in the process forget to move a negative sign with it or some other genius move that guarantees a careless error. SO:
    b. If you find yourself jamming your writing into a margin, over printed text or on staples, or if it starts trailing off into the breeze, stop and realign yourself [that takes another nanosecond], and get back on the right track!
2. If you are setting up equations, start them at the **top left** of the available space, then use your equal sign as a guiding line—i.e., place the equal sign for the next line of the equation directly below the first equal sign and work down from there. Once your equal signs start trailing off or, even worse, disappearing, it's a one-way ticket to *CrazyLand*!

2ⁿᵈ Ed. © ibidPREP llc

3. All your info should be listed in linear fashion either across or down your work space, and all info should be complete. Don't leave numbers or variables hanging in space. Make them be equal to *something!*

Do I Have to Do It Out?

I am not so great at listening to my own mind. Over the years, I have gotten better. I realize now that if I start thinking a lot about going to the corner to get a cup of coffee, it probably means I want a cup of coffee, and I should go get it.

If the tiny voice in your brain is starting to debate whether or not to do something, stop wasting time and DO IT! No one has ever suffered ill effects from writing out an equation. And if you think it might be a waste of precious time to do it, rest assured that it takes five times longer to debate with yourself whether or not to do it—and then you still probably have to do it anyway!

And please: even if you can't see how to solve a problem straight through from beginning to end, start with what you know how to do. Do the first couple of steps and see where that gets you. You'll be amazed at how often the next step becomes obvious when you do this. So just try! WHY THE BASICS

NINE BLOCKS

WHEN MY MOTHER LEARNED TO DRIVE SHE WAS DEATHLY AFRAID OF MAKING LEFT TURNS, SO SHE ONLY MADE RIGHT TURNS. THE ONLY PROBLEM WAS THAT SHE LIVED ON A ONE-WAY STREET AMONG A GRID OF OTHER ONE-WAY STREETS. THIS MEANT THAT WHEN SHE WAS ONE LEFT TURN AWAY FROM HER HOUSE, SHE HAD TO DRIVE NINE BLOCKS OUT OF HER WAY TO GET HOME!

I HAVE SAT AND WATCHED BOATLOADS OF STUDENTS WORK THROUGH PROBLEMS ONLY TO COME TO A DEAD HALT WHEN THEY NEEDED TO DO SOMETHING UNPLEASANT OR ANNOYING LIKE LONG DIVISION OR REWRITE NUMBERS IN ORDER OR PLOT POINTS ON A GRAPH OR DIVIDE BY π. INSTEAD OF PLOWING AHEAD, THEY TRY GUESSING, PLUGGING IN, WORKING BACKWARD, EYEBALLING THE NUMBERS OR IMAGINING STUFF IN THEIR HEADS. IN SHORT, THEY GO NINE BLOCKS OUT OF THEIR WAY INSTEAD OF MAKING ONE SCARY LEFT-HAND TURN.

It Doesn't Matter That It Doesn't Matter. It Matters.

For some reason many students do mental triage[2] on their math problems. They automatically decide what to bother reading and what not to bother doing. They decide which pieces of info or points of math "don't matter." Trust me, until you get to the very end of a problem and process everything in a question, YOU DO NOT GET TO DECIDE WHAT IS IMPORTANT.

Nuts & Bolts of Doing the MATH

1. Do NOT read the question all at once.
2. Read the question to the first comma or period—whichever comes first.
3. Translate each clause or sentence into math terms and equations as you read.
4. Draw any figures or write out any formulas as they are mentioned.
5. Make a plan of How to Solve and follow through by:
   a. Writing out all your work fully and neatly
   b. Labeling all terms
   c. FINISHING YOUR PROBLEMS [don't peek at answer choices halfway through]
6. Once you completely execute your approach, RE-READ the last part of the question. Be sure you're giving the answer that is called for!

---

[2] a process of prioritizing which problems get dealt with first and which get dealt with later or not at all.

2nd Ed. © ibidPREP llc

MUST KNOW

ARITHMETIC

2nd Ed. © *ibidPREP llc*

MUST KNOW MATH—ARITHMETIC

MUST KNOW TERMS

It's easy to speak any language if you know a few key basics. Learn these essential terms in order to start speaking better math:

- **SUM:**   The result of addition.
- **DIFFERENCE:**   The result of subtraction.
- **PRODUCT:**   The result of multiplication.
- **QUOTIENT:**   The result of division.
- **EVEN NUMBERS:**
  - Any whole number that can be divided by 2 without a remainder.
  - N.B.: When an odd number is divided by 2, the whole number remainder can only ever be 1.
- **ZERO:** Zero is an integer and it's even [when zero is divided by two the remainder is zero!] However, it is neither positive nor negative, and although you may divide zero by any number, you CANNOT divide any number by zero.
- **PRIME NUMBERS:**
  - Positive numbers that have only two distinct [different] factors: 1 and itself.
    2, 3, 5, 7, 11, 13, 17, 19, 23, 29, 31,etc....
  - 1 is NOT a prime number. [It only has one distinct factor {itself}, not two.]
  - All primes are odd numbers except 2, which for obvious reasons can be divided only by itself and one (there are no other numbers between them).
- **MULTIPLES**
  The whole number products of a number.
    E.g., the multiples of 12 are: 12, 24, 36, 48, 60, 72, 84, 96, etc.
    N.B.: The first multiple of every number is itself.
- **FACTORS**
  The factors of a number are those integers that can be multiplied with other integers to form that number.
    E.g., the FACTORS of 6 are 1, 2, 3 and 6.
- **DISTINCT**
  This simply means "different." As in, in the set {1, 2, 3, 3, 4}, there are five terms but only four DISTINCT numbers.
- **DIGITS**
  These are the individual numbers that compose bigger numbers—think of them as the letters that form bigger words or numbers. In other words, in the number 1,234 the digits are 1, 2, 3, and 4. The digit 1 is in the thousands place, the digit 2 is the hundreds place, and so on.
- **CONSECUTIVE**
  This simply means "in a row" or "one after the other." As in, the first five consecutive positive numbers are 1, 2, 3, 4, 5. Be careful, though; sometimes "one after the other" could mean different things. As in, the first five consecutive even numbers are 2, 4, 6, 8, 10.
- **INCLUSIVE**
  A series of numbers is said to be inclusive if the first and last terms in the series are part of the list.

    The set of integers 2-12 inclusive starts with 2 and ends with 12.

*When counting the number of terms in a list of **inclusive** terms, subtract the first from the last and add 1. E.g., *the number of terms from 4-14 inclusive is 11 {14 – 4 = 10 10 + 1 = 11; count the numbers on your fingers if you don't believe me!*

MULTIPLICATION TABLES

KNOW:

MULTIPLICATION TABLES THROUGH 12S

Especially your 9s and 12s tables.

	1	2	3	4	5	6	7	8	9	10	11	12
1	1	2	3	4	5	6	7	8	9	10	11	12
2	2	4	6	8	10	12	14	16	18	20	22	24
3	3	6	9	12	15	18	21	24	27	30	33	36
4	4	8	12	16	20	24	28	32	36	40	44	48
5	5	10	15	20	25	30	35	40	45	50	55	60
6	6	12	18	24	30	36	42	48	54	60	66	72
7	7	14	21	28	35	42	49	56	63	70	77	84
8	8	16	24	32	40	48	56	64	72	80	88	96
9	9	18	27	36	45	54	63	72	81	90	99	108
10	10	20	30	40	50	60	70	80	90	100	110	120
11	11	22	33	44	55	66	77	88	99	110	121	132
12	12	24	36	48	60	72	84	96	108	120	132	144

There are ways to make the multiplication tables easier. First, it helps to have a solid grip on adding. I can't tell you how many times I've seen students use their fingers to add 9 + 4. Don't get me wrong, using your fingers is far superior to saying "12." However, better still is KNOWING that 9 + 4 = 13.

Once you're comfortable with adding, let's go to the multiplication tables and start with the ONES [always start everything at ONE].

Stacking

The multiplication tables go only so far: what do we do with the really big numbers?!

The way to multiply big numbers is by stacking. You may have been taught some other methods, such as lattice, but you shouldn't use these methods on the test. You need to use **stacking**. Just in case you forgot how to stack, since you've been doing lattice for so long, here's a review!

Stacking is kind of like carrying in addition. Say you need to multiply 24 × 6.

$$\begin{array}{r} 24 \\ \times\ 6 \\ \hline \end{array}$$

We need to multiply 6 × 4 and also 6 × 2. We do 6 x 4 first [BEGIN ALL MULTIPLICATION AND ADDING IN THE ONES COLUMN], which equals 24. But where do we put the 2 and where do we put the 4? We put the **ones** number (in this case, the 4) under the TOTAL line into the ones column, and we "carry" the **tens** place number (in this case, the 2).

2nd Ed. © ibidPREP llc

Now we have this:

$$
\begin{array}{r}
\scriptstyle 2 \\
24 \\
\times\ 6 \\
\hline
4
\end{array}
$$

The next step is to multiply 6 × 2. We know that 6 × 2 is 12. Great. But what do we do with the 2 sitting on top of the other 2? We **add** it to the 12! So 12 + 2 = 14! What do we do with the 14? We put it under the line in front of what's already there.

Now we have:

$$
\begin{array}{r}
\scriptstyle 2 \\
24 \\
\times\ 6 \\
\hline
144
\end{array}
$$

And that's our answer! 144!

Let's try stacking one when we have two two-digit numbers.

$$
\begin{array}{r}
72 \\
\times\ 96 \\
\end{array}
$$

We need to multiply 2 × 6 first. That's 12.

$$
\begin{array}{r}
\scriptstyle 1 \\
72 \\
\times\ 96 \\
\hline
2
\end{array}
$$

Next, we multiply 6 × 7. That's 42. Then we add the 1 to 42, and we get 43. We put everything in the right place just as we learned above.

$$
\begin{array}{r}
\scriptstyle 1 \\
72 \\
\times\ 96 \\
\hline
432
\end{array}
$$

Now we are all done with the 6, and we need to move on to the **9**. Before we do anything, we put a **0** underneath the 2 because we're really multiplying by 90 not 9—so we add a zero to our answer.

$$
\begin{array}{r}
\scriptstyle 1 \\
72 \\
\times\ 96 \\
\hline
432 \\
0
\end{array}
$$

Next, we multiply the 9 by the 2 and be sure to carry the 1 in 18.

$$
\begin{array}{r}
\scriptstyle 1 \\
72 \\
\times\ 96 \\
\hline
432 \\
80
\end{array}
$$

Then we multiply the 9 by the 7, which is 63, and then we add the 1: 63 + 1 = 64, so:

$$
\begin{array}{r}
\scriptstyle 1 \\
72 \\
\times\ 96 \\
\hline
432 \\
6480
\end{array}
$$

Now we need to **add** this all together, so we put in another SUM [total] line.

$$
\begin{array}{r}
\scriptstyle 1 \\
72 \\
\times\ \ 96 \\
\hline
432 \\
+\ 6480 \\
\hline
6912
\end{array}
$$

And that's our answer! **6,912!**

STACKING PRACTICE

1. 25 × 6

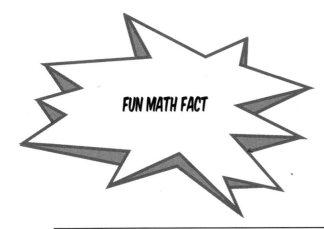

2. 42 × 7

3. 98 × 14

4. 27 × 79

5. 82 × 96

If you are picking through a bunch of numbers for an answer to a multiplication problem, you can always sort through the units digits first.

FUN MATH FACT

E.g., 4,382
$$\underline{\times\ \ \ 17}$$

A. 76, 786   B. 76, 494   C. 74, 952   D. 74,494   E. 73,328

In other words, start by multiplying the units digits. Then you'll know that whatever the answer is its unit digit must be a 4. That narrows your options down to B and D.

2nd Ed. © ibidPREP llc

FACTORS

The factors of a number are those numbers that can be multiplied by other numbers to form the original number.

E.g., the FACTORS of 6 are 1, 2, 3 and 6

Now that we know our times tables, we can start factoring. Factoring is an incredibly important skill for doing math. The best way to go about finding factors is to play bouncy-bouncy.

Place the number you want to factor [let's say 24] in the middle of the page or area you are writing in. Directly below that, on the left margin, write the number one [1] because 1 is a factor of all numbers. On the right margin, write the number you are factoring [24]. Then think of the next number after one that could go into your number. In this case TWO works. Just like when you write a list, write a comma after ONE and write TWO. Then, on the other side of the line, place a comma to the left of 24 and write TWO's pair. In this case it's TWELVE. Then you go up from TWO and keep seeing if each consecutive number is a factor of your number or not [check out our MULTIPLICATION TIPS AND TRICKS to help you with that!] By the time you get to the middle you will have covered all the numbers!

24

1,   2,   3,   4,   6,   8,   12,   24

Note: Do not forget that the first factor pair of every number is itself and one!

FACTORS
Find all the distinct factors of the following numbers.

1. 24   4. 15

2. 36   5. 60

3. 20

PRIME FACTORING

First of all, you remember what **prime numbers** are, right? Prime numbers are integers that only have **two** distinct factors: 1 and the number itself. Some examples of prime numbers are 2, 3, 5, 7, 11, 13 and 17. (1 is not a prime number because 1 only has ONE factor: 1).

You also remember what **factors** are, right? We just went over them! Factors are integers that multiply together to equal another number. For example, the factors of 12 are 1×12, 2×6, and 3×4.

Prime factorization involves finding which prime numbers multiply together to equal a number. There is only one set of prime factors for each number.

How does this work? As with all things, let's start with small, workable numbers. Let's try finding the prime factors of 12.

To factor it, let's start with the smallest prime number, which is 2. Can we divide 12 by 2? Yes.

$$12 = 2 \times 6$$

Since we want all the factors to be prime numbers, we must continue. 2 is a prime number, but is 6? No! So we have to break down 6.

$$6 = 2 \times 3$$

Both 2 and 3 are prime numbers, so we are done breaking down the 6 and, therefore, the factors of 12. Now we can put everything together:

$$12 = 2 \times 2 \times 3$$

When a number appears more than once in a prime factorization, it is best to express it with an **exponent**:

$$12 = 2 \times 2 \times 3 = 2^2 \times 3$$

Keep breaking down your factors until each factor is a prime number. Be sure to check this by multiplying your factors together! Also be sure to check that your factors are correct. ($2^2 \times 3 = 4 \times 3 = 12$, so we were correct.)

Let's try another example. Say we want to find the prime factorization of 49. Can we divide 49 by 2? No. So we try the next smallest prime number. Can we divide 49 by 3? No. So we keep trying the next smallest prime numbers until we get to one that is a factor:

$$49 = 7 \times 7$$

$$49 = 7^2$$

Let's try a third example. Say we want to find the prime factorization of 19. But wait, 19 is a prime number! So this is as far as we go. The answer is 19.

2ⁿᵈ Ed. © ibidPREP llc

The easiest way to make sure you get all the prime factors is to create a factor tree and circle your prime numbers as you discover them. Remember, don't rush to assume a number is prime just because it looks *fugly!*

Question: What is the prime factorization of 1,092?

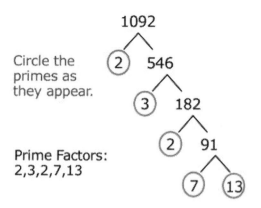

Circle the
primes as
they appear.

Prime Factors:
2,3,2,7,13

Answer: You may write your answer as—

$$2 \times 3 \times 2 \times 7 \times 13$$

Again however, it's neater and more formally correct to write your answer using exponents—

$$2^2 \times 3 \times 7 \times 13$$

PRIME FACTORIZATION
Find the prime factorization of the following numbers.

1. 147

2. 243

3. 48

4. 144

5. 66

6. 252

7. 250

8. 297

Division

Now that we're comfortable with multiplication and factoring, let's work on division. If you've mastered multiplication and addition, there's no part of division you can't handle.

What is division? Here's an example of a division problem written two different ways:

$$24 \div 8 \text{ and } 8\overline{)24}$$

In each case, 24 is the *dividend* and 8 is the *divisor*. The answer, which we haven't gotten to yet, is called the *quotient*.

So what is division asking us? It's asking us what number we'd have to multiply the *divisor* by in order to get the *dividend* or, as we say in English, how many times one number goes into another number.

In this case the answer is three: 8 times 3 equals 24. So three is the *quotient*.

But what do we do when we can't find the dividend or the divisor in our multiplication tables?? How can we divide then?

We do it step by step. Let's take the following problem:

$$693 \div 7$$

However, the best way to write this is the other way, like so:

$$\frac{1}{3}$$

Why? Because this makes it easier to do the subtraction we'll have to do. You'll see.

‡It's important to know your digits when you do this and remember how to multiply by ten.‡

First, we see if seven goes into the **first** digit, which is six. It does not [bummer], so we see if it goes into the first **two** digits: 69. Of course seven goes into 69! It doesn't go in **exactly**, but that doesn't matter: it just has to get close. Seven times nine gets us to 63 which is as close as we can get to 69 by sevens!

So we put a nine on the line above the nine in the TENs column. We put it there because we're really multiplying We then write 630 beneath 693, like so:

$$
\begin{array}{r}
9 \\
7\,\overline{)693} \\
-630 \\
\end{array}
$$

Now we have a subtraction problem: 693 – 630. Which equals what? 63. So we write that down below our subtraction problem.

2nd Ed. © ibidPREP llc

$$
\begin{array}{r}
9 \\
7\overline{)693} \\
-630 \\
\hline
63
\end{array}
$$

Now we have a NEW division problem: 63 divided by 7. You know this—you just did it! 7 goes into 63 nine times. We put this nine above the three to give us a quotient of 99!

$$
\begin{array}{r}
99 \\
7\overline{)693} \\
-630 \\
\hline
63 \\
-63 \\
\hline
0
\end{array}
$$

Now there's one more step! We have to check to make sure we did our work correctly. The best way to check your math is to do the reverse operation. In this case, we will MULTIPLY.

$$
\begin{array}{r}
99 \\
\times 7 \\
\hline
693
\end{array}
$$

But what about when it doesn't go into the number exactly any number of times? What do we do then? Then we have a remainder, which is explained below.

DIVISION PRACTICE
Solve the following division problems using long division.

1. 369 ÷ 3 =

2. 452 ÷ 4 =

3. 612 ÷ 6 =

4. 5,775 ÷ 5 =

5. 897 ÷ 9 =

6. 1213 ÷ 6 =

REMAINDERS

Remainder—the whole number amount left over when one number is divided by another.

Remainders are one of the first stops on the math highway. The point at which many students stop and say, "No thanks. I'm out." When you throw most kids 17 ÷ 4 the math gears grind to a halt and they look blankly at you and say, "You can't. It doesn't go in evenly."

While it is true that 17 ÷ 4 does not have a whole-number solution, 17 can absolutely be divided by 4. In fact, any number can be divided by any other number. The answer may not be pretty, but there will be an answer[1].

$$
\begin{array}{r}
4r1 \\
4\overline{)17} \\
-16 \\
\hline
1
\end{array}
$$

Fun Facts about Remainders

1. If a number goes evenly into another, the remainder is zero.
2. The remainder can never be equal to or greater than the divisor.
3. If the number being divided is less than the divisor, the remainder is equal to the number being divided.

$$5 \div 7 = 0 \, r5$$

INEQUALITIES

What's an inequality? Easy. It's the opposite of an equality. So what's an equality? You don't realize it, but you already know what an equality is: it's what you have when you have an equal sign. Here are some equalities[2]:

$$3 = 3$$

$$7 - 3 = 4$$

$$5 \times 3 = 15$$

Those are called equalities because what's on the left side of the equal sign has the same value as what's on the right side of the equal sign.

Inequalities, on the other hand, are what you have when what's on the left side of the equal sign is NOT equal to what's on the right side of the equal sign. In that case, we can't use an equal sign; we use something else instead: < or >.

Those are the two inequality signs. When do you use which?

---

[1] Except, of course, zero. No number may be divided by zero because zero cannot multiply with any number to get a value other than zero. That is why a fraction [which is a mini-division problem] with zero in its denominator is UNDEFINED.
[2] They are also known as "equations."

2nd Ed. © ibidPREP llc

The **big**, open part of the sign faces the **bigger** value and the **small**, pointy side of the sign faces the **smaller** value. Simple as that.

So:

$$3 > 2$$

$$6 < 2 + 5$$

$$7 - 3 < 5$$

Got it? Now try these practice problems.

INEQUALITY PRACTICE SET

1. 6 ___ 9

2. 7×6 ___ 41

3. $\dfrac{1}{3}$ ___ $\dfrac{1}{2}$

4. $2 + 5 - 6$ ___ $24 \div 12$

5. $\dfrac{1}{2} + \dfrac{1}{4}$ ___ $\dfrac{2}{3} + \dfrac{1}{6}$

6. $2 \div \dfrac{1}{4}$ ___ $10 \div 2$

MUST KNOW MATH—Average [Mean]

Sum of all numbers in a group divided by number of terms.

Any average problem can [and **MUST**] be written out as the formula:

$$AVG = \frac{\text{Sum of Terms}}{\text{Number of Terms}}$$

Most average [mean] problems will give you two out of the three variables in the formula above. Fill the numbers into their proper places in the formula **FIRST**. Then you'll be able to find the third number. Then proceed to the rest of the problem as given and as necessary.

MEDIAN:

Number that is the middle term of a set of numbers that have been put in ascending or descending order.

The median of the set {3, 2, 4, 5, 7, 4, 5} is 4 because the set in order looks like this: {2, 3, 4, 4, 5, 5, 7}. The number in the exact middle is 4.

If there is an even number of terms in the set, choose the **TWO** middle terms and find their mean.

E.g., the median of the set {3, 4, 4, 5, 6, 7} = 4.5 [4.5 is the average of 4 and 5, the two middle terms of the set].

MODE:

Number in a group that appears most often.

9, 12, 13, 13, 13, 14, 15, 18, 29 = mode of 13

2nd Ed. © ibidPREP llc

BASIC MEAN, MODE & MEDIAN

1. Stuart received the following scores on his math tests:

    97, 85, 92, 93, 89, 90.

    What was his mean score? _____

    What was his median score? _____

2. Mr. Norton got the following gas mileage during the last month:

    29 mpg, 25 mpg, 27 mpg, 25 mpg, and 24 mpg.

    What was his average mpg? _____

    What was the mode? _____

3. Find the mean, mode and median of each set of numbers:
    a. 9, 7, 12, 12 _____

    b. 3, 3, 5, 8, 7, 10 _____

4. If Stuart got 86, 72, 98 and 96 on his first four tests, at least how much would he have to get on his last to have an average of 90 for all five tests.

FRACTIONS

A fraction is a part of a whole. To get a part of a whole you must divide the whole. Therefore, a fraction is a divided whole.

A fraction is made of three parts: the numerator, the denominator and the dividing line.

The dividing line is like the knife that cuts the bread. It symbolizes that a whole, one, has been broken into parts.

The denominator represents the number the whole has been cut into. If the denominator is two, the bread has been cut into two pieces.

The numerator is the number of pieces we have. If we cut the bread into two pieces and we did not eat any, the numerator is two. If we eat one piece, the numerator is one—that is what we have left.

If the numerator equals the denominator, we always have one whole.

If the numerator is less than the denominator, we have less than one.

If the numerator is more than the denominator, we have more than one. For example, if we cut two breads in half (in two pieces each) we have four pieces, four halves: $\frac{4}{2}$. If we eat one of the four pieces we have three halves: $\frac{3}{2}$.

If the denominators are the same, we can easily add our pieces together. In other words, if I have two halves and you have one half and we put them together, we have three halves. We write it like this:

$$\frac{2}{2} + \frac{1}{2} = \frac{3}{2}$$

 2nd Ed. © ibidPREP llc

STUDATUTA'S FIRST RULE OF FRACTIONS

FIRST RULE OF FRACTIONS (AND THE ONLY ONE FOR NOW)

REDUCE FIRST

First and always reduce. One of the beauties of fractions is that they allow you to simplify your numbers and make your arithmetic easier, so reducing first makes your math easier and lowers your chance of making careless errors.

Now that you know how important it is to reduce, perhaps this is a good time to actually learn the proper way to do it:

How to Reduce #1

You may reduce the numerator and denominator [top & bottom of a fraction] within one fraction. We reduce by finding the GREATEST common factor of the numerator and denominator and then dividing the numerator and denominator by that factor.

$$\frac{5}{10} = \frac{5 \text{ divided by } 5}{10 \text{ divided by } 5} = \frac{1}{2}$$

Why? Because five is the greatest common factor of five and ten. It goes into five one time, and that leaves one as the numerator. It goes into ten two times, and that leaves two as the denominator.

Reducing makes it so much easier to multiply fractions. Once you've reduced your fractions, it's simple! You just multiply the numerators and the denominators!

So:

$$\frac{12}{48} \times \frac{9}{27} = \frac{\cancel{12}}{\cancel{48}} \times \frac{\cancel{9}}{\cancel{27}} = \frac{1}{4} \times \frac{1}{3} = \frac{1}{12}$$

Easy, right?

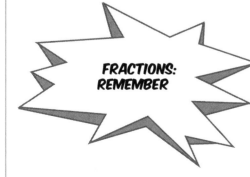

FRACTIONS: REMEMBER

The SMALLER the number in the denominator is, the LARGER the value of the fraction is. The larger the number in the denominator is, the SMALLER the overall number is:

$\frac{1}{2} > \frac{1}{5}$ because 2 < 5

$\frac{1}{100}$ is much smaller than $\frac{1}{5}$ because 100 is way bigger than 5.

Adding and Subtracting Fractions

This is the hardest thing you'll do with fractions, and with these you don't necessarily reduce right away. Let's take $\frac{1}{4}$ and $\frac{2}{3}$. If we want to add these together, we can't just combine numerators and denominators to make $\frac{3}{7}$. Why not? Because you can add or subtract fractions **ONLY** when the denominators are the **same**.

But, you say, being clever little students, the denominators *aren't* the same. That's true. So we have to *make* them the same. This is the opposite of reducing because usually we have to make the denominators bigger to make them the same.

What number should we make the denominators? The *lowest common multiple*, or the smallest number for which each denominator is a factor.

In this case the lowest common multiple is twelve.

$$\frac{1}{4} \times \frac{3}{3} = \frac{3}{12}$$

That's because we had to multiply four by three to get twelve. And, just like when we're reducing, we have to do the same thing to the numerator that we did to the denominator.

We can do the same thing to the other fraction. In this case, we just have to multiply the numerator and denominator by four.

$$\frac{2}{3} \times \frac{4}{4} = \frac{8}{12}$$

Now we're set to go!

$$\frac{1}{4} + \frac{2}{3} = \frac{3}{12} + \frac{8}{12} = \frac{11}{12}$$

So remember:
- If you are multiplying fractions, reduce them first, and then multiply across.
- And if you are adding or subtracting fractions, find a common denominator first, and then you're good to go!

Equivalents

$$\frac{1}{2} = \frac{2}{4} = \frac{3}{6} = \frac{4}{8} = \frac{5}{10} = \frac{6}{12}$$

$$\frac{1}{3} = \frac{2}{6} = \frac{3}{9} = \frac{4}{12} = \frac{5}{15} = \frac{6}{18}$$

$$\frac{1}{4} = \frac{2}{8} = \frac{3}{12} = \frac{4}{16} = \frac{5}{20} = \frac{6}{24}$$

$$\frac{1}{5} = \frac{2}{10} = \frac{3}{15} = \frac{4}{20} = \frac{5}{25} = \frac{6}{30}$$

 2ⁿᵈ Ed. © ibidPREP llc

FRACTION PROBLEMS—1

1. $\dfrac{1}{2} + \dfrac{2}{2} =$

2. $\dfrac{2}{4} + \dfrac{1}{4} =$

3. $\dfrac{3}{4} + \dfrac{3}{4} =$

4. $\dfrac{2}{4} + \dfrac{1}{2} =$

5. $\dfrac{3}{6} + \dfrac{2}{4} =$

6. $\dfrac{2}{6} + \dfrac{1}{3} =$

7. $\dfrac{1}{3} + \dfrac{4}{3} =$

8. $\dfrac{9}{9} + \dfrac{2}{18} =$

9. $\dfrac{1}{7} + \dfrac{3}{21} =$

10. $\dfrac{2}{6} + \dfrac{1}{4} =$

11. $\dfrac{4}{4} - \dfrac{1}{4} =$

12. $\dfrac{4}{3} - \dfrac{1}{3} =$

13. $\dfrac{2}{2} - \dfrac{3}{3} =$

14. $\dfrac{3}{2} - \dfrac{1}{2} =$

15. $\dfrac{3}{2} - \dfrac{2}{3} =$

16. $\dfrac{2}{2} - \dfrac{2}{2} =$

17. $\dfrac{18}{9} - \dfrac{4}{2} =$

18. $\dfrac{5}{6} - \dfrac{1}{3} =$

19. $\dfrac{5}{6} - \dfrac{1}{4} =$

20. $\dfrac{3}{4} - \dfrac{3}{8} =$

FRACTION PROBLEMS—2

1. If eight people are coming to dinner and half of them are vegetarians, how many people are vegetarians?

2. If a recipe calls for one quarter of a pound of meat for four people and eight people are coming to dinner, how many pounds of meat must you buy?

3. If eighteen lemons cost $3, how many lemons can you buy for $1?

4. One dollar is what fraction of three dollars?

5. $\dfrac{3}{4} =$

   A. $\dfrac{6}{9}$

   B. $\dfrac{3}{2}$

   C. $\dfrac{7}{14}$

   D. $\dfrac{12}{16}$

   E. $\dfrac{7}{8}$

6. Which is greatest?

   A. $\dfrac{3}{2}$

   B. $\dfrac{3}{3}$

   C. $\dfrac{3}{4}$

   D. $\dfrac{3}{5}$

   E. $\dfrac{3}{6}$

7. Which is least?

   A. $\dfrac{3}{17}$

   B. $\dfrac{3}{13}$

   C. $\dfrac{3}{8}$

   D. $\dfrac{3}{4}$

   E. $\dfrac{2}{17}$

8. A soup recipe yields 24 servings. It calls for 8 cups of water. If you want to make only 18 servings, how many cups of water will you need?

9. What is one-third of 15?

10. $\dfrac{1}{8} \times 1 =$

11. $\dfrac{1}{8} \times 8 =$

12. $\dfrac{2}{8} \times 4 =$

13. $\dfrac{1}{3} \times \dfrac{1}{3} =$

14. $\dfrac{1}{3} \times \dfrac{2}{3} =$

15. $\dfrac{1}{3} + \dfrac{2}{3} =$

16. $\dfrac{2}{4} \times \dfrac{2}{3} =$

17. $\dfrac{4}{2} \times \dfrac{2}{2} =$

2nd *Ed.* © *ibidPREP llc*

DIVIDING FRACTIONS

$$\frac{1}{2} \div \frac{3}{4} = \frac{\frac{1}{2}}{\frac{3}{4}}$$

Division is really just multiplying by opposites. So to divide by a fraction, you just multiply by its opposite. The opposite of a fraction is called its **reciprocal**. To find the reciprocal of a fraction, just flip the top and bottom.

E.g., the reciprocal of $\frac{3}{4}$ is $\frac{4}{3}$

Once you've found the reciprocal of the fraction you want to divide, then just multiply your numbers together!

$$\frac{1}{2} \div \frac{3}{4} = \frac{\frac{1}{2}}{\frac{3}{4}} = \frac{1}{2} \times \frac{4}{3} = \frac{4}{6} = \frac{2}{3}$$

DIVIDING FRACTIONS PRACTICE

1. $\frac{1}{2}$ divided by $\frac{1}{4}$

2. $\frac{1}{2}$ divided by $\frac{1}{3}$

3. $\frac{1}{4}$ divided by $\frac{1}{2}$

4. $\frac{1}{4}$ divided by 2

5. $\frac{1}{6}$ divided by $\frac{1}{3}$

6. $\frac{1}{6}$ divided by $\frac{1}{6}$

MIXED NUMBERS & IMPROPER FRACTIONS

1. Mixed numbers are numbers that combine whole numbers with fractions.

2. Improper fractions are fractions in which the numerator is greater than the denominator and so is greater in value than ONE.

In order to convert a **MIXED NUMBER** into an **IMPROPER FRACTION**:
- Multiply whole-number part of **MIXED NUMBER** with the denominator of the fraction.
- Add this product to the previous numerator of the fraction to form a new numerator.
- Place over denominator of fraction.
- That's all!

E.g., $3\frac{2}{5}$

- $3\frac{2}{5} \rightarrow$

- First make 3 into 5ths. Multiply $3 \times 5 = 15$, and put that over 5: $3 = \frac{15}{5}$

- Then add that to the $\frac{2}{5}$ part, so you get $\frac{15}{5} + \frac{2}{5} = \frac{15+2}{2} = \frac{17}{5}$

MIXED NUMBER TO IMPROPER FRACTIONS

1. $4\dfrac{3}{4} =$

2. $1\dfrac{1}{3} =$

3. $5\dfrac{3}{5} =$

4. $2\dfrac{1}{2} =$

5. $3\dfrac{9}{10} =$

6. $15\dfrac{4}{5} =$

In order to convert an **Improper Fraction** into a **Mixed Number:**

- Divide the numerator [top number] by the denominator [bottom number].
- The whole number result = the whole number part of your **Mixed Number.**
- The remainder = the numerator of your new [proper] fraction.
- The denominator of your new fraction = the same denominator as in the original **IMPROPER FRACTION**

$$\text{E.g., } \frac{25}{8} = 25 \div 8 = 3 \text{ Remainder } 1, \text{ so } \frac{25}{8} = 3\frac{1}{8}$$

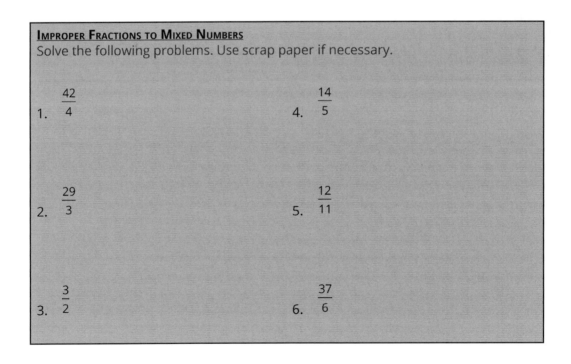

IMPROPER FRACTIONS TO MIXED NUMBERS
Solve the following problems. Use scrap paper if necessary.

1. $\dfrac{42}{4}$

2. $\dfrac{29}{3}$

3. $\dfrac{3}{2}$

4. $\dfrac{14}{5}$

5. $\dfrac{12}{11}$

6. $\dfrac{37}{6}$

2nd Ed. © ibidPREP llc

ADDING, SUBTRACTING, MULTIPLYING & DIVIDING FRACTIONS

Solve the following problems. Use scrap paper if necessary.

1. $\dfrac{2}{9}+\dfrac{4}{7}=$

2. $\dfrac{1}{8}+\dfrac{6}{7}=$

3. $\dfrac{15}{16}+\dfrac{4}{5}=$

4. $\dfrac{3}{5}-\dfrac{1}{2}=$

5. $\dfrac{11}{16}+\dfrac{1}{3}=$

6. $\dfrac{2}{3}-\dfrac{4}{7}=$

7. $\dfrac{7}{9}-\dfrac{4}{9}=$

8. $\dfrac{1}{4}+\dfrac{4}{15}=$

9. $\dfrac{3}{5}-\dfrac{1}{12}=$

10. $\dfrac{14}{15}+\dfrac{4}{15}=$

11. $\dfrac{17}{20}+\dfrac{3}{8}=$

12. $\dfrac{17}{20}+\dfrac{1}{15}=$

13. $\dfrac{3}{7}+\dfrac{9}{10}=$

14. $\dfrac{13}{16}-\dfrac{3}{16}=$

15. $\dfrac{1}{15}+\dfrac{3}{16}=$

16. $\dfrac{11}{12}-\dfrac{1}{10}=$

17. $\dfrac{11}{16}+\dfrac{4}{15}=$

18. $\dfrac{9}{16}-\dfrac{1}{10}=$

19. $\dfrac{2}{5}+\dfrac{9}{16}=$

20. $\dfrac{13}{20}+\dfrac{6}{7}=$

MULTIPLICATION AND DIVISION

1. $\dfrac{6}{7}\times\dfrac{11}{15}=$

2. $\dfrac{1}{9}\times\dfrac{7}{20}=$

3. $\dfrac{7}{9}\div\dfrac{1}{3}=$

4. $\dfrac{1}{7}\times\dfrac{4}{15}=$

5. $\dfrac{1}{16}\times\dfrac{4}{7}=$

6. $\dfrac{5}{9}\times\dfrac{9}{20}=$

7. $\dfrac{3}{16}\times\dfrac{4}{15}=$

8. $\dfrac{4}{5}\div\dfrac{2}{7}=$

9. $\dfrac{13}{20}\times\dfrac{15}{16}=$

10. $\dfrac{5}{6}\times\dfrac{5}{12}=$

11. $\dfrac{5}{12}\times\dfrac{2}{5}=$

12. $\dfrac{7}{12}\div\dfrac{1}{4}=$

13. $\dfrac{14}{15}\times\dfrac{4}{9}=$

14. $\dfrac{19}{20}\div\dfrac{7}{8}=$

15. $\dfrac{3}{5}\div\dfrac{2}{5}=$

16. $\dfrac{5}{9}\times\dfrac{2}{5}=$

17. $\dfrac{7}{12}\div\dfrac{4}{7}=$

18. $\dfrac{15}{16}\div\dfrac{13}{15}=$

19. $\dfrac{17}{20}\div\dfrac{4}{15}=$

20. $\dfrac{2}{7}\div\dfrac{17}{20}=$

Practice

HARDER FRACTIONS—DRILL SET

1. $\frac{1}{4} \times \left(\frac{1}{3} \div \frac{5}{9} \right) =$

2. $\left(\frac{1}{6} + \frac{2}{3} \right) \div \frac{9}{2} =$

3. $\left(\frac{3}{4} - \frac{1}{8} \right) \times \frac{8}{15} =$

4. $\left(\frac{6}{10} - \frac{3}{8} \right) \times \left(7 - \frac{8}{3} \right) =$

5. In lowest terms, the product of $\frac{8}{21}$, $\frac{7}{4}$ and $\frac{9}{8}$ is:

6. In lowest terms, the product of $\frac{9}{14}$, $\frac{5}{24}$ and $\frac{16}{25}$ is:

FRACTION WORD PROBLEMS

1. Leyla is painting a wall. If she paints $\frac{1}{4}$ of it yellow, $\frac{1}{3}$ of it orange and the rest of it blue, what fraction of the wall will be blue?

2. If one-half of the students in one class like pizza best and one-third of them like cheeseburgers best, what fraction of the students like something else best?

3. Mary has a bucket of golf balls. One-third of them are white, and one-sixth of the white balls are striped. What fraction of the whole bucket of balls are white, striped golf balls?

2nd Ed. © ibidPREP llc

DECIMALS

100,000 ‖ 10,000 ‖ 1,000 ‖ 100 ‖ 10 ‖ 1 ‖ .1 ‖ .01 ‖ .001 ‖ .0001 ‖ .00001

Ten's powers are ordered as if in a mirror on either side of one. There is a partner for every power, but there is only one one!

TENS & DECIMAL PLACES

One-hundred thousand, ten thousand, thousand, hundred, ten, one tenth, hundredth, thousandth, ten-thousandth, hundred-thou-sandth

---

Believe it or not, decimals, like their close cousins, fractions, were invented to make things *easier*, yet many students are as confused by decimals as they are by fractions. Decimals are really just a specific kind of fraction—just as percents are (more on those soon).

Multiply the Meat

Decimals and zeros in numbers confuse *everyone's* multiplication. The easiest way to perform this operation using numbers with zeros and decimals in them is to ignore the zeros and decimal points and just multiply the meat, i.e., the non-zero integers! Then, when you're done, put a decimal at the end of your number, and move it as needed by putting the zeros and the decimals back in. How?

Count the number of zeros in the two numbers you multiplied and add them onto your answer [moving the decimal to the right one place for each zero].

Count the number of decimal places in the two numbers you multiplied and move the decimal point to the left for each one. If the decimal ends up moving beyond your number, add a zero between the outermost digit and the decimal.

For example:

2,400 × .003

      Step One: Disregard the 0s and decimal places.

      Step Two: Add back in two 0s [taken off 2,400].

      Step Three: Move decimal point three places to the left.

So: 2,400 × .003 = 7.200

Practice

DECIMAL REVIEW

Please do the problems below WITHOUT your calculator. **After** you are finished you may check your work with your calculator.

Convert the fractions below to decimals:

1. $\dfrac{2}{10}$ = _____

2. $\dfrac{3}{100}$ = _____

3. $\dfrac{70}{1000}$ = _____

4. $\dfrac{15}{50}$ = _____

5. $\dfrac{22}{100}$ = _____

6. $\dfrac{22}{10}$ = _____

Adding and Subtracting Decimals:

1. 6.0389 – 0.78651 = _____

2. 2.89002 + 4.7939 = _____

3. 10.4098 – 1.989009 = _____

4. 5.8327 + 4.4072008 = _____

5. 6.93671 – 6.8784 = _____

6. 0.08876 + 0.00080221 = _____

Multiply the Meat:

1. 32,000 × 2,400 = _____

2. 170,000 × 14,000 = _____

3. 0.000012 × 4.3 = _____

4. 2.2 × 0.000045 = _____

5. 3,000 × 0.000016 = _____

6. 556,000,000 × 4.212 = _____

Convert the decimals below to fractions:

1. .08 = _____

2. .9 = _____

3. .006 = _____

4. .17 = _____

5. .095 = _____

6. .32 = _____

Multiplying and Dividing Decimals:

1. 1.2 × 0.08 = _____

2. .072 ÷ 6 = _____

3. 45 × 0.3 = _____

4. 5.2 ÷ 13 = _____

5. .0064 × 40 = _____

6. 1.10 ÷ 0.11 = _____

2nd Ed. © *ibidPREP llc*

PERCENTS

Percents act as a bridge between fractions and decimals. If you translate the word "percent" into math, you realize it means "divided by 100." So, 50 percent really means $50 \div 100$ which we know to write as $\frac{50}{100}$.

KNOW:

$\frac{1}{2} = .50 = 50\%$ $\frac{1}{6} = .1\overline{66} = 16.\overline{66}\%$

$\frac{1}{3} = .\overline{33} = 33.\overline{33}\%$ $\frac{1}{8} = .125 = 12.5\%$

$\frac{1}{4} = .25 = 25\%$ $\frac{1}{9} = .\overline{11} = 11.\overline{11}\%$

$\frac{1}{5} = .20 = 20\%$ $\frac{1}{10} = .10 = 10\%$

PERCENT AND AMOUNT

A big issue with students and percent questions seems to revolve around percent increase and percent decrease. What often confuses students here is that amount and percent are very different things.

Amount is a fixed number: Julia ordered 12 loaves of bread yesterday and 3 more than that today.

Percent is a fraction based on the ratio of the parts to a whole. 3 is what percent of 12?

Still, we are often sorely tempted to confuse the two...

EXAMPLE 1. Manuel wanted to buy a jacket that he saw in the store for $100. He waited and a week later the price of the jacket had increased 10%. He waited another week and this time when he returned to the store there was a sale and the jacket was 10% off the latest price.

How much was the jacket now?

If you said "$100," congratulations! You are absolutely normal. But wrong!

Remember: 10 percent of 100 [the original price that was raised] is going to be equal to a different [and smaller] amount than 10 percent of the later price, so you will actually be paying less than the original amount for the jacket after it has been raised and then goes on sale!

    Original price: $100

    10% of $100 = $10

    Price after first week [+10%] = $110

    10% of $110 = 11 {not 10!}

    So, the sale price will equal: $110 – $11= $99!

To determine the rate [percent] of increase or decrease if you're given the original and final amounts, just work backward.

A car originally sold for $24,000. At the end of the year, the car went on sale for $20,400. What percent off was the sale?

First, determine the **amount** of change.

$$24,000 - 20,400 = 3,600$$

Then determine what percent of the **ORIGINAL**[3] the amount of the change equals.

$$3,600 = \frac{x}{100} \cdot 24,000$$

$$3,600 = \frac{x}{1} \cdot 240$$

$$\frac{3,600}{240} = x$$

$$15 = x$$

SLIGHTLY COOL THING TO DO WITH PERCENTS

WHEN WE ARE TRYING TO FIGURE OUT PERCENT INCREASE OR DECREASE, MOST OF US FIGURE OUT WHAT AMOUNT OF THE ORIGINAL VALUE THE PERCENT INCREASE OR DECREASE IS, AND THEN WE ADD OR SUBTRACT THAT AMOUNT FROM THE ORIGINAL TO GET OUR NEW AMOUNT.

YOU MAY, HOWEVER, SAVE YOURSELF A STEP IN THAT PROCESS IF YOU ADD OR SUBTRACT THE PERCENT CHANGE FROM 100% [THE ORIGINAL PERCENTAGE] _FIRST_, AND THEN MULTIPLY THAT RESULT BY YOUR ORIGINAL AMOUNT.

EXAMPLE 1. A MEAL COST $28 BEFORE TAX. IF THE TAX ON THE BILL IS 8%, HOW MUCH DID THE MEAL COST AFTER TAX?

OLD WAY: 8% OF 28 = .08 × 28 = 2.24 ∴ AFTER TAX THE MEAL COST 28 + 2.24 = $30.24
NEW WAY: 8% + 100% = 108% ∴ AFTER TAX THE MEAL COST 28 × 1.08 = $30.24

EXAMPLE 2. A HOODIE COSTING $80 GOES ON SALE FOR 20% OFF. WHAT IS THE SALE PRICE OF THE HOODIE?

OLD WAY: 20% OF 80 = .20 × 80 = 16 ∴
THE SALE PRICE OF THE JACKET = 80 − 16 = $64

NEW WAY: 100% − 20% = 80% ∴
THE SALE PRICE OF THE JACKET = 80 × .80 = $64

---

[3] Percent increase and decrease are ALWAYS based on the original or starting amount you are given.

Here's a handy formula for figuring out percent change!

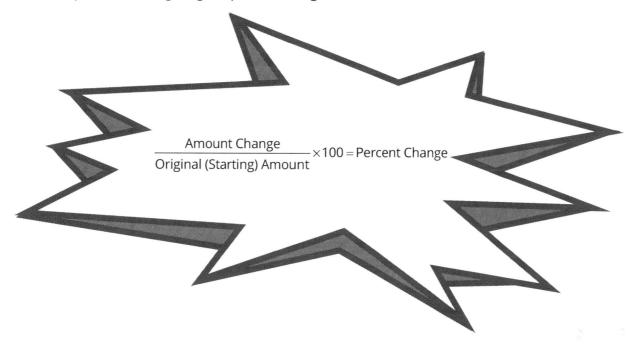

$$\frac{\text{Amount Change}}{\text{Original (Starting) Amount}} \times 100 = \text{Percent Change}$$

For example, Marge left 12 donuts on the counter. Homer ate three of them in two seconds. By what percent did the number of donuts decrease?

$$\frac{3}{12} \times 100 = \frac{1}{4} \times 100 = 25\%$$

You can also rework the formula in order to figure out the amount of change or even the original amount:

$$\frac{\text{Percent Change}}{100} \times \text{Original (Starting) Amount} = \text{Amount Change}$$

$$\frac{\text{Amount Change}}{\text{Percent Change}} \times 100 = \text{Original (Starting) Amount}$$

For example—

Bart ate 15% of the donuts Marge bought. If Marge bought 40 donuts, how many donuts did Bart eat?

$$\frac{\text{Percent Change}}{100} \times \text{Original (Starting) Amount} = \text{Amount Change}$$

$$\frac{15}{100} \times 40 = 6$$

Practice

PERCENTS WORD PROBLEMS

1. A class contains 30 students and 60% of the students in the class wiggle in their seats. How many students wiggle?

2. There are 25 people in a waiting room, 60% of them are sick and 80% of the sick people are making odd noises. How many sick people are making odd noises?

3. If 80% of a class of 50 students have brown hair and 20% of those students have curly hair, how many students in the class do not have curly brown hair?

4. Rebekah bought a house for $45,000. In three years its value increased to $72,000. What is the percent increase?

5. Last year the prison housed 1,200 inmates. This year the number decreased to 960. What is the percent decrease?

$$1,200 \quad 960 \qquad 960 = \frac{80}{100} = \frac{8}{10} =$$
$$-960 \over 240 \quad 1,200 \qquad 1,200$$

6. Last semester the college enrolled 15 students in its tutoring program. This year there are 27 students who need help. What is the percent increase?

7. Candy bars were 10 cents in 1972, and now they are 65 cents. What is the percent of increase?

8. The value of the inventory at the dollar store increased from $46,400 to $52,200 from one year to the next. What is the percent increase in the value of the inventory?

9. The price of a sofa increased from $520 to $582.40. What is the percent increase?

PERCENT/AMOUNT REVIEW

1. Find the percentage increase:
From $2,000 to $3,000

2. Find the percentage decrease:
From $75 to $60

3. Find the percentage increase:
From $48,000 to $60,000

2nd Ed. © ibidPREP llc

ADDITION IS THE SAME AS SUBTRACTION, MULTIPLICATION IS THE SAME AS DIVISION, & ROOTS ARE THE SAME AS EXPONENTS.

SUBTRACTING IS REALLY JUST ADDING A NEGATIVE.

$$8 - 5 = 8 + (-5) = 3$$

DIVIDING A NUMBER BY A DIVISOR IS THE SAME AS MULTIPLYING A NUMBER BY THE INVERSE OF THE DIVISOR.

$$16 \div 4 = 16 \times \frac{1}{4} = \frac{16}{4} = 4$$

TAKING THE ROOT OF A NUMBER IS THE SAME AS TAKING A NUMBER TO A FRACTIONAL POWER.

$$\sqrt[3]{125} = 125^{\frac{1}{3}}; \quad 7^{\frac{1}{4}} = \sqrt[4]{7} \; ; \text{ ETC.}$$

THE ONLY THING "WRONG" WITH PEMDAS IS THAT ADDITION DOESN'T NECESSARILY HAVE TO GO BEFORE SUBTRACTION BECAUSE THEY'RE THE SAME THING! THEREFORE, JUST DO WHICHEVER OF THE TWO COMES FIRST. THE SAME IS TRUE FOR MULTIPLICATION/DIVISION AND EXPONENTS/ROOTS.[38]

[38] **PEMDAS—P**arentheses, **E**xponents [roots], **M**ultiplication, **D**ivision, **A**ddition, **S**ubtraction

Practice

PEMDAS—PRACTICE

1. $9 - 1 \times 4 =$ 5

2. $(8 - 5) + 3.8 =$ 6.8

3. $7 + 8 \times 7 \div 2 =$ 35
   56 28

4. $6 \times (6 \div 3)^2 =$ 24

5. $(49 \div 7^2) \times 5 =$ 5

6. $(18 \div 6 + 2) \times \dfrac{7+3}{5} =$ 10
   5   $\frac{10}{5}$

7. $((8 \times 2)^2 + 5) \div (9 \div 2 + 4.5) =$ 29
   16^2
   29
   16
   ×16
   160
   96
   256

8. $7 + 8 \cdot 2 =$ 23

9. $(16 - 5) \times 9 + 3 =$ 102

10. $30 - 7 \cdot 8 \div 2 =$ 2

11. $(3^2 + 3) \div 3 =$ 4

12. $6 \times 8 \div 2 - 1 =$ 23
    48
    24

13. $(24 \div 4 + 2^2) \times (6 + 3)/(12 \div 2) =$ 15
    6   4
    9
    $90 \div 6 = 15$

2nd Ed. © ibidPREP llc

BASIC ARITHMETIC

1. $0.98 + 45.102 + 32.3333 + 31 + 0.00009$
   A. 368.573
   B. 210.536299
   C. 109.41539
   D. 99.9975
   E. 80.8769543

2. $0.12 \div 10$
   A. 12
   B. 1.2
   C. 0.12
   D. 0.012
   E. 0.0012

3. $(9 \div 3) \times (8 \div 4)$
   A. 1
   B. 6
   C. 72
   D. 576
   E. 752

4. $6 \times 0 \times 5 =$
   A. 0
   B. 2
   C. 11
   D. 25
   E. 30

5. $7.95 \div 1.5 =$
   A. 2.4
   B. 5.3
   C. 6.2
   D. 7.3
   E. 7.5

6. $-32 + 7 =$
   A. -25
   B. 25
   C. -26
   D. 26
   E. 27

7. $-37 + -47 =$
   A. 64
   B. -84
   C. 65
   D. -75
   E. -66

8. $41\% =$
   A. 4.1
   B. .41
   C. .041
   D. .0041
   E. .00415

EXPONENTS

One of the great [not] things about math is that as soon as you get multiplication slightly sorted out [3 × 2 = 6], they change things and introduce exponents. Then, all of a sudden something that looks like 3 × 2, namely 3^2, doesn't equal 6; now it equals 9! Even though 2 × 2 and 2^2 both equal 4? A lot of students, understandably, bow out at this point and simply decide to bail on exponent questions whenever they arise.

However, the good thing about exponents on standardized tests is they fall under that heading of SCARY TOPICS/EASY QUESTIONS.

So, if you just hang in and remember a few basic rules about exponents, then you should be rewarded with a not too difficult question to get right.

The basic rules of exponents are listed below, but the most important thing to remember is that taking a number to a power simply means multiplying it by itself that number of times.

$4^3 = 4 \times 4 \times 4 = 64$

A square root is the number that, times itself, equals the number you are taking the root of. In better words, if you multiply the square root of a number by itself [square the square root], you will get the original number. Put an even better way: $\sqrt{x} \cdot \sqrt{x} = x$.

Everyone knows that $\sqrt{9} = 3$, but most students freak out when they see things like $\sqrt{2}$. They freak out for a couple of reasons, but mostly because $\sqrt{2}$ is a hideous irrational number that threatens the fabric of human existence. [Ok, maybe I went a little far there.] Happily, on this test, you don't have to deal with 1.414213562... just $\sqrt{2}$, which is why it was invented in the first place—to symbolize a long, hideous number that no one else wants to deal with either. Treat it like a variable.

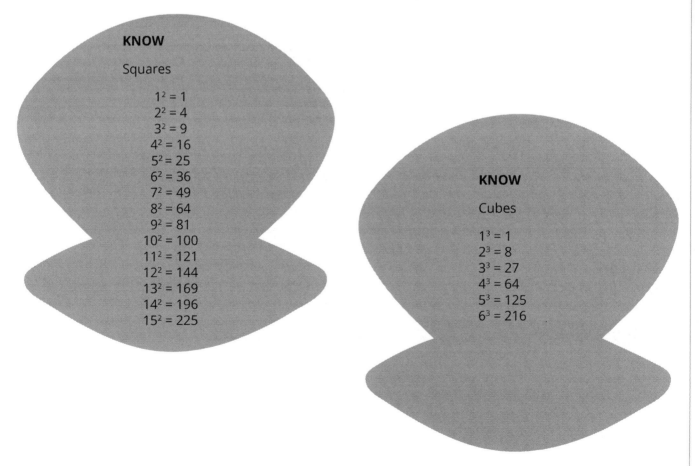

KNOW

Squares

$1^2 = 1$
$2^2 = 4$
$3^2 = 9$
$4^2 = 16$
$5^2 = 25$
$6^2 = 36$
$7^2 = 49$
$8^2 = 64$
$9^2 = 81$
$10^2 = 100$
$11^2 = 121$
$12^2 = 144$
$13^2 = 169$
$14^2 = 196$
$15^2 = 225$

KNOW

Cubes

$1^3 = 1$
$2^3 = 8$
$3^3 = 27$
$4^3 = 64$
$5^3 = 125$
$6^3 = 216$

2ⁿᵈ Ed. © ibidPREP llc

Exponent Rules

Number to a power times a number to a power

To solve a number to a power times a number to a power, ADD the exponents:

$5^3 \times 5^4 = 5^{3+4} = 5^7$

Number to a power divided by a number to a power

To determine a number to a power divided by a number to a power, SUBTRACT the exponents:

$$\frac{7^9}{7^4} = 7^{9-4} = 7^5$$

Number To A Power Taken To A Power

To determine a number to a power taken to a power, MULTIPLY the powers:

$$(5^3)^4 = 5^{3 \times 4} = 5^{12}$$

A number to a power times a different number to the same power

To determine a number to a power times a different number to the same power, MULTIPLY THE BASES and LEAVE THE EXPONENTS ALONE:

$$4^3 \times 5^3 = (4 \times 5)^3 = 20^3$$

A fraction to a power

When you take a fraction to a power, remember to take the numerator and the denominator to that power:

$$\left(\frac{2}{3}\right)^4 = \frac{2^4}{3^4} = \frac{16}{81}$$

Negative exponents

This is REALLY confusing. Negative exponents have NOTHING to do with negative numbers. A number taken to a negative exponent equals the inverse of that number. [Flip it and put it under 1.]

$$5^{-3} = \frac{1}{5^3} = \frac{1}{125}$$

A number to a power plus that same number to the same power, plus itself again, plus itself...

is just equal to the number of times you are adding that number times itself:

$$4^3 + 4^3 + 4^3 + 4^3 = 4(4^3) = 4^1(4^3) = 4^{1+3} = 4^4$$

The square root of a fraction...

is equal to the square root of the top and the bottom:

$$\sqrt{\frac{9}{25}} = \frac{\sqrt{9}}{\sqrt{25}} = \frac{3}{5}$$

Practice

SQUARES AND CUBES THE UBERDWEEB TEST MAKERS
LOVE

There are few things the geeks who make these tests get more excited about than the fact that negative numbers squared become positive. The second thing they love, love, love is that a number between zero and one gets SMALLER when it gets squared. Here are some other annoying, er, amazing facts they like to exploit.[5]

"FUN" FACTS

"FUN" FACTS

- NEGATIVE NUMBERS SQUARED become POSITIVE.
- A number between zero and one gets SMALLER when it gets squared or cubed.

$$\left(\frac{1}{2}\right)^2 = \frac{1}{4} \text{ and } \left(\frac{1}{4}\right)^3 = \frac{1}{64}$$

- A number less than -1 gets SMALLER when it's cubed.

$$-2^3 = -8 \; ; \; -2 > -8$$

- A number between -1 and 0 gets BIGGER when it's cubed.

$$\left(-\frac{1}{4}\right)^3 = -\frac{1}{64} \text{ [no matter how it may seem, } -\frac{1}{64} \text{ is}$$

$$\text{GREATER THAN } -\frac{1}{4} \text{]}$$

[5] make use of, take advantage of

2ⁿᵈ Ed. © ibidPREP llc

EXPONENTS—PRACTICE

Express answer in exponent form

1. $5^3 \times 5^4 =$ 5^7

2. $(3^4)^2 =$ 81

3. $5^4 + 5^4 + 5^4 + 5^4 + 5^4 =$ 25^{20}

4. $3^3 \times 5^3 =$ 15^6

5. $(6^3)^4 \times 6^5 =$ 222^9

EXPONENTS—DRILL SET

1. Simplify $\dfrac{(3)^3}{(2)^3} + \dfrac{(5)^2}{(4)^2}$ 25

   A. $\dfrac{79}{8}$

   B. $\dfrac{79}{16}$

   C. $\dfrac{29}{16}$

   D. $\dfrac{16}{29}$

   E. $\dfrac{8}{79}$

2. Simplify $(1)^4 + (2)^3 + (3)^2 + (4)^1$
   A. 24
   B. 22
   C. 20
   D. 12
   E. 2

   $1 + 8 + 9 + 4 = 22$

3. Simplify $\dfrac{(4)^3}{(2)^2} + (2)^3 \times (3)^2$
   A. 144
   B. 88
   C. 80
   D. 72
   E. 56

   $\dfrac{64}{4}$ $16 + 8 = 24 \times 9$

MUST KNOW

ALGEBRA

2nd Ed. © ibidPREP llc

How to Solve for x!

All You Have To Do Is...

Algebra is a great tool for solving problems with unknown quantities in them. A quantity is just a number of things, and those things can be anything from doorknobs to people's ages to pickles. In pre-algebra, which many of you may be doing already, students set up problems and then try to solve them by sticking numbers into a blank where the unknown number would be. That's an *okay* way of going about things, but if it were actually an ideal method, humankind would never have progressed to **algebra**. If we put an "x" in place of the blank in our equations, all kinds of magic is possible—including solving the problem quickly!

The "x" in an equation is called a variable because its value can vary[1]! When you are moving around your x, think of it as a bottle of ketchup: if you have one bottle of ketchup and you add it to two bottles of ketchup, you get three bottles of ketchup!

1 Bottle of Ketchup + 2 Bottles of Ketchup = 3 Bottles of Ketchup

$1x + 2x = 3x$

It's the same for multiplication:

3 Bottles of Ketchup × 4 = 12 Bottles of Ketchup

$3x \times 4 = 12x$

(Note that we don't × use for multiplication in algebra because it is too easily confused with the x we use for our variable.)

It also works for division:

10 Bottles of Ketchup ÷ 5 = 2 Bottles of Ketchup

$10x \div 5 = 2x$

(Note that it's better to turn division problems into fractions in algebra, so make friends with fractions.)

Equations with x

The goal in equations with one variable is to get x [or whatever single variable you're solving for] alone on one side of the equal sign—everything that gets put onto the other side ends up being the value of x.

To do this:

Combine like terms

Although you've heard this phrase before, you may not have entirely grasped precisely what it means. It means:

a. Move all the x's to one side and all the numbers to the other. Add, subtract, multiply and divide all the x's with each other and all the numbers with themselves. Then:

b. Put all the x's on one side of the equal sign and all the variables on the other.

Putting the variables and numbers together with one another is not that hard, but moving terms across the equal sign may be. The reason we move terms and variables is so that we may get x [or whatever we're solving for] alone on one side of the equation. If we do that, then naturally everything on the other side of the equal sign will be what x is equal to! In order to avoid making the same mistakes most kids make again and again, we're going to peel away using a little process called SADMEP.

---

[1] change

SADMEP

You all know about PEMDAS. However, very few of you, perhaps none of you, have ever heard of SADMEP. I never had either, and, in fact, I thought I made it up [a quick Google search relieved me of that delusion].

It merely means the order of operations in reverse, and you use it to keep in mind the process by which you move terms across the equal sign to peel away to x. So, first, if there's anything attached to x by addition or subtraction, do the reverse to it to move it. Then divide away coefficients, take roots to powers or take the roots of powers, and, last, undo parentheses!

$$\text{e.g. } 2(4+x)^2 - 3 = 47$$

$$\underline{+3 = +3} \qquad \text{Subtraction!}$$
(Same as Addition)

$$2(4+x)^2 = 50$$

$$\frac{2(4+x)^2}{2} = \frac{50}{2} \qquad \text{Division!}$$
(Same as Multiplication)

$$(4+x)^2 = 25$$

$$\sqrt{(4+x)^2} = \sqrt{25} \qquad \text{Roots!}$$
(Same as Exponents)

$$(4+x) = 5$$

Parentheses!

$$4+x = 5$$

$$\underline{-4 \qquad = -4} \qquad \text{Addition!}$$

$$x = 1$$

Yes, Backsies

The only way this whole algebra she-bob works is if you remember that if you do it to one side of the equation you have to do it to the other. [If you give your brother a piece of Halloween candy, he darn well better give you one, no?] Once you have moved all the numbers to one side, you can go ahead and do the same with any terms [remembering, of course, that just plain x means $1x$].

Once you have become aware of the process involved in solving algebraic equations, the best thing to do is to practice solving for x over and over in every way imaginable. Even more than in most other math problems, writing out your steps here, clearly and neatly aligned, is vital. It's amazing how often students who have routine difficulties doing basic arithmetic try to do complete algebra steps in their heads. This is a GREAT way to make careless mistakes [adding when you should be subtracting a term is also an enduring classic careless error!]

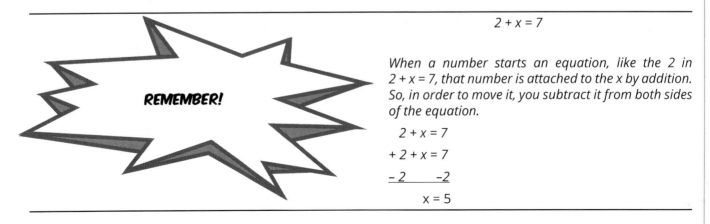

$$2 + x = 7$$

REMEMBER!

When a number starts an equation, like the 2 in $2 + x = 7$, that number is attached to the x by addition. So, in order to move it, you subtract it from both sides of the equation.

$$2 + x = 7$$
$$+ 2 + x = 7$$
$$\underline{- 2 \qquad -2}$$
$$x = 5$$

2nd Ed. © ibidPREP llc

Solve for "x"—Drill Set

Solve each of the equations below for "x" or "y."

1. 8y = 64

$y = 8$

2. 12y = 108

$y = 9$

3. 1 – y = –8

$(-(-8) = y = -9$

4. 8y = 32

$y = 4$

5. 5y + 2 = 7

$7 - 2 = 5$
$5 - 5 = 0$ $y = 5$

6. 7 – y = 4

$7 - 4 = 3$
$y = 3$

7. 4y + 10 = 58

$58 - 10 = 48$ $y = 12$
$48 ÷ n = 12$

8. 5 – y = –2

$5 - (-2) = 7$ $y = 7$

9. 8y + 12 = 108

$108 - 12$ 96 $y = 12$
96 8
12

10. 12 + y = 23

-12 $y = 11$

11. –6 + y = 13

$y = 19$

12. 4y – 8 = 16

$16 ÷ 8 = \frac{8}{4}$ $y = 2$
2

13. 7y = 7

$7 - 7 = 0$ $y = 1$

14. 4y + 10 = 26

$26 ÷ 16 = \frac{4}{4}$ $y = 4$
-10

15. x – 4 = 10

$4 + 10 = 14$
$x = 14$

16. 2x – 4 = 10

$10 + 4 = 14$ $x = 4$
$14 ÷ 2 = 7$

17. 5x – 6 = 4x + 6

$+6 = 13$ 12
$x = 12$

18. 4x + 3 = 2 + 6(x – 4)

$4x + 3 = 2 + 6x - 24$
$3 = 14 + 2x - 24$
$3 = 2x - 22$

$25 = 2x$
-12.5

WORDS TO MATH

Now we can do word problems!

A lot of the math on this test seems a lot harder than it is because it's given to you in words instead of numbers. But fear not! We will teach you to isolate phrases and the best way to deal with all the screwy phrasing[2]. The best way is to turn words into math as quickly as possible. Here are some words translated into math. Learn this handy lexicon[3], so you won't get as easily thrown by the test's weird terminology.

Let's do an example:

If George [G] is three times Martha's [M] age, and Martha is 4 years younger than Bill [B], then how old will George be when Bill is 10 years old?

Breaking it down and translating words to math:

If George [G] is three times Martha's [M] age,

STOP!   G = 3M

and Martha is 4 years younger than Bill,

STOP!   M = B – 4

then how old will George be when Bill is 10 years old?

B = 10

In this problem we are trying to get to George [G] from Bill [B].

Often with word problems, it works best to start with the last piece of info and work backward!!

M = B – 4

Then, since B = 10

M = 10 – 4 = 6

M = 6

Now we can use our first piece of knowledge and solve for *G!*

G = 3M and M = 6, so

3M = 3(6)

G = 18

---

[2] wording
[3] dictionary, word list

        2nd Ed. © ibidPREP llc

ALGEBRA WORD PROBLEMS

1. Paul is selling lucky rabbit's feet for $2.50 each plus a one-dollar shipping and handling fee. If he receives a total of $35, how many rabbit's feet did he sell?
   - A. 10
   - B. 11
   - C. 12
   - D. 13
   - E. 14

2. Michael buys $5.40 worth of lollipops for 12 cents each. He then sells each one for 15 cents each. How much profit does he earn?
   - A. $0.75
   - B. $1.35
   - C. $3.10
   - D. $5.40
   - E. $6.75

3. Stan sells cookies for 25 cents each. If the money he receives for all sales is at least $8 but less than $9, which of the following could NOT be the number of cookies he sold?
   - A. 32
   - B. 33
   - C. 34
   - D. 35
   - E. 36

4. A basic pizza comes with cheese and one free topping and costs $15. If each additional topping is 75 cents, how many total toppings are on a pizza that costs $18? (Note: cheese does NOT count as a topping.)
   - A. 3
   - B. 4
   - C. 5
   - D. 6
   - E. 7

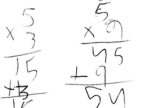

5. Brenda makes smoothies for a health-food store. She puts three kinds of fruit into each smoothie, and each smoothie costs $5. Customers can also add a shot of wheat grass for $1. If she sells a total of $99 worth of smoothies one day, which of the following could be the number of shots of wheat grass she sold?
   - A. 3
   - B. 9
   - C. 12
   - D. 16
   - E. 18

6. Sally buys $3.12 worth of seashells. If each seashell had been a penny more expensive, she would have been able to purchase two fewer seashells than she did. How many did she actually buy?
   - A. 12
   - B. 24
   - C. 26
   - D. 39
   - E. 52

Percent Word Problems

Many percent problems are expressed as word problems. If you remember that certain words can be replaced with math signs, you're in business.

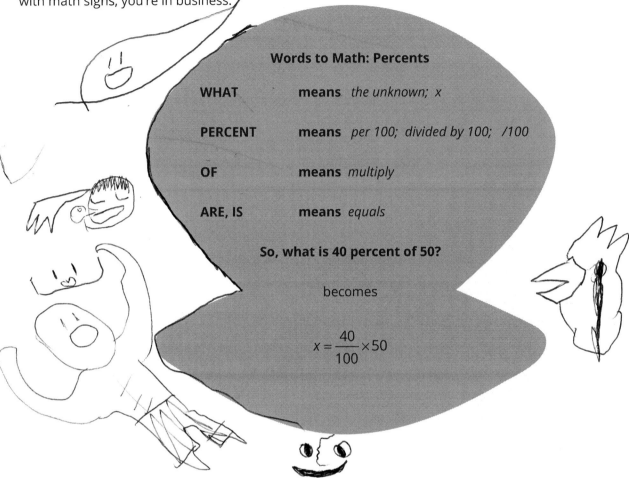

Words to Math: Percents

WHAT   **means** *the unknown; x*

PERCENT   **means** *per 100; divided by 100; /100*

OF   **means** *multiply*

ARE, IS   **means** *equals*

So, what is 40 percent of 50?

becomes

$$x = \frac{40}{100} \times 50$$

E.g.,   80% of a class of 200 are nose pickers. How many are nose pickers?

80%: $\frac{80}{100}$ [PER means divided by & CENT means 100—change all percents to fractions with a denominator of 100]

To solve this problem, REDUCE FIRST!

$$\frac{80}{100} \times 200 = 160$$

E.g., what is 30% of 90?

Translate words to math and you get:

$$[\text{What}] \; x \; [\text{is}] = [30\%] \; \frac{30}{100} \; [\text{of}] \times [90] \; 90 = \frac{3}{1} \times 9 = 27$$

Although there are many ways to solve percent problems, please try the following using the fractional, words-to-math approach!

PERCENTS—DRILL SET

1. What percent of 20 is 30?

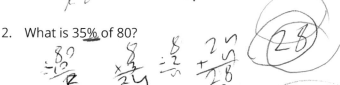

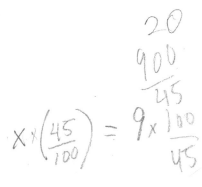

2. What is 35% of 80?

3. 45% of what is 9?

4. Suppose you bought something in Dogtown that was priced at $6.95, and the total bill after tax was $7.61. What is the sales tax rate in Dogtown? (Round answer to one decimal place.)

5. Suppose a certain item used to sell for 75 cents a pound, you see that it's been marked up to 81 cents a pound. What is the percent increase?

6. A computer software retailer increased the wholesale price of his goods by 40% to determine his selling price. Find the selling price of a computer game that cost the retailer $25 wholesale.

7. A golf shop pays its wholesaler $40 for a certain club and then sells it to a golfer for $75. What is the rate of increase?

8. A shoe store uses a 40% markup on cost. Find the cost of a pair of shoes that sells for $63.

9. An item originally priced at $55 is marked 25% off. What is the sale price?

10. An item that regularly sells for $425 is marked down to $318.75. What is the rate of decrease?

11. Growing up, Schmul lived in a tiny country village. When he left for college, the population was 840. He recently heard that the population had grown by 5%. What is the present population?

12. Your friend diets and goes from 125 pounds to 110 pounds. What was her percentage weight loss?

MUST KNOW

GEOMETRY

2nd Ed. © ibidPREP llc

WORDS TO MATH: STILL APPLIES, BUT MORE SO

Just as with general word problems, it is vital in geometry problems that you translate words into math as you go and not try to take in the whole problem at once. Many times you will be setting up equations just as in algebraic word problems. However, with geometry problems, it's very important that instead of simply creating equations, you put down formulas as you go. There are very few formulas the Hunter Test requires that you know, but as with all their basics, they want you to know them inside and out! You must learn them by heart because nothing in your text is going to tell you WHEN or WHERE to apply them, or even what they are!

Fill in Figures

When you are given a geo problem with a figure above it, always, *always* fill in everything you know about the figure and everything you are given about the figure BEFORE you start to tackle the question itself. Most of the time in the process of filling in the info you will solve the problem!

Solve for your angle (or whatever) last

Just as students feel compelled to go after the hardest-looking part of the question first, they also usually feel compelled to go after the answer first. Who wants to spend any more time than necessary on a problem? Of course, that usually leads to a bigger problem and more time wasted—especially in geometry problems in which you are meant to solve for an angle inside a figure. Usually the figure will give you one or two actual angle or side values, a few additional unknowns and the unknown you need to solve for. The ONLY way to find your variable will be to figure out ALL the other unknowns first. In fact, one way I keep my students from going after their variable first is to cover the question and just make them figure out everything they can about the figure given. Once they do that, I uncover the question, and all they have to do is provide the right answer from their quiver[1] of knowledge.

GEOMETRY

From now until high school, there will not be too much geometry that you will be required to know. However, if you learn very well the few things that you are required to know, then you will be in great shape for whatever geometry questions come your way for a long time to come!

The Basics

There are THREE DIMENSIONS that we can see:

1. **Length**
2. **Width**
3. **Height**

Shapes and objects with **two dimensions** are essentially flat [if they rise or have any thickness at all, they're not really 2D]: paper, screens [even though things projected on them might *look* 3D], maps, floors, streets, rectangles, triangles, circles, etc.

Shapes and objects with **three dimensions** rise, at least slightly, from their 2D bases. E.g., cans, cones, pyramids, people, trees, cars, etc.

---

[1] a case for holding arrows

Polygons

Polygons are 2D [flat] shapes made of intersecting line segments. They are generally named for the number of sides they have.

Triangles—Triangles are polygons with three sides ["tri" means three!] and three interior angles. The sum of the three angles in a triangle **always** equals 180°.

Equilateral Triangle—In an equilateral triangle all sides are equal and all angles are equal. Since all angles are equal and the three interior angles of a triangle add up 180° to then each angle in an equilateral triangle equals 60°.

Quadrilaterals—Quadrilaterals have four sides and four interior angles. The sum of the four angles in a quadrilateral equals 360°. There are many kinds of quadrilaterals. Some of them you probably know.

Trapezoid—A trapezoid has two sides that are parallel.

Parallelogram—A parallelogram has two pairs of parallel sides and each pair of opposite angles is equal.

Rhombus—A rhombus is a special kind of parallelogram. All its sides are equal, but all its angles do not have to be. If a rhombus has all equal angles, then those angles are 90°, and the rhombus is a square!

Rectangle—A rectangle is a special kind of parallelogram. It has two pairs of equal sides and each pair of opposite corner angles is equal, AND all those corner angles are 90°.

Square—A square is a special kind of rectangle [which is a special kind of parallelogram]. A square is a rectangle whose sides are all equal to each other.

2ⁿᵈ Ed. © ibidPREP llc

Pentagon/Hexagon/Heptagon/Octagon...

A pentagon is a five-sided polygon.

A hexagon is a six-sided polygon.

A heptagon is a seven-sided polygon.

An octagon is an eight-sided polygon.

If a polygon has all equal sides and all equal interior angles, then it is called a ***regular*** polygon.

TRIANGLES

1. The sum of the angles of a triangle = 180°.
2. In a right triangle the side opposite the largest angle (and therefore the longest) is the hypotenuse.
3. In similar triangles all angles are congruent to their counterparts in the other triangle and all sides are in equal ratios to one another.

Some Triangles

An **isosceles** triangle has two equal sides and two equal angles opposite them.

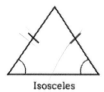

Isosceles

An **equilateral** triangle has three equal sides and three 60° angles.

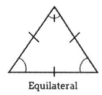

Equilateral

In a **right*** triangle, the side opposite the 90° angle [and therefore the longest] is the hypotenuse—"c."

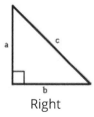

Right

*Careful though; as much as we wish it were the case, not every triangle is an equilateral or right triangle. Don't assume it is unless that info is given.

CIRCLES

Every time you are given a fact about a circle—its area, circumference, etc.—write it down as an equation!

Circles

- The **central angle** of a circle measures 360°.
- **One revolution** of a circle is equal to the **circumference** of that circle.
- **The diameter** is the **longest chord** that can be drawn in the circle—it passes through the center. It is equal to two times the radius.
- The **radius** is a line drawn from the center to the circumference of a circle. It is **one-half** the **diameter**.
- The **circumference** of a circle is the distance a **360°** arc around the circle covers [think of it as the perimeter of the circle].
- The **circumference** of a circle [its perimeter] = **πd = 2πr**
- The **area of a circle** = **πr²** [if you get area and circumference of circles confused, remember area always has the square in it: square feet, square meters, r²].

Diameter of a circle = 2 × radius

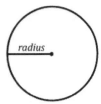

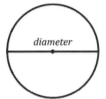

AREA

Area is the space inside a shape.

The two main areas you need to know are the area of a rectangle and the area of a triangle. The area of a square is the same as the area of a rectangle because a square is a rectangle. It is a special rectangle: one with all sides equal!

2ⁿᵈ Ed. © *ibidPREP llc*

Area of a Rectangle = Length x Width or Base x Height

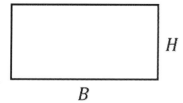

The area of a triangle is similar to the area of a rectangle; it's just half the base x height because:

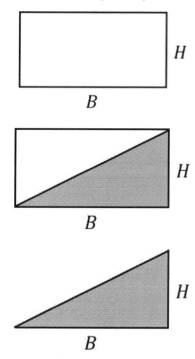

Area of a Triangle = ½ base x height (A = ½B x H)

Example: Twins Stacy and Tracy share a fabulous loft bedroom that is 15 feet by 20 feet. Unfortunately, they fight all the time. If Stacy splits the room in half diagonally and forbids Tracy from setting foot on her side, how big will each twin's part of the room be?

Perimeter

Perimeter is the distance around a shape. E.g., if you walk around your playground, how far do you walk?

Perimeter of a Rectangle = Side + Side + Side + Side **or** 2 times Length + 2 times Width

or 2(Length + Width)

Perimeter of a Triangle = Side + Side + Side

How To Do Geo—Part 2

Fill in Pictures—

If you are given a picture and given information about that picture, be sure to fill that information in on the figure so you get a clear idea of what's going on in that picture. It REALLY helps!

Make Like a Gunfighter and DRAW!

If you are NOT given a picture, make your life easier and simply draw one!

You would be surprised how many students skip this step, but it makes solving the problem SO MUCH EASIER if you can see what's going on.

E.g., The most popular ride at Landfill Land is the Deep Sludge Coaster. One car holds 12 rows of screaming kids. If each row holds 3 riders, what is the largest number of screaming fourth graders that can ride at one time?

Draw a diagram below with information from the question:

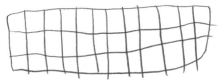 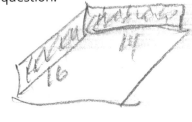

Now, do the math to find the answer.

Fill in Formulas!

Geometry problems are MUCH easier to solve if you write down the formulas for the specific shapes as those things are mentioned. Once you write out that formula, then it's just a matter of filling it in as you go. It's sort of like following a recipe. If you have the right recipe and follow the steps, you can't screw up!

Fortunately, on a lot of geometry problems they give you the correct formulas, so you just need to remember to fill in the information for them as you go.

NOW... Let's put it all together! Use diagrams, formulas and math to solve the following problem.

E.g., Rona has a mandrake garden that is 3 feet wide and 9 feet long. She wants to enclose her garden with a row of roses. If rose edging costs $40/yard, how much will it cost her to do this?

Perimeter = 2 Length + 2 Width

1 Yard = 3 Feet

2nd Ed. © ibidPREP llc

AREA AND PERIMETER—DRILL SET

1. A rectangular photo measures 8 inches by 6 inches. If the photo is framed with a two-inch wooden frame, what is the difference between the area of the photo with the frame and the area of the photo?
   A. 168 square inches
   B. 120 square inches
   C. 72 square inches
   D. 48 square inches
   E. 22 square inches

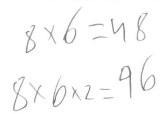

2. In the figure to the right, all angles shown are right angles. What is the perimeter of the figure?
   A. 50
   B. 50
   C. 30
   D. 20
   E. Cannot be determined

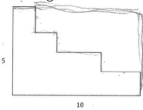

3. What is the area of the trapezoid ABCD below if the combined areas of right triangle BFD and right triangle ACE are 15?
   A. 50
   B. 45
   C. 30
   D. 25
   E. Cannot be determined

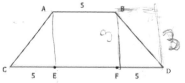

4. The figure to the right has a perimeter of 60. What is the length of $\overline{BC}$?
   A. 10
   B. 14
   C. 16
   D. 18
   E. Cannot be determined

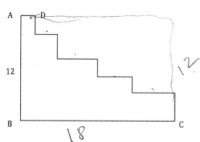

5. A rectangular yard measuring 16 feet by 14 feet. is to be surrounded by a 3 foot-wide hedge. What will be the area of that hedge?
   A. 440 square feet
   B. 224 square feet
   C. 216 square feet
   D. 194 square feet
   E. 160 square feet

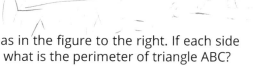

6. Four equilateral triangles are arranged as in the figure to the right. If each side of the four triangles measures 5 inches, what is the perimeter of triangle ABC?
   A. 60 inches
   B. 40 inches
   C. 30 inches
   D. 25 inches
   E. 20 inches

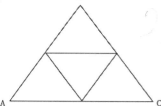

3D Geometry

So now that you're finally comfortable with all the 2D geometry they're going to throw at you, we have to take it to the next level: the third dimension!

Now is a good time to review just what is meant by two dimensions and three dimensions. Two-dimensional geometry is everything you've done so far with us. A two-dimensional shape is one with only two dimensions (duh). This means that a rectangle has only length and width. Length is one dimension, width the other.

Adding a third dimension to the rectangle would make it a 3D shape. What is the third dimension? Height.

Now that the rectangle has height, it's not just flat. It's the difference between a flat sheet of paper (2D) and a box (3D).

Now that we've got this third dimension (height), our shape has a new property called **volume**. Volume is simply how much space an object takes up. So the volume of my pencil would be much, much smaller than the volume of my house. Each exists as a 3D object, but the house takes up much more space than the pencil.

How do we measure this volume? We sort of use the same units we used for length and width: things like meters, inches, miles, etc. With those, if we had a rectangle that was 6 inches by 4 inches, the area would be 24 square inches. That's because each of those inches would have a length and a width (like a square). However, with 3D shapes, we now would get 24 cubic inches, or 24 in^3. Each unit of measurement is now 3D as well.

Volume of a Box [Rectangular Prism]

Just as we find the area of a rectangle by multiplying the TWO DIMENSIONS of the shape with each other [length × width], we find the VOLUME of a box by multiplying the THREE DIMENSIONS with each other

$$\textbf{Length × Width × Height}$$

Surface Area of a Box

The surface area of a box is the area of all of the faces of the box added together. Imagine how much wrapping paper would be needed to cover the shape!

$$\textbf{2LW + 2LH + 2WH}$$

2nd Ed. © ibidPREP llc

3D GEOMETRY—DRILL SET

1. A rectangular prism has a volume of 360 cubic centimeters. The height of this prism is 6 cm, and its width is 5 cm. Find the surface area.
   A. 300
   B. 324
   C. 360
   D. 432
   E. 720

2. Determine the surface area of a cube with a volume of 343.
   A. 49
   B. 252
   C. 294
   D. 307
   E. 343

3. Beppe needs to excavate soil to build his new pool. If the dimensions of the pool will be 15 feet by 30 feet by 9 feet deep, and it costs $10 per cubic yard to excavate, how much will the excavation cost, in dollars?
   A. $720
   B. $900
   C. $1,500
   D. $10,500
   E. $11,200

4. Minnie needs to bake a cake that will fit into a one-cubic-foot box. She knows to add one-tenth of a gram of sugar for every cubic inch of cake. How many grams of sugar will she need to add?
   A. 1.2
   B. 2.4
   C. 14.4
   D. 86.4
   E. 172.8

5. A rectangular prism has a surface area of 448 . Its length is 14 cm and its width is 6 cm. Find its height.
   A. 5
   B. 6
   C. 7
   D. 8
   E. 9

Practice

GEOMETRY REVIEW

1. Jill's bedroom is exactly 15 feet by 18 feet. If Jill wants to put a carpet on the floor, how much carpeting is needed?
   A. 33 square feet
   B. 270 square feet
   C. 715 square feet
   D. 829 square feet
   E. 1,080 square feet

2. How many sides does a quadrilateral have?
   A. 2
   B. 3
   C. 4
   D. 5
   E. Any number of sides greater than 3

3. What is the area of the figure to the right?
   A. 4 square units
   B. 8 square units
   C. 16 square units
   D. 24 square units
   E. 64 square units

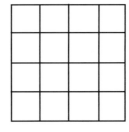

4. Amy's room is 768 square feet. Which of the following could be a correct measurement of Amy's room?
   A. 15 feet by 35 feet
   B. 34 feet by 41 feet
   C. 22 feet by 32 feet
   D. 24 feet by 32 feet
   E. 24 feet by 44 feet

5. Paul measured the area of a square to be 121 ft². What is the perimeter of this square?
   A. 132 feet
   B. 120 feet
   C. 44 feet
   D. 22 feet
   E. None of the above

2nd Ed. © ibidPREP llc

SPECIAL HUNTER

MATH PROBLEMS

Special Hunter Word Problems!

Now that we've covered the Hunter math basics, we can turn and face some of the special kinds of problems that might pop up on the test. Although we will show you ways to solve these problems, we can't stress enough that you will need to be prepared to find ways to solve problems on your own using the good, solid basics we've reviewed—and you must make sure you're answering the right question! Many Hunter questions involve extra, sometimes unexpected, steps!

Hunter students are encouraged to find creative solutions, to take risks and try things. The best way to do this in math is to be confident in your approach and careful in your execution. If you think writing out a list of numbers and then picking out the terms you need will do the trick, then do it! And take the time to do it right.

The main challenge with these problems is to feel comfortable taking an *empirical* approach—using trial and error and putting numbers out there to see how they behave. Though you may be a great student and used to knowing how to do things, these problems won't necessarily have a preset way to do them—that's up to you to find!

Number Knowledge

On most of these tests, there will be a question or two asking you about the properties of some unknown numbers. It may be something like "four-digit number WXYZ has all of the following conditions," and they will then list a few conditions. The conditions will require you to know your math words: if you know that XYZ is divisible by nine, you had better remember what divisible means. So go back to your Must Know Math if you don't know such words!

Fortunately, this is a multiple choice test, and this gives you an advantage: there are only five possibilities for WXYZ. But how to figure out which one?

Usually, the best way is to test the five choices to see if they satisfy the conditions. However, to do this efficiently, it is important to really master a lot of the properties of numbers. For example, any number that is divisible by three will add up to a multiple of three. Huh?

An example: 15. 15 is obviously divisible by 3. However, the sum of its digits (5 + 1), is six. Six is also a multiple of three. This works for **ANY** number divisible by three.

Another way to solve these is, if they're given as addition problems and you are given letters in the place of digits, your answer is either going to come from examining the behavior of the digits in the ones place or the last place given. It's all about carrying!

There are more tricks like this in **Appendix C.** It is important that you become as comfortable with them as possible because they can save you a lot of time on these problems.

Practice

NUMBER KNOWLEDGE 1

The problems below feature topics that you've learned about algebra and word problems but also test your knowledge of the in's and out's of your MUST KNOW MATH. Don't be afraid to get creative!

1. Please evaluate the following expression:

$$\frac{\dfrac{5}{3} - \dfrac{3}{8}}{\dfrac{3}{4} - \dfrac{3}{8}} =$$

A. $\dfrac{23}{18}$

B. $\dfrac{40}{9}$

C. $\dfrac{8}{3}$

D. $\dfrac{24}{9}$

E. $\dfrac{31}{9}$

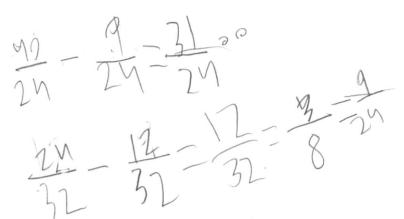

2. How many positive two-digit numbers increase by 27 when you reverse their digits?
   A. 4
   B. 5
   C. 6
   D. 7
   E. 8

3. What four-digit number can ABCD represent if:
   The four digits are 3, 5, 7 and 8.
   The number formed by the digits AB is divisible by 2 without remainder.
   The number formed by the digits ABC is divisible by 11 without remainder.
   A. 7,853
   B. 3,857
   C. 3,578
   D. 5,873
   E. 8,753

2nd Ed. © ibidPREP llc

4. When the 58th **odd** natural number is subtracted from the 108th **even** natural number, what is the result? [Natural numbers are counting numbers: 1, 2, 3, 4...]
   A. 50
   B. 54
   C. 97
   D. 101
   E. 115

5. WXYZ is a four-digit number composed of the digits 6, 7 and 8. The following statements about WXYZ are true:
   i.   Either the 6, 7 or 8 is used twice and the other two are used once.
   ii. YZ is divisible by three.
   iii. XYZ is also divisible by three.
   Which of the following is WXYZ
   A. 6,787
   B. 6,687
   C. 8,867
   D. 6,778
   E. 7,768

6. Each of the following is a factor of 90 EXCEPT:
   A. 5
   B. 6
   C. 15
   D. 16
   E. 45

7. If A is the set of prime numbers and B is the set of two-digit positive integers whose units digit is 7, how many numbers are common to both sets?
   A. none
   B. two
   C. four
   D. five
   E. six

NUMBER KNOWLEDGE 2

1. If the positive difference between 5.4 and 2.08 is multiplied by .38, the result is:
   A. .988
   B. 1.2616
   C. 2.94
   D. 3.9312
   E. 6.464

2. When a certain odd number is divided by 5 the remainder is 4. Which digit must be in the units place of the odd number?
   A. 1
   B. 3
   C. 5
   D. 7
   E. 9

3. In the expression below, each letter represents a one-digit number. Where the same letter appears, it represents the same number in each case. Each distinct letter represents a different number. What number must replace C?

$$\begin{array}{r} AAA \\ AAB \\ +ABC \\ \hline 1{,}051 \end{array}$$

   A. 0
   B. 1
   C. 3
   D. 4
   E. 7

4. Let an IBID number be defined as one in which the sum of the *distinct* factors of the number not including the number itself is greater than the number. Which of the following is an IBID number?
   A. 15
   B. 16
   C. 18
   D. 21
   E. 27

5. Which of the following is not a factor of the sum of all prime numbers less than 18?
   A. 1
   B. 2
   C. 6
   D. 29
   E. 58

6. PQRS is a four-digit number composed of 1, 2, 4 and 5. The following statements are true about PQRS:
   i.   PQRS is divisible by six but QR is not.
   ii. RS is divisible by nine.
   Which of the following could be PQRS?
   A. 1,254
   B. 1,245
   C. 4,125
   D. 1,425
   E. 5,124

2nd Ed. © ibidPREP llc

MIXED RATES

Mixed-rate problems are among the hardest problems you'll face on this test, and certainly the hardest algebra. What is a mixed-rate problem? One that's like this:

If I can paint one-quarter of a room in an hour, and you can paint one-sixth of a room in an hour, how long will it take us to paint it together?

The first step is to figure out our **combined rate**. That is, how much of the room will we paint together in one hour? We find that by adding:

$$\frac{1}{4} + \frac{1}{6} = \frac{5}{12}$$

That is how much of the room we will paint in an hour. And, luckily, the number of hours it will take us to paint the room is just the **reciprocal** of our **combined rate**! The reciprocal works because if together they do 5/12 of the job, then multiplying that part of the job by its reciprocal gives you one whole room. So, it will take $\frac{12}{5}$ hours to paint the whole room!

The whole secret is to figure out how long it takes to complete 1 job no matter what the job is.

$$\frac{5}{12} \text{ of the room} \times \frac{12}{5} \text{ hours} = 1 \text{ painted room}$$

We can apply this strategy to all sorts of problems: first we figure out what can be done for a given unit (one hour, say, or one minute) and then we can figure out how long it takes to complete the whole task.

MIXED RATES

1. Marcus can paint one-quarter of a house in an hour and Larry can paint one-fifth of a house in an hour. How long will it take them to paint the whole house if they work together?

    A. $2\frac{1}{5}$ hours

    B. $2\frac{2}{9}$ hours

    C. $2\frac{3}{8}$ hours

    D. $3\frac{1}{9}$ hours

    E. $3\frac{1}{2}$ hours

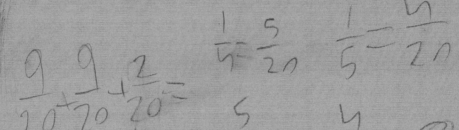

2. Brenda, Linda and Mary are hired to build a tree house, which they complete in four hours. They are paid a total of $107.50 for the job. They decide to distribute the money such that each of them receives the same hourly rate. How much should Mary receive if she arrived an hour and fifteen minutes late?

    A. $24.50
    B. $26.75
    C. $27.50
    D. $33.00
    E. $35.25

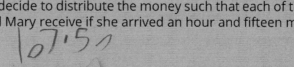

3. Martina can mow $\frac{1}{6}$ of a lawn in one hour and Bob can mow $\frac{1}{4}$ of the same lawn in one hour. How long will it take them to mow the lawn together?
    A. 2 hours
    B. 2 hours and 15 minutes
    C. 2 hours and 24 minutes
    D. 2 hours and 30 minutes
    E. 2 hours and 36 minutes

4. A recipe for chocolate cookies calls for 2.5 cups of sugar and produces 36 cookies. How much sugar will be required to produce 84 cookies?
    A. 5 cups

    B. $5\frac{1}{3}$ cups

    C. $5\frac{1}{2}$ cups

    D. $5\frac{2}{3}$ cups

    E. $5\frac{5}{6}$ cups

5. Three dogs knock over a 101 ounce bag of food and begin to eat it. Those three begin eating at the same time, but a fourth dog doesn't start until an a minute and a half later. If they all eat ten ounces a minute, how long will the fourth dog be eating before all the food is gone?
    A. 1.2 minutes
    B. 1.4 minutes
    C. 1.5 minutes
    D. 1.75 minutes
    E. 2 minutes

6. John, Max, Lucas and Steven are running a lemonade stand. John is there for six and one half hours, Max is there for three and one half hours, Lucas is there for two and one-half hours, and Steven is there for one-half hour. If they receive a total of $260 and want everyone to get paid the same hourly rate, how much more money will Lucas receive than Steven?
    A. $10
    B. $20
    C. $30
    D. $40
    E. $80

2nd Ed. © ibidPREP llc

PATTERNS

Finding Patterns Intellectually[1]

Some problems in math require that you know a formula or a set of relationships in order to be able solve them—like many geometry problems. Other problems require that you figure out the formula or pattern involved. A good way to discover a pattern is the way scientists do it.

- Create a hypothesis
    - Make a guess as to how you think the pattern might be formed
- Test the hypothesis through trial and error
    - Try your pattern or the pattern given on every answer choice
- Be thorough
    - Don't poop out after trying two or three answers and guess "D" out of laziness. Get to "E"!

Often in these problems, the hypothesis is given to you. Then it is merely a question of testing the various possible solutions offered.

All of these patterns involve basic math operations. Most of us like to test addition and multiplication first,;however, don't be afraid of trying subtraction and division. More important, try to be able to see and test for patterns that might COMBINE operations [add one then multiply by two, etc.]

PATTERN PROBLEMS

1. Which of the following sequences of numbers follows the pattern "add 7" if the first number is 16?
    - A. 16, 22, 29, 36, 43, 50
    - B. 16, 23, 31, 38, 45, 52
    - C. 16, 24, 30, 37, 44, 51
    - D. 16, 23, 30, 37, 44, 51
    - E. 16, 23, 31, 38, 45, 52

2. Write a number sequence of at least six numbers whose pattern is "subtract 6" when the first number is 99.

3. Which of the following sequences does NOT follow a consistent pattern?
    - A. 82, 70, 58, 46, 34, 22
    - B. 128, 64, 32, 16, 6, 3
    - C. 13, 19, 26, 32, 39, 45
    - D. 4, 8, 12, 16, 20, 24, 28
    - E. 100, 87, 74, 61, 48, 35

4. Which number goes in the blank: 16, 32, 48, ___, 80, 96?

5. Write a sequence of at least six numbers who pattern is "add 9" when the first number is 23.

---

[1] Having an idea and testing it!

Finding Patterns Empirically[2]

Some questions provide the format of a series and it's up to you follow it through to see how it behaves. You must write out the pattern and SEE what you have empirically—you will not be able to do these in your head!

Series, Sequences & Patterns

These are the problems in which you are asked to find what date something will fall on, the order of beads in a necklace, letters in a code, numbers in a sequence, etc. There are a few things to remember with these problems:

1. They are made to seem as if you'll have to do a lot of calculations in order to figure them out—wrong!
2. If the pattern is not given, and if you get going from the beginning long enough to see a pattern [see box below], you won't have to do a hundred calculations.

Example: if Eddy makes a necklace with beads colored blue, yellow, red in that order and he needs 100 beads to complete the necklace, what color will the final bead be?

$$1, 3, 9...$$

Example: every term in the sequence above is determined by multiplying the preceding term by three. Based on the sequence, what will the units digit of the 51st term be?

THE LONGEST JOURNEY STARTS WITH THE FIRST STEP[3]

WHAT WORKS FOR CHINESE PHILOSOPHY WORKS FOR MATH—EVERY SEQUENCE STARTS WITH THE FIRST TERM AND EVERY TRIAL STARTS AT ONE. WHEN YOU'RE FACTORING, START WITH ONE; EVEN THOUGH YOU KNOW WHAT IT IS, IT STILL COUNTS!

THIS PRINCIPLE WORKS ON MANY LEVELS:

1. YOU CANNOT GET TO THE FINAL TERM UNLESS YOU GO THROUGH THE FIRST TERM.

2. YOU CANNOT BEGIN TO SEE A PATTERN UNLESS YOU LAY IT OUT FROM THE BEGINNING.

3. WHAT WORKS FOR SMALL NUMBERS WORKS FOR BIGGER NUMBERS, AND SMALLER NUMBERS ARE EASIER TO WORK WITH.

---

[2] Figuring stuff out by experience, observation or experiment.
[3] Attributed to Lao-Tzu, founder of Taoism, a great Chinese religious philoso-   phy

2nd Ed. © ibidPREP llc

SERIES, SEQUENCES & PATTERNS PROBLEMS

$$648, 108, ...$$

1. In the sequence above, each term after the first term is $\frac{1}{6}$ of the term preceding it. What is the fifth term in this sequence?

    A. $\frac{1}{3}$

    B. $\frac{1}{2}$

    C. 3

    D. 6

    E. 12

2. The first term of a sequence is 24. The second term is 16. The third term and each term thereafter is the average (arithmetic mean) of the two terms immediately preceding it. What is the value of the first term in the sequence that is not an integer?

3. The first two terms of a sequence are 1 and 2, and all the following terms in the sequence are produced by subtracting the next to last term from the last term in the series. What is the 50th term in the sequence?

$$x, 13, 43, y, z, 1213$$

4. In the above sequence, each term after the first term, x, is 4 more than 3 times the previous term. What is the sum of $x + z$?

$$-3, 6, 3...$$

5. In the sequence above, each odd term (e.g., –3) is multiplied by –2 to find the next term. Each even term (e.g., 6) is subtracted by 3 to find the next term. What is the *absolute* value of the 12th term?
    A. -33
    B. -30
    C. 63
    D. 126
    E. 129

6. Paulina is making a Legos tower. She starts with 2 whites, 3 reds and 5 blues, in that order, and repeats that pattern until she runs out of Legos. If the last piece is red, which of the following could be the number of Legos in the tower?
    A. 42
    B. 44
    C. 46
    D. 48
    E. 50

Serial Numbers

A Way to Start

If you are given a number/sequence formed by a series of numbers in a pattern [all the multiples of 5, all even numbers, etc.] and then asked to find what the 46th digit [e.g.] might be, start lining up the digits in rows and columns. Put all the single digits first, then all the teens, 20s, 30s, etc., in separate rows. Then count the number of digits in each row and put that number at the end of the row, then add them up to get to the digit you're looking for!

What is the 46th digit in the number formed by putting together all the even numbers in a row starting from 2:

24681012141618....

Ready? Go!

4 digits: 2, 4, 6, 8

10 digits: 10, 12, 14, 16, 18

10 digits: 20, 22, 24, 26, 28

10 digits: 30, 32, 34, 36, 38

10 digits: 40, 42, 44, 46, 48

<u>**2 digits: 50**</u>

So, the 46th digit = 0!

GIVEN PATTERNS

1. A number begins: 36912151821242730… If the pattern continues, what will the 57th digit of the number be?
   A. 0
   B. 1
   C. 3
   D. 5
   E. 9

2. What is the 104th digit in the following sequence: 246810121416182022…
   A. 1
   B. 2
   C. 4
   D. 6
   E. 8

3. What is the 185th digit in the following sequence: 1324354657687981091110…
   A. 3
   B. 4
   C. 5
   D. 6
   E. 7

4. Mika read *The Giver* last night. She started on page 18 and finished at the end of page 113. How many pages did she read?
   A. 93
   B. 94
   C. 95
   D. 96
   E. 97

5. What is the difference of the 22nd multiple of three and the 22nd odd term?
   A. 66
   B. 43
   C. 26
   D. 23
   E. 21

6. What is the quotient of the 54th even number and the fifth odd number?
   A. 108
   B. 99
   C. 59
   D. 12
   E. 6

PERMUTATIONS AND PROBABILITY

These topics are great examples of partial knowledge being a dangerous thing. Chances are, when you see the words combination and permutation you start trying to remember which is which and what are those formulas you were taught.

The good news is that you don't need to remember any of that. Most combination and permutation questions are not called that. Usually you are asked to figure out how many *arrangements* or permutations of a number of items or events you can have.

Possibility × Possibility × Possibility: Arrangement problems usually come down to possibility times possibility, with limited possibilities going first. What the heck does that mean? Here we go:

   a.   Find the number of possible combinations of outfits you can wear over a three-day weekend if you have five different outfits.

      i.   Figure how many possible outfits you have to choose from on Saturday (5). Now that you've chosen one outfit for Saturday, how many outfits do you have to choose from for Sunday? (4), and how many do you have to choose from for Monday? (3)

      ii.   Take your possibilities for each day and multiply them together. That is your total number of possibilities:

$$5 \times 4 \times 3 = 60$$

   b.   If there are **limits** to the possibilities, **begin with the limited selections first**. If there are 5 people in a car but only 2 of them can drive, how many different seating arrangements can there be?

      i.   Figure out how many possible drivers there are to choose from, since that is the limited role (2). Now that one slot has been filled, how many people are there to choose from for the passenger seat? (4!); how many for the first back seat? (3); how many for the middle back seat (2); and how many for the last back seat? (1).

      ii.   Your total number of possibilities is:

$$2 \times 4 \times 3 \times 2 \times 1 = 48$$

Probability: Probability always equals:

$$\frac{\text{Your Events}}{\text{All Events}}$$

except when you're looking for fewest times you need to do something in order to have your event occur. In those questions, always do the probability of the worst case scenario.

In other words, if I have 10 blues cards and 10 red cards and I wanted to know what is the fewest number of cards I'd have to pick to guarantee that I will pick at least one blue card, I determine my answer by assuming I have the worst luck in the world and pick all red cards first:

Not Your Event + One instance of your event

In this case that would be:

10 + 1 {One instance of your event} = 11

Now you try:

In a deck of 52 cards with 13 in each of two red suits and two black suits, what is the fewest number of cards that you must pick to guarantee that you will pick one card of each color?

PERMUTATION & PROBABILITY

1. At Thanksgiving, there are eight cousins and they all want to give each other a hug. How many total hugs will be given?
   A. 22
   B. 23
   C. 24
   D. 26
   E. 28

2. A jar holds 16 marbles. 3 of them are red, 2 are blue, and the rest are cat's eye marbles. How many marbles must be drawn to be sure to have at least two cat's eye marbles?
   A. 2
   B. 7
   C. 8
   D. 14
   E. 16

3. A standard deck of cards is made up of only four suits, each of which appears 13 times. If a deck is missing all the cards of one suit, at most how many cards must be dealt to be sure to know which suit is missing?
   A. 3
   B. 13
   C. 26
   D. 27
   E. 39

4. In an effort to help a class of six students get to know each other better, a teacher has insisted that each student lend a favorite book to every other student. How many total books will be loaned?
   A. 15
   B. 21
   C. 25
   D. 30
   E. 120

5. A soccer team has 11 players. At practice, the coach demands that each player make a pass to—or receive a pass from—every other player on the team. How many total passes will be made?
   A. 10
   B. 11
   C. 55
   D. 66
   E. 110

PERMUTATIONS & ARRANGEMENTS

1. How many different positive three-digit integers can be formed if the hundreds digit must be 7, the tens digit must be greater than 1, and the integer is even?
   A. 32
   B. 35
   C. 40
   D. 175
   E. 409

2. There are 7 girls and 5 boys in a group. One boy and one girl are the leaders. How many different pairs of leaders are possible?
   A. 2
   B. 7
   C. 12
   D. 35
   E. 70

3. In how many different ways can six people stand in line if the tallest person stands third in line?

4. The digits 1,2,5,7 and 9 will be used <u>without repetition</u> to form different four-digit numbers. Of all such numbers, how many are less than 5,000?
   A. 24
   B. 36
   C. 48
   D. 120
   E. 240

5. A man walks across the park each day. Each day he enters the park at the West Gate, and goes first to the lake along one of four paths. When he leaves the lake, he goes to the zoo, choosing from five possible paths. He then goes to the East Gate along one of eight different routes. After how many days will it be until the man has to repeat a route across the park?

6. Six different bands are playing at the musical festival, bands A, B, C, D, E, and F. Bands E and F are the most popular and must be the last two bands to perform. In how many different orders can the bands perform?

7. A starting team in the new sport of Cartlop consists of a forward, a defender and a goalie. If there are 5 forwards on the team, 4 defensemen and 2 goalies, how many different starting lineups can the coach make?

8. Wilbur still needs to choose 1 wide receiver and 1 running back for his fantasy football team. He has 8 wide receivers and 3 running backs to choose from. How many different selections of a WR and RB are possible?
   A. 3
   B. 8
   C. 11
   D. 24
   E. 48

2nd Ed. © *ibidPREP llc*

ARRANGEMENT PROBLEMS—THESE ARE GREAT FOR DIAGRAMMING!

Here are two examples of sequence problems, one easier and one slightly harder:

Example 1
Thomas has arranged five items of clothing on his bed to wear to a job interview: a tie, a shirt, a belt, cuff links and pants. The items are arranged from farthest left to farthest right.
   1) The tie is directly to the left of the shirt.
   2) There are more than two items in between the belt and shirt.
   3) The cuff links are next to the belt.
What position are the pants in?
A. Left
B. Middle
C. Second from right
D. Right
E. Cannot be determined from the information given.

Here's how we go about solving it:

Begin breaking down the problem with the first sentence...

   • **Thomas has arranged five items of clothing on his bed.**
Right away we know to create five dashes on your paper.

—   —   —   —   —

Continue by looking at the three pieces of information given. We are trying to figure out the arrangement of Thomas's clothing **before** answering the question, so we don't get misled by false answers. Look at the pieces of information and see if one of them (it may not be the first one) enables us to immediately draw any conclusions. Keep in mind that this is not always possible. In this case, we can use information piece #2 to infer several of the clothing items' placements.

   • **There are more than two items in between the belt and shirt.**
Fill in what we know already [what is possible]:

(B)   (B)
(S)   (S)
—   —   —   —   —

Since there are more than two items between the belt and shirt, in other words **at least three items**, the belt and shirt must be on the farthest left and farthest right or farthest right and farthest left, respectively.

Using information piece #1 together with #2, we can deduce which edge each clothing item will be on:

   • **The tie is directly to the left of the shirt.**

B   T   S
—   —   —   —   —

If the tie is directly to the left of the shirt, the shirt has to be on the farthest right and the belt on the farthest left.

Using information piece #3, we can deduce the final order of the clothing items **before we've even looked at the question!**

- **The cuff links are next to the belt.**

B	C		T	S
—	—	—	—	—

Therefore, the pants are in the middle.

B	C	P	T	S
—	—	—	—	—

NOW FIND OUT WHAT THE QUESTION IS ASKING:

- **What position are the pants in?**

REFER to the order we created to evaluate each of the answer choices below, and we can't go wrong!

A. left
B. middle
C. second from right
D. right
E. Cannot be determined from the information given.

The answer is B.

As diagrammed above, the problem looks long, but if we give ourselves a decent-sized rectangle of room on the page, we'll have plenty of space and time! Worry not.

2nd Ed. © ibidPREP llc

ARRANGEMENT

1. There is a race in Indianapolis with four drivers, Brittney, Bubba, Jennifer and Darren. No two drivers finished at the same time. The following statements are true:
    1) Brittney came in last.
    2) Exactly one driver finished between Darren and Brittney.
    3) Jennifer did not come in third place.
   Who won the race?
   A. Brittney
   B. Bubba
   C. Jennifer
   D. Darren
   E. Cannot be determined from the information given.

2. There is a litter of five kittens named Monet, Lily, Curly, Hank and Sparkles. Hank is not as fluffy as Monet or Lily. Sparkles is fluffier than Curly. Which of the following must be true?
   A. Lily is the fluffiest kitten.
   B. Sparkles is the fluffiest kitten.
   C. Either Hank or Curly is the least fluffy kitten.
   D. Monet is either the fluffiest or the least fluffy kitten.
   E. Lily is fluffier than Monet.

3. Jacob, Lucille, Mario and Blanche were the only four contestants in the Team Icarus flying contest, in which people compete to see whose engineless device can fly the farthest. The following statements are true:
    1) Mario's device flew farther than Jacob's.
    2) Lucille's device did not fly as far as Blanche's.
   Based only on the information above, which of the following is necessarily true?
   A. Jacob's device flew the shortest distance.
   B. Blanche's device flew farther than Jacob's.
   C. If Lucille finished third, Mario was the winner.
   D. If Blanche was the winner, Lucille came in second.
   E. If Mario came in second, Blanche was the winner.

4. Four Soviet snipers are holed up in the rubble of Stalingrad. Their names are Ivan, Dmitry, Alyosha and Vladimir. Dying of hunger, they decide to hunt rats to eat. The following statements are true:
   1) Ivan killed the second-most rats.
   2) Vladimir killed fewer rats than Dmitry but more than Alyosha.

   Which of the following is the ranking of the rat hunters, starting with the most successful?
   A. Vladimir, Ivan, Dmitry, Alyosha
   B. Dmitry, Ivan, Vladimir, Alyosha
   C. Dmitry, Ivan, Alyosha, Vladimir
   D. Vladimir, Ivan, Alyosha, Dmitry
   E. Cannot be determined from the information given.

5. Two brothers, Adam and Boden, and three sisters, Misty, Summer and Hazel, attend a ball game and sit in five consecutive seats. The following statements are true:
   1) Misty sits to the left of Adam, who is in the middle.
   2) Boden sits next to Summer but not his brother.
   3) Hazel sits next to Adam.

   Which of the following is the order of their seats from left to right?
   A. Misty, Hazel, Adam, Boden, Summer
   B. Hazel, Misty, Adam, Summer, Boden
   C. Misty, Hazel, Adam, Summer, Boden
   D. Boden, Summer, Adam, Hazel, Misty
   E. Cannot be determined from the information given

     2nd Ed. © ibidPREP llc

COMBINED SETS

On this test you will probably see a problem that requires you to make sense of a lot of confusing data.

For example:

There are three horses at a ranch—Sweyn, Lars and Jonsson—and a group of sixth graders come to learn how to ride. 38 students ride Sweyn, 25 ride Lars, and 33 ride Jonsson. If each student rode exactly two horses, how many students are in the class?

Questions like these seem really hard because it's difficult to turn these words into math. There aren't any of our must know terms, so how are we going to make an equation? Well, if we think it through, we can figure out how many total horse rides there were: to get that number we just add up the three numbers we were given:

$$38 + 25 + 33 = 96$$

So there were 96 horse rides taken at the ranch. And we also know that each student went on exactly two rides! Therefore, we can just divide 96 by 2!

$$96 \div 2 = 48$$

There were 48 students on the field trip.

So, to review: when we recognize that we have a combined set problem like this, we add up the total (of whatever we're counting) and divide by the number of events each member participated in. That gives us the total number of participants (students or whatever)!

Practice

COMBINED SETS PROBLEMS

1. On a school trip to Crazyland Amusement Park, a class of sixth graders goes on four rides, Twisted Tornado, Raucous Roller Coaster, Majestic Mountain, and Spinning Teacups. 20 students ride Twisted Tornado, 30 ride the Raucous Roller Coaster, 25 ride the Majestic Mountain, and 15 ride the Spinning Teacups. If each student rides exactly two rides, how many students are in the class?
    A. 15
    B. 25
    C. 45
    D. 55
    E. 90

2. A group of rowdy high school students attend a music festival. The bands Garbage, Slime, Angst and Vengeance perform. Each student manages to attend exactly three performances. If 11 students see Garbage, 60 see Slime, 47 see Angst, and a whopping 101 see Vengeance, how many high school students attended the music festival?
    A. 60
    B. 73
    C. 107
    D. 112
    E. 219

3. At a local high school, students are required to read two of the following four authors over the summer: R.L. Stine, Raymond Chandler, Patricia Highsmith, and James M. Cain. If 51 students read R. L. Stine, 32 read Raymond Chandler, 41 read Patricia Highsmith, and 32 read James M. Cain, how many students are at the high school?
    A. 44
    B. 48
    C. 78
    D. 84
    E. 156

4. At a little league baseball game the concessions stand sells hot dogs, cheeseburgers, cups of French fries and cups of onion rings. They only sell items in pairs, so each customer gets exactly two of the items. If the stand sells 37 hot dogs, 41 cheeseburgers, 27 cups of French fries and 39 cups of onion rings, how many total customers did they have?
    A. 56
    B. 64
    C. 72
    D. 144
    E. 1,156

5. At the TriBeCa film festival, four movies are being shown one day: Kid with Bike in the Rain, Love Among Bullets, Matchstick Tower and Lothario. Each critic sees exactly three movies. 41 critics see Kid with Bike in the Rain, 20 critics see Love Among Bullets, 35 see Matchstick Tower, and 45 see Lothario. How many critics attended the festival?
    A. 43
    B. 47
    C. 54
    D. 96
    E. 141

2nd Ed. © ibidPREP llc

PROBABILITY

Probability is one of those scary-looking topics that turns out to be redunkulously simple. Remember:

$$Probability = \frac{Number\ of\ Your\ Event}{Number\ of\ All\ Events}$$

As with all the things we're trying to figure out, let's try understanding this with the simplest example first. A coin toss works perfectly.

What are the chances of getting a heads on a coin toss?

$$Probability\ of\ Tossing\ a\ Heads = \frac{Number\ of\ heads}{Number\ of\ sides} = \frac{1}{2}$$

NOTE—If multiple parties are working toward a single goal, the sum of the probabilities of all parties must equal one.

E.g., Joe, Mary and Helvetica are running in a race. If Joe has a one-in-three chance of winning the race and Mary has a one-in-two chance of winning the race, what is the chance that Helvetica will win?

Here's how to set it up:

Probability of each participant winning: $J = \frac{1}{3}$, $M = \frac{1}{2}$, $H = x$

All probabilities together = 100%, or 1 out of 1 [someone has to win the race], so

$J + M + H = \frac{1}{1}$, *so*

$$J + M + H = \frac{1}{3} + \frac{1}{2} + x = 1$$
$$\frac{2}{6} + \frac{3}{6} + x = 1$$
$$\frac{5}{6} + x = 1$$

$x = \frac{1}{6}$ *Therefore, the chances that Helvetica will win the race are one in six* $[\frac{1}{6}]$.

Practice

4, 6, 10, 12, 15, 18, 20, 24

1. A number is selected at random from the list above. What is the probability that the number selected will be a multiple of both 4 and 6?

    A. $\frac{1}{8}$

    B. $\frac{1}{4}$

    C. $\frac{1}{2}$

    D. $\frac{3}{4}$

    E. 1

Food Preferences of Students

	School A	School B
Like Hamburgers	50	60
Like Pizza	70	20

2. The table above shows students classified according to what school they go to and their food preference. If a student is picked at random from either school, what is the probability that he or she likes burgers AND attends School A?

    A. $\frac{1}{20}$

    B. $\frac{1}{5}$

    C. $\frac{1}{4}$

    D. $\frac{5}{12}$

    E. $\frac{5}{6}$

3. There are 12 pairs of socks in a drawer. Five pairs are gray, three are black and the rest are white. If one pair of socks is taken at random from the drawer, what is the probability that it is white?

    A. $\frac{1}{12}$

    B. $\frac{1}{8}$

    C. $\frac{1}{3}$

    D. $\frac{1}{2}$

    E. $\frac{2}{3}$

2nd Ed. © ibidPREP llc

4. A bag of marbles contains only yellow, blue and green marbles. There are 4 yellow marbles and 2 blue marbles, and $\frac{1}{3}$ of the marbles are green. If a marble is picked out of the bag at random, what is the probability that it will be blue?

A. $\frac{1}{9}$

B. $\frac{1}{6}$

C. $\frac{2}{9}$

D. $\frac{1}{4}$

E. $\frac{1}{3}$

5. David chooses numbers from two hats, one red and one blue. The red hat contains all even digits greater than zero, and the blue hat contains all odd digits greater than zero. The numbers picked are used to form fractions. The red number is the numerator, and the blue number is the denominator. What is probability that David's fraction will be greater than $\frac{1}{2}$ but less than 1?

BACKSOLVING

Occasionally on this test there may be a few math problems best solved with methods you have yet to learn. However, this fact does not mean you have to get these questions wrong or blindly guess at them. You can find the right answer using the knowledge you've learned from our math section **and** the occasional shortcut.

One of these shortcuts is called **backsolving**. Although 90% of the time on standardized tests, you're much better off ignoring multiple choice answers, there are times when you have to use them. Certain algebra questions on the Hunter Test may be best solved using the answer choices.

George spent five dollars on gumballs. If they had been a nickel cheaper each, he would have been able to purchase five more gumballs. How much were the gumballs?
   A. 20 cents
   B. 25 cents
   C. 30 cents
   D. 35 cents
   E. 40 cents

Though it is possible to set this question up as an equation to solve, it may be safe to assume you don't know how [it would require polynomials!] Fortunately, the test has kindly narrowed down all possible answers to five, and one of them must be correct! The simplest thing to do then is test the choices and see what works.

If you've ever looked closely at most multiple choice math answers, you may have noticed that they are almost always in size order. Since they are in size order, it's generally best to start with the middle choice. That way if you test a value and it turns out to be wrong, you'll need to test only one more to find the answer. Why? Because if C is too high, there will be only two lower ones remaining. Testing one of those, you'll either find the right answer or another one that it isn't. [So if "C" is too high and "A" is too low, it must be "B"!]

30 cents is in the middle, so we'll test that one.

$$5.00 \div 0.30 = 16.7$$

When gumballs are 30 cents, George can buy 16 of them. If this is the correct price, George *has* to be able to buy 21 gumballs when they cost 25 cents each. Again, we test:

$$5.00 \div 0.25 = 20$$

So we can now say for sure that C is not the right answer, and therefore we have to try another choice. We should try one of the *lower* prices because, at lower prices, a nickel difference in price will result in a bigger change in the number of gumballs

Since we already know how many gumballs George can buy at 25 cents each (20), let's try answer choice B. If B is correct, George has to be able to buy exactly 25 gumballs at twenty cents each. So we test it:

$$5.00 \div 0.20 = 25$$

It works! This means that B is the correct answer. Solving it this way, we turned a problem that is supposed to require polynomials (whatever the heck they are!) into a problem that's simple division, which you mastered ages ago.

Backsolving is how you play math on your home court!

 2nd Ed. © ibidPREP llc

REMEMBER: Backsolving is **NOT** to be used except as an absolute last resort. It takes much longer than creating equation and solving them.

Keep backsolving in the back of your mind. It *can* work on all kinds of problems. Even better, you can use backsolving as a way to check your work.

<u>**BACKSOLVING PROBLEM SET**</u>

1. The units digit of a two-digit number is two times the tens digit. If the digits are reversed, the resulting number is nine less than twice the original number. What is the original number?
    A. 12
    B. 24
    C. 36
    D. 39
    E. 48

2. It is Valentine's Day and Molly is receiving many valentines at school. In each period, she receives twice as many valentines as she did in the period before. If she receives 252 valentines in the whole day, how many did she receive in her third-period class?
    A. 1
    B. 2
    C. 4
    D. 8
    E. 16

3. Out of a total of 79 games, a basketball team won 51 more games than it lost. How many games did the team lose?
    A. 12
    B. 14
    C. 16
    D. 28
    E. 65

DISTANCE PROBLEMS AND COMBINED DISTANCE

Any time you see a distance problem, BAM!, write down :

$$D = RT : \text{Distance} = \text{Rate} \times \text{Time}$$

and if you remember that then you also know:

$$R = D/T : \text{Rate} = \text{Distance} \div \text{Time}$$

$$T = D/R : \text{Time} = \text{Distance} \div \text{Rate}$$

Then you can just fill in any information you're given and solve for what's missing:

1. If your family drove 20 miles per hour for 3 hours and 30 miles per hour for 2 hours, how many total miles did your family drive?

2. If your family drove 60 miles per hour over the course of a 150-mile trip, how long did you travel for?

3. If your family drove a 200-mile trip in 2 hours and 20 minutes, how fast were you driving?

4. If your family drove 30 miles per hour for 6 hours, 40 mph for 5 hours and 50 mph for 4 hours, what is your total distance and what is your average speed for the entire trip?

[Careful here: remember that average is the TOTAL/NUMBER OF TERMS, and since miles per hour is the TO-TAL miles divided by TOTAL hours, you can't just add up the three rates and average those because you spend different amounts of time driving at the different rates.]

COMBINED DISTANCE AND RATE PROBLEMS

Sometimes you may be asked various questions about people starting out at two different points and travelling toward each other.

The first thing to remember about distance problems is that:

$$\text{Distance} = \text{Rate} \times \text{Time}$$

Sometimes you may be asked what happens when two people head out at the same time or at different times or to cover the same distance or to meet coming from opposite directions. The important thing to remember for vehicles moving in opposite directions is that the point at which they would meet [or pass] is the same as the time at which their two distances would add up to the total distance!

If one vehicle leaves at a different time from the other but is going faster than the other, you simply need to set up the two distance formulas as equal but make sure you adjust their times to account for their difference.

1. Train A leaves Boston traveling at 80mph and heads to New York at the same time that Train B leaves New York and heads to Boston traveling at 60mph. If their starting time was 11 a.m. and the two cities are 280 miles apart, at what time did they pass each other?

2ⁿᵈ Ed. © ibidPREP llc

SPANISH STEPS PROBLEM

HERE'S ONE OF THOSE PROBLEMS THAT LOOKS A LOT HARDER THAN IT IS.

IF THE SPANISH STEPS [A VERY FAMOUS OUTDOOR STAIRCASE IN A ROMAN PLAZA, SEE RIGHT] ARE 120 FEET TALL AND 240 FEET LONG, HOW MANY FEET OF CARPETING WOULD IT TAKE TO COVER THE STEPS FROM THE BOTTOM OF THE PLAZA TO THE TOP?

IT IS EASY TO GET SUPER REVVED UP BY THIS PROBLEM AND TRY DUSTING OFF YOUR TRIG, CURSING ME ["THAT JERK SAID THERE WAS NO TRIG ON THE HUNTER TEST!"], WHIPPING OUT YOUR SLIDE RULE [NEVER MIND WHAT THAT IS] OR JUST FLEEING. HOWEVER, IF YOU LOOK CLOSELY AT THE DRAWING, YOU MIGHT NOTICE THAT ALL YOU HAVE TO DO IS CARPET THE HORIZONTAL TOPS OF THE STEPS AND THE VERTICAL FRONTS OF THE STEPS. IF YOU CONNECT ALL THE HORIZONTALS [FLATTENING THEM], YOU REALIZE

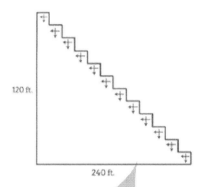

YOU HAVE THE LENGTH OF THE STEPS. IF YOU CONNECT ALL THE VERTICALS, YOU HAVE THE HEIGHTS. SO:

YOU WOULD SIMPLY NEED 120 FEET + 240 FEET = 360 FEET OF CARPETING TO CARPET THE SPANISH STEPS!

Practice

RATIO PROBLEMS

1. Margaret had five gerbils when she was 7 years ol Every year after that, there were five times as many gerbils as the year before. What is the ratio of how many gerbils she had when she was 10 to when she was 13?

   A. $\dfrac{1}{5}$

   B. $\dfrac{1}{25}$

   C. $\dfrac{1}{125}$

   D. $\dfrac{1}{625}$

   E. $\dfrac{1}{3125}$

2. Travis bought an antique at an auction. He later sold it at another auction to Karen for 45% more than he originally paid. Karen later sold it to Madeline for 25% more than she paid. At about what percentage of the original price did Karen sell the painting to Madeline?

   A. 95
   B. 180
   C. 200
   D. 215
   E. 240

3. The world's biggest brownie is cut into 2 pieces, and each piece is cut into 20 squares. What percent of the original brownie is each of the squares?

   A. 0.25%
   B. 1%
   C. 1.25%
   D. 1.75%
   E. 2.5%

4. If a car depreciates in value by 15% after one year, 20% of what was left after two years, and 25% of that remainder after three years, what percentage of the original value remains?

   A. 10%
   B. 23.3%
   C. 36.2%
   D. 51%
   E. 76%

2nd Ed. © ibidPREP llc

5. Over the course of a week, a book store sells four times the number of books it sold on the previous day. After four days, the amount of toys sold on the 4th day would equal what fraction of all toys sold over those four days?

A. $\dfrac{64}{85}$

B. $\dfrac{60}{80}$

C. $\dfrac{1}{5}$

D. $\dfrac{1}{4}$

E. $\dfrac{1}{3}$

6. Jeffery starts collecting baseball cards when he is 8 years old. Every year after that, he has four times as many baseball cards as the year before. What is the ratio of how many baseball cards he had when he was 9 to how many baseball cards he had when he was 13?

A. $\dfrac{1}{4}$

B. $\dfrac{1}{16}$

C. $\dfrac{1}{64}$

D. $\dfrac{1}{256}$

E. $\dfrac{1}{1024}$

WORD PROBLEMS—TIME AND MONEY
1. Mr Pup bought exactly $14 worth of cans of dog food. If the cans had cost 15 cents less each, she would have bought 30 more can How much did each can cost?
   A. 20 cents
   B. 25 cents
   C. 30 cents
   D. 35 cents
   E. 40 cents

2. Kathy, Ann, and Karen buy notebooks at the store to get ready for the school year. Together, they spend $7.80. Kathy gets six notebooks, Ann gets six notebooks, and Karen gets three notebooks. How much did each notebook cost?
    A. 50 cents
    B. 52 cents
    C. 54 cents
    D. 56 cents
    E. 58 cents

3. Pedro has 95 cents in 26 coins with at least one quarter. How many nickels does he have?
    A. 1
    B. 2
    C. 3
    D. 4
    E. 5

4. Samuel spent $96 on baseballs from Expensive Balls. If he had bought baseballs from Cheap Balls, the baseballs would have been $2.00 cheaper each, and he could have bought four more baseballs. How many baseballs from Expensive Balls did Samuel buy?
    A. 12
    B. 13
    C. 14
    D. 15
    E. 16

5. Joan has $1.30 in 34 coins with three nickels. How many dimes does she have?
    A. 1
    B. 2
    C. 3
    D. 4
    E. 5

6. Robert gets into a taxi that has him pay $1.88 for the first mile he travels, and $1.16 for each mile thereafter. What is the greatest number of miles that Robert could travel for $10.00?
    A. 7
    B. 8
    C. 9
    D. 16
    E. 18

7. Timothy solves 4 English problems in 2.5 minutes, 2 minutes, 1 minute, and 2 minutes respectively. How quickly must he solve another 6 problems, on average, so that his average time to solve a problem is 105 seconds?
    A. 75 minutes
    B. 1 minute
    C. 1.5 minutes
    D. 1.66 minutes
    E. 2.25 minutes

2nd Ed. © ibidPREP llc

8. Adam's painting company can paint buildings at the rate of 2 months per building. If they have painted 6 ½ buildings, how many days have they been working? (Assume every month has 30 day)
   A. 150
   B. 245
   C. 375
   D. 390
   E. 410

9. Two trains depart at the same time from Town A and Town B, heading toward each other. The first is travelling at 65 miles an hour and the other at 35 miles an hour. If the distance between the two towns is 900 miles, how far from each other are they two hours before they meet?
   A. 80 miles
   B. 100 miles
   C. 120 miles
   D. 140 miles
   E. 160 miles

10. Ofelia reads different passages in 1 minute, 2.5 minutes, and 1 minute respectively. How quickly must he read another 7 passages, on average, so that his average time to read a passage is 125 seconds?
    A. 115 seconds
    B. 120 seconds
    C. 125 seconds
    D. 130 seconds
    E. 135 seconds

11. Lakisha's book company can produce new books at the rate of 5 months per book. If they have produced 3 ½ new books, how many days have they been working? (Assume every month has 30 day)
    A. 355
    B. 390
    C. 425
    D. 475
    E. 525

12. Two trains depart at the same time from City X and City Y, heading toward each other. The first is travelling at 55 miles an hour and the other at 35 miles an hour. If the distance between the two cities is 630 miles, how far from each other are they one hour before they meet?
    A. 90 miles
    B. 100 miles
    C. 110 miles
    D. 120 miles
    E. 130 miles

IRREGULAR SHAPES

If you see a circle with a shaded *yin* area within it, do not freak thinking that you were taught the area of a *yin* sign and forgot, or weren't paying attention, or should have been taught it by your tutor. Instead, please try to **see the shape as the sum or difference of shapes you do know** the area of -- circles, triangles, rectangles and that's it. The entire visual world can be broken down into those shapes when drawing **or** doing geometry. It is nice to work with an alphabet that has only three letters!

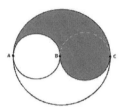

You may see the symbol as:

The area of half the big circle + half the area of the shaded little circle – half the area of the unshaded little circle

OR

you may simply see the shaded area as:

half the area of the circle

To see that:
- Draw a diameter of the circle.
- Notice that is the diameter of the smaller shaded circle.
- Take the part of the shaded little circle that is below the diameter and remove it
- Replace it in the gap from the unshaded little semicircle *above* the diameter.
- The large semicircle is now completely shaded in!

2ⁿᵈ Ed. © ibidPREP llc

AREA & PERIMETER OF REGULAR & IRREGULAR SHAPES

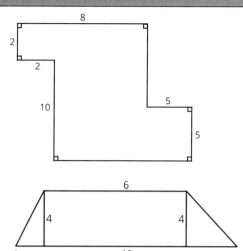

1. What is the perimeter of the figure to the right?
    A. 32
    B. 50
    C. 99
    D. 100
    E. 101

2. Find the area of the figure to the right.
    A. 36
    B. 24
    C. 48
    D. 60
    E. 72

3. Jondo wants to build a pool that has two adjoining square sections, one for himself and one for his kids. The kids' pool will have a side the length of one-third the length of a side of the adult pool. The area of the adult pool will be 100 square yards. What will the perimeter of the entire pool be in feet?

    A. $46\dfrac{2}{3}$

    B. 120
    C. 140
    D. 360
    E. 1200

COMBINED SHAPES—AREA AND PERIMETER—DRILL SET

1. A seamstress is sewing a band onto a square piece of fabric as shown in the picture. If the swatch originally had an area of 36, what is the area of the band?
    A. 12
    B. 10
    C. 8
    D. 6
    E. 4

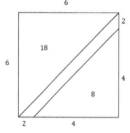

2. A square of area 64 has a triangle removed as shown in the figure. What is the area of the removed piece?
    A. 48
    B. 36
    C. 32
    D. 24
    E. 16

3. Wendy is making a rectangular patio that is 27 feet x 21 feet. If she builds a second one for her front yard with each dimension one-third shorter, what will be the combined area of the two patios?
    A. 819 square feet
    B. 630 square feet
    C. 315 square feet
    D. 160 square feet
    E. 128 square feet

4. Triangle ABC has a height of six. Triangle ACD has an area of 12. $\overline{CD}$ is one-fifth the length of $\overline{BE}$. What is the area of triangle ABE?
    A. 120
    B. 60
    C. 40
    D. 30
    E. 20

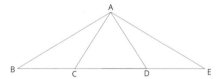

5. Robbie the Robot's face is made from a piece of sheet metal that has a perimeter of 10 feet. The height of Robbie the Robot's face is one foot less than the length of his face. His eyes are cutout squares with sides of 6 inches, and the cutout area of his mouth is twice the area of one of his eyes. If a drop of epoxy paint covers 120 square inches, how many drops of epoxy are needed to paint Robbie the Robot's face?
    A. 1
    B. 6
    C. 7
    D. 9
    E. 12

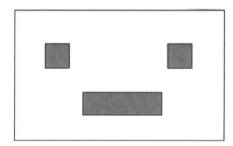

2nd Ed. © *ibidPREP llc*

2nd Ed. © ibidPREP llc

HOW TO AVOID EXAMICIDE

PART III—TAKING THE TEST: BEFORE & AFTER

1. EVERYONE LIES ABOUT HER SCORES—

Keep in mind: no matter how well you do on your tests [unless you score perfectly], it will always seem like everyone else has done better. Things will seem this way for two very good reasons:

- Kids who do well on their tests are much more likely to talk about their scores than kids who don't.

- Also, kids who don't score well on their tests are much more likely to lie about their scores.

2. IF YOU RUN INTO PEOPLE YOU KNOW BEFORE YOU TAKE YOUR TEST, DO NOT TALK TO THEM!

The only motive other students have in speaking to you right before a test is to give you some of their anxiety. How much your friends love and support you doesn't matter; everyone is in survival mode, and everyone is just trying to unload anxiety as quickly and easily as possible. Short of throwing up, making other people nervous seems to help best. So kids will tell other kids things like "Did you hear there might be Roman Numerals on this test?" or "Did you hear that there might be poetry in the Reading Comprehension this year?" all in the hopes of seeing that burst of fear in their best friends' eyes. It doesn't even matter that you tell yourself they're full of baloney—it's too late—you just got a dose of their anxiety right into your veins. In order to avoid this happening, smile and wave to your friends and acquaintances before a test, but DO NOT engage them in conversation. Talk to them AFTER the test.

2nd Ed. © ibidPREP llc

HOW TO AVOID EXAMICIDE

3. THE TODDLER & THE THRESHOLD

When my sons were just starting to walk, their balance was incredibly precarious. They toddled down our hallways, perilously[42] swaying from foot to foot until they reached the threshold to the living room. Invariably, stepping on and over that tiny threshold was, for them, akin to climbing Mount Kilimanjaro. That little bump would upset their tentative[43] balances, and they'd come crashing down on their diapered rears.

While you're taking the test, if you hit a bump, you must be more resilient than a toddler, if only because you have no diapered butt to fall on. If you see a new kind of math problem or there's a reading passage the meaning of which completely eludes you, DON'T FREAK. Just take your best shot at it:

- ELIMINATE bad answers,
- GUESS, and then
- MOVE ON and FORGET ABOUT THAT PROBLEM!

Don't let one tough question ruin the rest of the test—put it out of your mind.

---

[42] dangerously
[43] uncertain, faltering

CHAPTER SIX
GAME DAY

Ok—You've Learned The Material And The Test, Now Let's Play!

At Last—Studatuta's Guide to Guessing

How to Guess

As I've gotten older and crankier, I have become less interested in teaching kids how to guess because, for the most part, it's really much more productive for me to spend my time teaching them how not to have to guess.

However, in spite of everyone's best efforts, sometimes there are those questions that we just can't figure out. In those situations, we need to grab our guts and guess! Below is a summary of some of the ideas I have touched upon throughout this book and a few new ideas on how to guess and how not to guess.

Six Steps to Better Guesses

These guidelines are not always right, nor are they meant to overrule any answers you may have figured out on your own. These are just some ideas of what to do if you have no idea what to do!

1. In math: Close is Wrong! Unless you are rounding to begin with, if you get an answer, and your answer isn't among the answer choices, DON'T guess the number that's closest to your answer. Pick any other number.
2. In math: on a hard problem that you don't know how to solve, do not just guess the answer that turns out to be the sum or product of the numbers in the question. Don't "just" do anything.
3. In general: if you are a lousy guesser, figure out what your guess normally would be and then pick something else.
4. In general: don't plan to "come back later." Guess right away, but put a little "g" next to the questions you guess on [in your test book, not your answer sheet]. That way, you can go back, but only if you really need to and have the time.
5. In general: do not waste time guessing. Instead of "thinking" about your guess, flip a coin in your head, pick that answer, and MOVE ON!
6. In general: guessing should be fun [about as fun as anything ever is on these tests]. Don't overthink it; just relax and pick one!

Don't Change Your Game!

So you've remembered to get a good night's sleep, eat a good breakfast and relax, and now at last you're ready to take your test. Now remember: play exactly the same way you've practiced. DO NOT change your game just because "now it's real!"

Veal Parmigiana

When the proctor calls "Five minutes," it is almost impossible not to react as if she just said, "Five seconds until the ceiling collapses!" It might help, however, if you pretend she's saying "Veal Parmigiana" instead and react accordingly. Mmmmm, Veal Parmigiana.

REMEMBER: There is NOTHING to be gained by going faster at the end of a section. For most tests the questions at the end are harder, so going faster will only improve your chances of getting them wrong. Better to take your time and get two correct than to rush and get five wrong.

Besides:

Five Minutes Is a Very Long Time

Sit and watch the clock for five minutes. It will feel like an eternity. Try doing it for just a minute. You will be amazed.

2nd Ed. © ibidPREP llc

It's Not Roulette!! [and Roulette Isn't Roulette]

If you've ever been to a casino [and if you have, I don't want to know about it], you might remember that next to most roulette wheels are LED displays that list the last dozen or so prior winning numbers from that table. They might as well give you the last 12 winning numbers from the roulette wheel three tables away or from a casino down the street. Prior results HAVE NO STATISTICAL EFFECT on future results. The odds are exactly the same for getting three 5's in a row as they are for getting 3, 4, 5 or ANY RANDOM COMBINATION OF NUMBERS.

So: DO NOT WASTE ANY TIME LOOKING AT YOUR PREVIOUS ANSWERS AND USING THEM AS A GUIDE FOR YOUR NEXT ANSWER. DO NOT LOOK FOR PATTERNS OR TRY TO FIGURE OUT WHAT THE TEST MAKERS WERE UP TO. Doing so is a waste of precious time and brainpower.

For example:

You've just answered three questions, and they were all "D." On your next question, the answer you want to pick is ALSO "D." You freak out and decide something must be wrong—there can't be that many "D's"—so you talk yourself out of the fourth "D." The only problem here is, even if it were impossible to have five "D's" in a row, how do you know which is the wrong "D"? Kid logic always seems to have it that the last "D" must be wrong. It absolutely does not have to be.

The Letter: Here's What I Send to All My Students Before Their Tests. Now I'm Sending It to You.

To all my geniuses:

I just wanted to write you with a few things to be aware of come test day and the night before.

The night before, please relax. It is not the time to try to learn or review anything. Before dinner you might want to review your formulas, but then have some pizza, watch a movie and go to bed at a decent hour, but not too early that you're tossing in bed.

Test morning, please arrive on time and make sure you have with you: Pencils, Snack and Brain.

When you show up that cold Friday morning in January to take your test at Hunter, be prepared. You're going to be faced with very long lines all the way around TWO blocks! Parents and caregivers will be asked to stand on one side of the sidewalk, students on the other. Everyone will be really nervous—especially parents and caregivers. Please remember, everyone else is nervous too; rise above it!

Walk into the school like you own the place. Float above everyone's nervous energy. Whatever silly, annoying questions kids and grownups are fretting about, DO NOT ENGAGE. Everything will be sorted out, and you will be in your seat shortly.

If you see anyone you know before the test, try not to speak with him or her too much. As much as your friends love you, they will mostly be looking to offload anxiety onto you. No one needs more anxiety.

Remember—Don't change what you've been doing! If your test seems different from those you have been practicing on, it's probably nerves. Just keep going until you start to feel comfortable. If an early question seems hard, it does not mean that all the others ones will be harder—sometimes it's just difficult to get going. If the test truly is different, just Remain Clam! That means it will be different for EVERYONE! Our tests and practice are based on our past knowledge of the test AND what little there is on the website. If things have changed, go with it, especially on math. Feel free to invent and try stuff. You know enough now to be resourceful!

Also remember—No matter what kind of essay prompt they throw at you, answer something! Even if the question doesn't make sense, write that and try to interpret it in your own way. E.g.:

> "If by asking 'Do whales jump to the moon?' you mean
> can grown-ups learn to reach for new heights, then...."

And also, also remember: It doesn't matter if you hit a bumpy patch—it matters how you respond to it!

When in doubt: guess and don't obsess, forget about it, and move on! All the questions afterwards are far more important!

You have practiced, you know the test...Now go out there, stick to your game plan and ace the test!!!

Go get 'em!
Studatuta

Test Taking and Time— More Thoughts!

WHEN I WAS WISE

I GOT TO THE TURNSTILES. MY TRAIN WAS ALREADY IN THE STATION, DOORS OPEN. I TOOK OUT MY WALLET TO GET MY METROCARD, BUT IT WASN'T IN ITS USUAL PLACE. FOR SOME REASON, I DID NOT RIFLE THROUGH MY WALLET LIKE A MADMAN AS I WOULD HAVE DONE THE OTHER 99% OF THE TIME. INSTEAD I SAID TO MYSELF, "THE TRAIN IS ALREADY GONE. PUT IT OUT OF YOUR MIND. WHAT IS THE MOST EFFICIENT WAY TO FIND THE CARD?" WITH A WEIRD POISE, I STOPPED, TOOK THE BUSINESS AND CREDIT CARDS OUT OF MY WALLET AND SYSTEMATICALLY FLIPPED THROUGH THEM. IN SECONDS, I FOUND THE METROCARD, SLID IT THROUGH THE TURNSTILE AND GOT ON THE TRAIN!

WHEN I WAS NOT SO WISE

I TOOK THE WRONG SUBWAY LINE TO MEET A FRIEND IN LOWER MANHATTAN. THE STOP I ENDED UP GETTING OFF AT WAS NOT FAR FROM MY DESTINATION, BUT LOWER MANHATTAN IS FULL OF TINY, WINDING STREETS. I WAS ALREADY RUNNING LATE, SO I RUSHED OUT OF THE SUBWAY. AT THE EXIT WAS A LARGE "YOU ARE HERE" MAP OF THE NEIGHBORHOOD. I PAUSED FOR A NANOSECOND AND THOUGHT ABOUT STUDYING THE MAP. MY UN-CLAM MIND SHOUTED, "YOU DON'T HAVE TIME TO READ THE MAP!!" SO I DIDN'T.

OF COURSE, I GOT LOST. INSTEAD OF TAKING ONE MINUTE TO READ THE MAP AND ENDING UP MAYBE FIVE MINUTES LATE, I RUSHED AND ENDED UP 20 MINUTES LATE!

Subway Stories

OUTRO

When I started tutoring, I was just a few years older than my students. I was a fine, if rough, writer and painter, and a wildly undisciplined and fairly indifferent math student. Now, I am more often than not a few years older than my students' parents, a somewhat more polished writer and artist, and a really excellent basic-math kind of guy. In spite of how everyone likes to yammer about "kids nowadays," I can honestly say that kids are the same. Mostly, as far as I can tell, only the nature of distractions has changed. Otherwise, the song remains the same: some students are engaged, some are checked out, some are only interested in hanging out. For many, education is something you get through or at best a means to an end. For others, it's a job: a responsibility you tend to during the day and evenings, and nothing more. In my experience, the rarest creature of all is the engaged student.

The engaged student is interested in the material either because she finds it interesting or because it *might* be interesting. The engaged student doesn't decide this is boring or that is boring or that isn't me. The engaged student samples *everything*, gives it a fair shake and moves on or not. The engaged student doesn't just learn stuff for a test and then do a memory dump the next day. The engaged student actually learns stuff.

As much as this book has been an appeal to students to *REMAIN CLAM!* on their tests, it has also [not so secretly] been an appeal to students to engage: to face the work in front of them head-on and not spend all their time trying to find a way around it. I hope this book has inspired students to read in depth and write out and complete equations, to admit when they don't know something and figure it out, look it up or ask someone!

The payoff for all this engagement is more than just a guarantee of marvelous scores on your tests; it is also a great way to learn how to use your mind—now and beyond these tests. So, by all means:

Engage!! [and *REMAIN CLAM!]*

2nd Ed. © *ibidPREP llc*

CHAPTER SEVEN

THE ANSWERS

READING

ANNE OF GREEN GABLES—PG. 67
1. E
2. C
3. B
4. A
5. D
6. E

A SMALL BOY VISITS A MAMMOTH CAVE—PG. 50
1. B
2. C
3. A
4. E
5. B
6. C
7. B

WATCHING A CRAFTSMAN—PG. 53
1. A
2. E
3. C
4. C
5. A
6. B

FOG—PG. 57
1. E
2. D
3. D
4. C
5. D

THE MOON LANDING HOAX CONSPIRACY—PG. 59
1. D
2. B
3. E
4. B
5. A
6. D
7. C

ANNIE BESANT—AN AUTOBIOGRAPHY—PG. 61
1. D
2. B
3. A
4. E
5. C

BED IN SUMMER—PG. 41
1. A
2. B
3. B
4. C
5. A

VESPERS—PG. 42
1. B
2. C
3. A
4. E
5. C

DRAMATIC TEXT: PETER PAN SCENE—PG. 45
1. D
2. A
3. E
4. B
5. C
6. E
7. A

ANNE OF GREEN GABLES—PG. 67
1. B
2. D
3. A
4. E
5. E
6. C

GRAMMAR

QUOTATION PRACTICE—PG. 90
1. noun
2. proper noun
3. noun
4. adjective
5. verb/noun
6. verb
7. adverb
8. adverb
9. adjective
10. adjective
11. proper noun
12. noun
13. proper noun
14. adjective
15. noun
16. proper noun
17. proper noun
18. proper noun
19. adverb
20. proper noun

Part B
For
And
Nor
But
Or
Yet
So

HOMOPHONE PRACTICE—PG. 95
1. Darrin likes to eat, to drink and to fly kites.
2. The way Bobby, my brother, talks, you would think he's from a different country.
3. Tomorrow will be July 4, 2020.
4. My favorite date is Wednesday, November 22, 1961.
5. Mr. Getz, my principal, also teaches math, science and gym.
6. Noah, shine the light over here, so I can see you better.
7. The kids were wearing fuzzy, wool hats over their big, round heads.
8. Even though you saved your money, you still do not have enough for a bicycle.
9. Since you are late, we had to start without you.
10. If you don't finish the project by tomorrow, you won't get a good grade on it.
11. Before we moved to the city, we had many animals on our farm.
12. Providing that you study for the test, I am sure you will do well.
13. No, there is not enough time to play a game of Monopoly before we leave.
14. Before we leave, we need to turn off all the lights.
15. Well, if you must choose the red dress, I guess that is all right with me.
16. The light, fluffy lemon cake was the hit of the party.
17. A new highway was built, so motorists can move around

the city more smoothly.

18. However, we have tried to find our dog for two days.
19. Well, do you want to be a squirrel instead?
20. The last time you told me a lie, I believed you, but not this time.

POSSESSION—2—PG. 89

1. Sam isn't coming to the library with us.
2. Don't you want something to eat?
3. We've been working on this project all month.
4. It's starting to feel like spring.

COMPOUND WORD QUESTIONS—PG. 96

1. She'd
2. Couldn't
3. Won't
4. He's
5. We'd
6. I've
7. You're
8. We'll
9. Shouldn't
10. She's
11. It's
12. I'd
13. That'll
14. Who's
15. Didn't
16. They're
17. He'd
18. We're
19. Wouldn't
20. They'd
21. I'm
22. You'll
23. That'd
24. She'll
25. You'd
26. That's
27. What're
28. He'll
29. It'd
30. I'll

CHAPTER THREE—PG. 73

1. All the boys' bicycles are gone.
2. The dancer's dress was made of silk.
3. Did the cat eat the Smith family's food off of the table?
4. Marta plays on the girls' basketball team.
5. Matthew and Marsha's toys are all over the floor.
6. The hero's arrows aimed for the villain's heart.
7. The family of dragons breathed fire on the heroes' shields.
8. The heroes' horses' heads were covered in flameproof armor.
9. The boys went to the girl's party and danced with her friends.
10. Some of the girl's friends danced while her other friends played Frisbee.
11. Unfortunately, it was the girl's dog's Frisbee.
12. The girl's dog chased its Frisbee, much to all her friends' fear.

POSSESSION—1—PG. 89

1. Its
2. Theirs
3. Mine
4. Her
5. Yours
6. His, mine
7. Their
8. Its
9. Your; ours
10. My
11. Its
12. Hers
13. Their
14. Our
15. Their
16. Hers
17. Its
18. Mine
19. Our
20. Your
21. His
22. Hers
23. His
24. Its

CAPITALIZATION—PG. 98

1. I like to go to McDonald's on Tuesdays after soccer practice.
2. Meredith says it is silly for me to go to McDonald's after soccer because fast food is not healthy.
3. My mom said after I finished my homework I could watch SpongeBob.
4. At soccer practice, I hurt my ankle, so I am going to see the doctor on Wednesday morning.
5. I go to Sunshine Elementary School, and my teacher's name is Mr. Oliver.
6. My favorite book is The Star-Bellied Sneeches by Dr. Seuss.
7. One day I want to go to Africa and see a real tiger.
8. For dinner last night I ate pizza from Domino's.
9. This weekend I need to study for my spelling test before I play video games.
10. I made my favorite stuffed animal at Build a Bear, and I named her Daisy.

HOMOPHONE PRACTICE—1—PG. 103

1. Which...Witch
2. There....their...They're
3. Too...to...two
4. write...right
5. It's....its
6. Whether...weather

CLASSIFY PARTS OF SPEECH PRACTICE—PG. 89

1. two, one
2. sole
3. whether
4. it's
5. you're
6. here
7. our
8. than
9. pedal
10. some
11. dye
12. pears

Fraction Word Problems—pg. 180

1. A lot
2. every day
3. cannot
4. All together
5. some time
6. Everyday...sometime

MATH

Stacking Practice—pg. 162

1. 150
2. 294
3. 1,372
4. 2,133
5. 7,872

Factors—pg. 163

1. 1, 2, 3, 4, 6, 8, 12, 24
2. 1, 2, 3, 4, 6, 9, 12, 18, 36
3. 1, 2, 4, 5, 10, 20
4. 1, 3, 5, 15
5. 1, 2, 3, 4, 5, 6, 10, 12, 15, 20, 30, 60

Prime Factorization—pg. 165

1. 3, 7, 7
2. 3^5
3. 2^4, 3
4. 3^2, 2^4
5. 2, 3, 11
6. 2^2, 3^2, 7
7. 2, 5^3
8. 3^3, 11

Division Practice—pg. 167

1. 123
2. 113
3. 102
4. 1,155
5. 99 r 6
6. 202 r 1

Inequality Practice Set—pg. 169

1. <
2. >
3. <
4. <
5. <
6. >

Basic Mean, Mode & Median—pg. 171

1. 91, 91
2. mean = 26; mode = 25
3. a. mean = 10; median = 10.5; mode =12
   b. mean = 6; median = 6; mode = 3
4. 98

Fraction Problems—1—pg. 175

1. $\dfrac{3}{2}$
2. $\dfrac{3}{4}$
3. $\dfrac{3}{2}$
4. 1
5. 1
6. $\dfrac{2}{3}$
7. $\dfrac{5}{3}$
8. $\dfrac{10}{9}$
9. $\dfrac{2}{7}$
10. $\dfrac{7}{12}$
11. $\dfrac{3}{4}$
12. 1
13. 0
14. 1
15. $\dfrac{5}{6}$
16. 0
17. 0
18. $\dfrac{1}{2}$
19. $\dfrac{7}{12}$
20. $\dfrac{3}{8}$

Fraction Problems—2—pg. 175

1. 4
2. 0.5 pounds
3. 6
4. $\dfrac{1}{3}$
5. D
6. A
7. E
8. 6 cups
9. 5
10. $\dfrac{1}{8}$
11. 1
12. 1
13. $\dfrac{1}{9}$
14. $\dfrac{2}{9}$
15. 1
16. $\dfrac{1}{3}$
17. 2

Dividing Fractions Practice—pg. 177

1. 2
2. $\dfrac{3}{2}$
3. $\dfrac{1}{2}$
4. $\dfrac{1}{8}$
5. $\dfrac{1}{2}$
6. 1

Mixed Number to Improper Fractions—pg. 178

1. $\dfrac{19}{4}$
2. $\dfrac{4}{3}$
3. $\dfrac{28}{5}$
4. $\dfrac{5}{2}$

5. $\dfrac{39}{10}$
6. $\dfrac{79}{5}$

Improper Fractions to Mixed Numbers—pg. 178

1. $10\dfrac{1}{2}$
2. $9\dfrac{2}{3}$
3. $1\dfrac{1}{2}$
4. $2\dfrac{4}{5}$
5. $1\dfrac{1}{11}$
6. $6\dfrac{1}{6}$

Adding, Subtracting, Multiplying & Dividing Fractions—pg. 179

1. $\dfrac{50}{63}$
2. $\dfrac{55}{56}$
3. $\dfrac{139}{80}$
4. $\dfrac{1}{10}$
5. $\dfrac{49}{48}$
6. $\dfrac{2}{21}$
7. $\dfrac{1}{3}$
8. $\dfrac{31}{60}$
9. $\dfrac{31}{60}$

10. $\dfrac{6}{5}$
11. $\dfrac{49}{40}$
12. $\dfrac{11}{12}$
13. $\dfrac{93}{70}$
14. $\dfrac{5}{8}$
15. $\dfrac{61}{240}$
16. $\dfrac{49}{60}$
17. $\dfrac{229}{240}$
18. $\dfrac{37}{80}$
19. $\dfrac{77}{80}$
20. $\dfrac{211}{140}$

Multiplication and Division—pg. 179

1. $\dfrac{22}{35}$
2. $\dfrac{7}{180}$
3. $\dfrac{7}{3}$
4. $\dfrac{4}{105}$
5. $\dfrac{1}{28}$
6. $\dfrac{1}{4}$
7. $\dfrac{1}{20}$
8. $\dfrac{14}{5}$
9. $\dfrac{39}{64}$

10. $\dfrac{25}{72}$

11. $\dfrac{1}{6}$

12. $\dfrac{7}{3}$

13. $\dfrac{56}{135}$

14. $\dfrac{38}{35}$

15. $\dfrac{3}{2}$

16. $\dfrac{2}{9}$

17. $\dfrac{49}{48}$

18. $\dfrac{225}{208}$

19. $\dfrac{51}{16}$

20. $\dfrac{40}{119}$

HARDER FRACTIONS—DRILL SET—PG. 180

1. $\dfrac{3}{20}$

2. $\dfrac{5}{27}$

3. $\dfrac{1}{3}$

4. $\dfrac{39}{40}$

5. $\dfrac{3}{4}$

6. $\dfrac{3}{35}$

FRACTION WORD PROBLEMS—PG. 180

1. $\dfrac{5}{12}$

2. $\dfrac{1}{6}$

3. $\dfrac{1}{18}$

DECIMAL REVIEW—PG. 182

Converting fractions to decimals
1. 0.2
2. 0.03
3. 0.07
4. 0.3
5. 0.22
6. 2.2

Converting decimals to fractions

1. $\dfrac{8}{100}$

2. $\dfrac{9}{10}$

3. $\dfrac{6}{1000}$

4. $\dfrac{17}{100}$

5. $\dfrac{95}{1000}$

6. $\dfrac{32}{100}$

Adding and Subtracting Decimals

1. 5.25239
2. 7.68392
3. 8.420791
4. 10.2399008
5. 0.05831
6. 0.08956221

Multiplication and Division of Decimals

1. 0.096
2. 0.012
3. 13.5
4. 0.4
5. 0.256
6. 10

PERCENTS WORD PROBLEMS—PG. 186
1. 18
2. 12

3. 42
4. 60%
5. 20%
6. 80%
7. 550%
8. 12.5%
9. 12%

PERCENT/AMOUNT REVIEW—PG. 186
1. 50%
2. 20%
3. 25%

PEMDAS—PRACTICE—PG. 188
1. 5
2. 6.8
3. 35
4. 24
5. 5
6. 10
7. 29
8. 23
9. 102
10. 2
11. 4
12. 23
13. 15

BASIC ARITHMETIC—PG. 189
1. C
2. D
3. B
4. A
5. B
6. A
7. B
8. B

EXPONENTS—PRACTICE—PG. 193
1. 5^7
2. 3^8
3. 5^5
4. 15^3
5. 6^{17}

EXPONENTS—DRILL SET—PG. 193
1. B
2. B
3. B

SOLVE FOR "X"—DRILL SET—PG. 199
1. 8

2. 9
3. 9
4. 4
5. 1
6. 3
7. 12
8. 7
9. 12
10. 11
11. 19
12. 6
13. 1
14. 4
15. 14
16. 7
17. 12
18. 12.5

ALGEBRA WORD PROBLEMS—PG. 201
1. A
2. B
3. E
4. C
5. B
6. C

PERCENTS—DRILL SET—PG. 203
1. 150%
2. 28
3. 20
4. 9.5%
5. 8%
6. $35
7. 87.5%
8. $45
9. $41.25
10. 25%
11. 882
12. 12%

AREA AND PERIMETER—DRILL SET—PG. 213
1. C
2. C
3. C
4. D
5. C
6. C

3D GEOMETRY—DRILL SET—PG. 215
1. B
2. C
3. C

4. E
5. C

GEOMETRY REVIEW—PG. 216
1. B
2. C
3. C
4. D
5. C

NUMBER KNOWLEDGE 1—PG. 220
1. E
2. C
3. B
4. D
5. B
6. D
7. D

NUMBER KNOWLEDGE 2—PG. 221
1. B
2. E
3. A
4. C
5. C
6. A

MIXED RATES—PG. 223
1. B
2. C
3. C
4. E
5. B
6. D

PATTERN PROBLEMS—PG. 225
1. D
2. 99, 93, 87, 81, 75, 69, 63, etc.
3. B
4. 64
5. 23, 32, 41, 50, 59, 68, 77, 86

SERIES, SEQUENCES & PATTERNS PROBLEMS—PG. 227
1. B
2. 18.5
3. 2
4. 406
5. D
6. B

GIVEN PATTERNS—PG. 229
1. A
2. E
3. C
4. D
5. D
6. D

PERMUTATION & PROBABILITY—PG. 231
1. E
2. B
3. D
4. A
5. C

PERMUTATIONS & ARRANGEMENTS—PG. 231
1. C
2. D
3. 120
4. C
5. 160
6. 48
7. 40
8. D

ARRANGEMENT—PG. 235
1. C
2. C
3. E
4. B
5. C

COMBINED SETS PROBLEMS—PG. 238
1. C
2. B
3. C
4. C
5. B

PROBABILITY—DRILL SET—PG. 240
1. B
2. C
3. C
4. C
5. $\dfrac{3}{10}$

BACKSOLVING PROBLEM SET—PG. 243
1. C
2. E
3. B
4.

Ratio Problems—pg. 246

1. C
2. B
3. E
4. D
5. A
6. D

Word Problems—Time and Money—pg. 247

1. D
2. B
3. C
4. A
5. D
6. B
7. D
8. D
9. B
10. E
11. E
12. A

Area & Perimeter of Regular & Irregular Shapes—pg. 251

1. B
2. A
3. A

Combined Shapes—Area and Perimeter—Drill Set—pg. 251

1. B
2. C
3. A
4. B
5. B

2nd Ed. © *ibidPREP llc*

APPENDIX A

READING COMPREHENSION–

NUTS & BOLTS

NUTS & BOLTS OF READING COMPREHENSION

1. Read the passage.

2. Keep reading until you've got your Two T's. Usually you'll know your Theme and Thesis by the first few sentences of the second paragraph, but sometimes the author doesn't spit them out until much later. Hang in!

   a. Make sure you are clear on what the topic [THEME] truly is: just because they're talking about *bananas*, it doesn't mean that the topic is really *bananas*.

   b. Make sure you are clear on what the author's viewpoint [THESIS] is: i.e., look for the "but." Just because the author writes "most people think bananas," it doesn't mean the author thinks "bananas." In fact he probably thinks "not bananas."

3. Once you've established what the "but" and/or author's point is, you will see that **every** body paragraph is designed to support that point.

4. Occasionally, authors will devote a body paragraph to a contrary example—something that seems to contradict their point of view. Authors do this in order to:

   a. Seem fair—they want to create the appearance of examining all sides of an argument and demonstrating their awareness of them, or

   b. Strengthen their point—by raising and then ultimately dismissing or diminishing contrary points of view, authors hope to reinforce the strength of their own point of view.

5. Every passage makes one and only one point, and most of the questions hinge on your being aware of what that point is.

6. Answering the questions:

   a. Read the question,

   b. Paraphrase the question so as to be sure you know what it's asking,

   c. Determine **your** answer to the question. If you don't have one, look back to the passage. Don't flip back to the question until you've figured something out. Then:

   d. Once you have an answer in mind:

      i. Read the answers given.

      ii. Eliminate any answers that seem wrong outright.

      iii. If you find the answer during your first read-through of the answers—pick it.

      iv. If you don't find the answer you want but have one or two choices left, look closely at the remaining answers and try to find one or two words in an answer that would make it **wrong.**

      v. If you are still left with more than one answer choice, pick the answer that seems qualified the most [some, often, occasionally, etc.] **and** the most like previous answers to other questions in the section, and then,

      vi. Move on! Don't spend too much time on a question you're totally clueless about. The longer you spend on a reading comprehension question, the more likely you are to waste time, energy and points. If you don't know the answer, guess and GTHOOT![45]

---

[45] Get the Heck Out of There!

Appendix B
Essay Process & Structure

2nd Ed. © ibidPREP llc

Essay Process: Structure and Tips

1. Read the topic.
2. Think about the topic.
   a. Ask yourself what it really means.
   b. Cast about your mind for anything (historical, literary, personal—anything that makes your point) that has to do with the topic. It is not important whether it seems like a positive or negative example—just be **specific.**
3. Based on your examples, decide which point will be either easier or more interesting to make. Remember, ***any*** example can be used to make any point of view. You don't have to be "right" as long as you are consistent. Your examples don't necessarily have to be from literature or history, but they do have to be on point. Personal anecdotes should be used sparingly.
4. Begin writing:
   a. Intro Paragraph:
      i. [Sentence 1] **<u>WHAT</u>** YOU BELIEVE—Your opinion of the topic. It is not necessary to say "I believe...." You can just make a statement: *It is not true that...*
      ii. [Sentence 2] **<u>WHY</u>** YOU BELIEVE IT— *It is not true **because...***
      iii. [Sentence 3] **<u>HOW</u>** YOU WILL SET ABOUT PROVING YOUR WHY. *History and literature have clearly shown topic to be false....*
      iv. [Sentence 4] Introduce your examples. *The lessons of **WWII** and **Macbeth** provide clear examples of where history and literature prove topic false....*
   b. Paragraph 2—Example 1
      i. Example 1 proves that topic is false because...
      ii. Specific Example "A" from text or incident.
      iii. Specific Example "B" from text or incident.
      iv. *As shown in Specific Example "A" and "B," Example 1 proves topic false.*
   c. Paragraph 3 — Example 2
      i. Connect to Example 2 and then show how it further proves point....
      ii. Specific Example "A" from text or incident.
      iii. Specific Example "B" from text or incident.
      iv. *As shown in Specific Example "A" and "B," Example 2 proves topic false.*
   d. Paragraph 3a— Example 3 [if you have a good third example and time, use it. If not, just mention it as additional proof in conclusion along with any other possible examples you might have].
   e. Paragraph 4—Conclusion
      i. *As shown above through history and literature, the topic is obviously false.*
      ii. *It is obviously false because of the "because" stated above* [Paragraph 1, Sentence 2] *and proved with the examples above.*
      iii. *Although some may say it is true because of **"some contrary reason,"** this reason only serves to make topic even more false because **"some reason of your own to contradict the contrary."***
5. **Reread** what you've written.
   a. Make sure there are no blatant grammatical errors.
   b. Make sure that the essay is reasonably legible.
   c. Make sure that paragraphs are clearly delineated

APPENDIX C

MULTIPLICATION & DIVISION TIPS

Multiplying by 2

Most everyone can multiply an even number by 2 fairly comfortably, but we often get stuck when multiplying an odd number by 2. One good approach is to simply double an even number just above or below your number and then add or subtract two.

E.g., 2 × 19
Think of (2 × 20) and subtract 2, so
2 × 19 = (2 × 20)–2 = 40 – 2 = 38

E.g., 2 × 37
Think of (2 × 36) and add 2, so
2 × 37 = (2 × 36) + 2 = 72 + 2 = 74

Of course you may also double the ten's digit and then double the one's digit:
2 × 37 = (2 × 30) + (2 × 7) = 60 + 14 = 74

Dividing by 2

Just as with multiplication, most of us can divide an even number by two fairly easily but have trouble dividing an odd number by two. One thing to keep in mind is that there are only ever two remainders possible when dividing by two: zero and one. An even number divided by two always has a remainder of zero, and an odd number divided by two always has a remainder of one (which becomes 0.5 if we continue dividing), so the best way to divide an odd number by two is to go to the even number below your number, divide that number by two, and add to your answer!

E.g., 45 ÷ 2

Think of (44 ÷ 2) and add .5, so

45 ÷ 2= (44 ÷ 2) + .5 = 22 + .5 = 22.5

Is a Number Divisible by 3, 6 or 9?

3

To determine if a number is divisible by 3, simply add all the digits in the number. If their sum is a multiple of 3, then the number is a multiple of 3.

E.g., 2,132
The digits of 2,132 are 2, 1, 3 and 2, and their sum is 2 + 1 + 3+ 2 = 8, SO 2,132 IS NOT divisible by 3.

E.g., 366
The digits of 366 are 3, 6 and 6, and their sum is 3 + 6 + 6 = 15; 15 is a multiple of 3, so 366 IS divisible by 3.

6

A number is a multiple of 6 if the number is even and its digits add up to a multiple of 6.

E.g., 846
The digits of 846 are 8, 4 and 6, so 846 is divisible by 6 because 8 + 4 + 6 = 18, and 846 is an even number.

E.g., 1,942
The digits of 1,942 are 1, 9, 4 and 2 so 1,942 is NOT divisible by 6 because 1 + 9 + 4 + 2 =16, and 16 is not a multiple of 6.

9

A number is a multiple of 9 if its digits add up to a multiple of 9.

The digits of 17,658 are 1, 7, 6, 5 and 8, so 17,658 IS divisible by 9 because 1 + 7 + 6 + 5 + 8 = 27, and 27 is a multiple of 9.

Multiplying by 9

To multiply a single-digit number by 9, simply make the ten's digit of the product one less than the number you're multiplying 9 by, and then make the one's digit whatever adds to the ten's digit to make 9. That sounds much harder than it is.

In other words, in 9 × 7, the ten's digit would be 6 [one less than 7] and the one's digit would be 3 [because 6 + 3 = 9], so 9 × 7 = 63!

NERD FACT: The digits of the first 20 multiples of 9 [except 99] all add up to 9!

Multiplying and Dividing by 5

All multiples of 5 have a units digit of 0 or 5.

To multiply a number by 5, simply multiply the number by ten and divide it by 2.
        In 24 × 5, 24 becomes 240, which is then divided by 2 to give the product 120!

To divide a number by 5, simply divide the number by 10 and multiply that by 2!
        In 245 ÷ 5, 245 becomes 24.5, which is then multiplied by 2 to give the quotient 49!

Multiplying and Dividing by 11

The first nine multiples of 11 are simply that number repeated: 11 × 2 = 22, 11 × 3 = 33, 11 × 4 = 44, etc.

To multiply a two-digit number by 11, simply split that number and put the sum of its digits in between the original digits.

E.g.   15
           ×11
split the 15 to make it   1__5
then take 1 + 5 [6] to make   165

Other examples—

$$
\begin{array}{r}
27 \\
\times 11 \\
\hline
2\_7 \\
\end{array}
$$

$2 + 7 = 9$, so   297

$$
\begin{array}{r}
35 \\
\times 11 \\
\hline
3\_5 \\
\end{array}
$$

$3 + 5 = 8$, so   385

When the sum of the digits of the number is greater than 10, simply carry the 1 as you would in regular addition.

$$
\begin{array}{r}
94 \\
\times 11 \\
\hline
9\_4 \\
\end{array}
$$

$9 + 4 = 13$, so 3 becomes the middle digit and 1 gets added to 9 to make 10:   1,034

Acknowledgments

Translating more than two decades of teaching into a coherent form that includes equations and illustrations has proven a vast undertaking. Many people have helped make this book and the others in the series possible. Among them, in no particular order, are Ian Fiedorek, Paul Ketchum, Audrey Moyce and the great and powerful Beth Servetar. Over and above the brilliant contributions of all these wonderful people, I am grateful to all my students past and present who have allowed me into their amazing minds long enough to learn how to teach them better.

Also available:

Remain Clam! Test Taking & the Student Mind: 4th Grade Common Core Edition

Remain Clam! Test Taking & the Student Mind: Middle School Workbook Edition

Remain Clam! Test Taking & the Teenage Mind: 7th Grade Common Core Edition

Remain Clam! Test Taking & the Student Mind: SHSAT Edition

Remain Clam! Test Taking & the Teenage Mind: SAT Edition

Remain Clam! Test Taking & the Teenage Mind: ACT Edition

About the Author

Stuart Servetar is from Brooklyn, NY. He grew up in Rockland County, NY, and attended Wesleyan University in Middletown, CT, where he studied English Literature. After briefly studying fine art at Pratt Institute, Stuart settled in New York City to write, paint and eventually tutor. When the Berlin Wall came down, Stuart headed to Eastern Europe and lived in Prague for a number of years. There he painted, taught English and was the food critic for *The Prague Post.* Upon returning to New York City, Stuart continued to paint and became the art critic for *The NYPress.* From there he wrote art criticism for a number of local, national and international publications. He also resumed tutoring. In 2006, Stuart formed ibidPREP in order to bring his approach to tutoring and test prep to a wider cross-section of students. Today, ibidPREP offers classes and individual tutoring throughout the New York/New Jersey metropolitan area.

101517

2nd Ed. © ibidPREP llc

Made in the USA
Middletown, DE
02 November 2018